Globalization and European Welfare States

Challenges and Change

D0264013

Edited by

Robert Sykes
Bruno Palier
and
Pauline M. Prior

Consultant Editor: Jo Campling

palgrave

First published 2001 by
PALGRAVE
Houndmills, Basingstoke, Hampshire RG21 6X5 and
175 Fifth Avenue, New York, N.Y. 10010
Companies and representatives throughout the world

PALGRAVE is the new global academic imprint of St. Martin's Press LLC
Scholarly and Reference Division and Palgrave Publishers Ltd (formerly
Macmillan Press Ltd).

ISBN 0-333-79018-9 hardback
ISBN 0-333-79239-4 paperback

This book is printed on paper suitable for recycling and
made from fully managed and sustained forest sources.

A catalogue record for this book is available from the British Library.

Library of Congress Cataloging-in-Publication Data
Globalization and European welfare states : challenges and change / edited by
Robert Sykes, Bruno Palier, and Pauline Prior; consultant editor Jo Campling.
    p. cm.
Includes bibliographical references and index.
ISBN 0-333-79018-9
    1. Public welfare–Europe. 2. Welfare state. 3. International cooperation.
4. Europe–Social policy. I. Sykes, Robert. II. Palier, Bruno. III. Prior,
Pauline. IV. Campling, Jo.
HV238.G56 2000
361.6'5'094–dc21   00-048302

10   9   8   7   6   5   4   3   2   1
10   09   08   07   06   05   04   03   02   01

Printed in China

For Lucas Palier

Contents

List of Figures and Tables

Foreword

Globalization has become increasingly invoked as a ready explanation for all manner of developments and problems. It is perhaps even more frequently used to justify certain policies both between and within countries. A particular merit of this book is its refusal to accept the conventional wisdom on 'globalization'. Firmly rejecting the process as a given, it makes a strong case for a much more differentiated view of globalization. The central question posed by the editors is: how far, and in what ways, has the process of globalization been implicated in recent changes to European welfare states? The answers throw much light on the ways in which powerful actors, including global agencies, have shaped government as well as public perceptions of the phenomenon of globalization. It is not surprising that the concept and the process are socially and politically constructed, but the ways in which different models of globalization are shaped, circulated and indeed sold across countries deserve to be better known and taken into account by both policymakers and analysts.

The country chapters in the second part of the book provide valuable indications of the uses to which the 'imperative of globalization' has been put by different governments. The book as a whole helps us to understand how and why certain logics of globalization have become more dominant and influential than others. While these have been seen as demanding policies of welfare retrenchment in many countries, some governments have perceived the issues very differently and devised solutions which may be described as more welfare-friendly. This variety of responses to the problem of globalization revealed by the analyses from across Europe is one of the strengths of the study. It indicates alternative options which can usefully inform both policy and research.

The Social Policy Association (SPA) was founded over a generation ago to bring together teachers, researchers, practitioners and students to support the development of the study of social policy and administration. Over this time comparative social policy has become one of the strongest areas of growth. In recent years the SPA has been more active in its international work in a variety of ways, supporting the establishment of the European Social Policy Research Network and taking other initiatives to facilitate and improve contact, exchange and research among those working in social policy across many countries. The study day on globalization where scholars from many countries discussed many of the topics developed in this book was organized and supported by the SPA. It is very good to have such an excellent outcome.

ADRIAN SINFIELD
President of the Social Policy Association

Acknowledgements

Many people have helped the editors and authors in the preparation of this book. They include family, friends, colleagues and students and are too numerous to name – we would like to thank them all for their support, encouragement and professional input.

We would also like formally to thank the World Bank, UNICEF, UNESCO and EUROSTAT, and the OECD for statistics and other materials used in various chapters of the book. Every effort has been made to trace all the copyright-holders of statistical and other materials referred to in the book, but if any have been inadvertently overlooked the publishers will be pleased to make the necessary arrangement at the first opportunity.

We would also like to acknowledge the fact that a great deal of the research was carried out with funding gained from many different sources. Pauline Prior would especially like to thank Peter Kennealy at the European University Institute at Florence for the financial and academic support of the EUSSIRF project. Bruno Palier would especially like to acknowledge the role in developing his thinking of two forums: the European forum of the Jean Monnet Center chaired by Yves Meny 'Recasting the Welfare State in Europe' in 1998–9 under the direction of Martin Rhodes and Maurizio Ferrera, and the European network of researchers Cost A15 project 'Globalization, Europeanization and the Reforms of European Welfare Systems', chaired by Denis Bouget. He would also like to thank Mariane Berthod, former head of Mire (Mission Recherche from the French Ministry of Social Affairs) for providing many incentives to develop research in the area of welfare state reform and globalization. Robert Sykes would especially like to thank Linda for her support, especially when this book seemed to be driving her partner to distraction.

Last and not least, we must thank the UK Social Policy Association for providing financial support for the study day on 'Globalization and the European Welfare States' in July 1999 out of which this collective enterprise has had its long, but eventually fruitful, gestation.

ROBERT SYKES
BRUNO PALIER
PAULINE M. PRIOR

Notes on the Contributors

Santiago Álvarez is Senior Lecturer in Public Economics at the University of Oviedo, Spain. He is a member of the International Institute of Public Finance and the Institute of Fiscal Studies (London) and his research areas include social policy, tax theory, public choice and Spanish public sector and fiscal federalism.

John Clarke is Professor of Social Policy at the Open University. Drawing on a background in culture studies, his interests have centred on the political, ideological and organizational conflicts around social welfare. Much of his recent work has addressed the role of managerialism in the remaking of welfare systems. Recent publications include *The Managerial State* (1997), co-authored with Janet Newman, and *New Managerialism, New Welfare?* (2000), co-edited with Sharon Gewirtz and Eugene McLaughlin. He has also written on US culture and politics including *New Times and Old Enemies: Essays on Cultural Studies and America* (1991).

Mary Daly is Professor of Sociology at the Queen's University of Belfast. A native of the Republic of Ireland, she has previously worked there as well as in Germany and Italy. She has published widely on comparative social policy and on sociological topics relating to Ireland. Her main research interests currently lie in how welfare states affect gender relations, the sociology of the family, poverty and social inequality. She is the author of *The Gender Division of Welfare* (2000).

Bob Deacon is Professor of Social Policy at the University of Sheffield and Director of the Globalism and Social Policy programme (GASPP: http://www.stakes.fi/gaspp) which is based at Sheffield and STAKES (National Research and Development Centre), Helsinki. Among his recent publications are *Global Social Policiy: International Organizations and the Future of Welfare* (1997), and he is the founding editor of the journal *Global Social Policy*. He is a member of the International Advisory Board of the ILO's Programme on Socio-Economic Security and has worked on aspects of globalization and social policy in association with WHO, UNRISD, UNDP, UN Secretariat, EU and World Bank programmes.

Zsuzsa Ferge (née Kecskeméti) was born in Budapest in 1931, and is an economist who has worked in the field of social statistics, sociology and social policy. She was appointed Professor of Sociology at Eotvos University in Budapest in 1988. She founded the first department of social policy in Hungary in 1989 where she is still teaching. Her main area of interest in research and teaching have been social structure, social inequal ities and poverty, and the social impact of economic and political transitions. She has held a number of Visiting Professorships at French, English and American universities. She is a member of the European Academy and of the Hungarian Academy of Sciences and holds an honorary degree from Edinburgh University.

Norman Ginsburg is Professor of Social Policy at the University of North London. He has written *Class, Capital and Social Policy* (1979) and *Divisions of Welfare* (1992), as well as papers and articles on housing and urban policy, on European and comparative social policy, and on race, ethnicity and social policy. He has been a member of the editorial collective of the journal *Critical Social Policy* since it started in 1980. He is involved in research on urban regeneration processes, housing privitization and social policy globalization.

Ana M. Guillén is Associate Professor of Sociology at the University of Oviedo, where she teaches comparative social policy. She has written extensively on welfare state development, health policy and comparative social policy (published in English, Spanish, Italian, French and Greek). She is author of *La construcción politica del sistema sanitario español: de la postguerra a la democracia* (2000). She co-authored with Manos Matsaganis 'Testing the "Social Dumping" Hypothesis in Southern Europe: Welfare Policies in Greece and Spain during the last 20 years' (*Journal of European Social Policy*, 10, 2 2000) In 1998–9, she was a Jean Monnet Fellow and participant in the European University Institute's *European Forum: Recasting the European Welfare State.*

Colin Hay is Reader in Political Analysis in the Department of Political Science and International Studies at the University of Birmingham. He is the author of *Re-stating Social and Political Change* (1996), *The Political Economy of New-Labour* (1999), and *Post-war British Politics in perspective* (1999) with D. Marsh *et al.*, and co-editor with D. Marsh of *Demystifying Globalization* (2000), and *Theorising Modernity* (1999), with M. O'Brien and S. Penna.

Pekka Kosonen is a Senior Research Fellow of the Academy of Finland and Associate Professor in the Sociology of Law in the University of Helsinki. He has studied structural changes in the Finnish society and has compared Nordic welfare states as well as Nordic economic policies. He was the co-ordinator of the research program 'Finland and European Integration', 1990–5. His research topic deals with globalization and small welfare states, in particular Denmark, Finland, Ireland and New Zealand. Recent publications include 'The Scandinavian Welfare Model in the New Europe', in Boje and Olsson (eds) *Scandinavia in a New Europe* (1993), and 'Activation, Incentives and Workfare in Four Nordic Countries' in *Comparing Welfare States in Nordic Europe and France* (2000).

Bruno Palier is Chargé de Recherches at CNRS in the Centre d'Etudes de la vie Politique Française (CEVIPOF), at the Institut d'études politiques de Paris. He specializes in the comparison of social protection reforms in Europe. He is a member of the Management Committee of the European network, Cost A15 'Reforming the Welfare Systems in Europe', and co-ordinator of the forthcoming working paper series for the International Labour Office on *The Extension of Social Protection*. He was responsible for the Mire programme *Comparing Social Welfare Systems in Europe*. His most recent publications include 'Defrosting the French Welfare State', in the journal *West European Politics* (2000) and 'From the Cradle to ... Where? Current Pension Policy Trends in Western Europe' (co-authored with Giuliano Bonoli) in the *Yearbook of European Administrative History* (2000).

Pauline M. Prior lectures in social policy at Queen's University, Belfast. With a background in social services training and management, her main areas of research interest are mental health policy, the impact of wider political and economic structures on national social policies, comparative social policy and the interrelationship between gender and health. Her publications include *Mental health and politics in Northern Ireland* (1993), *Gender and Mental Health* (1999) and a number of articles on different aspects of mental health policy.

Robert Sykes is Principal Lecturer in Social Policy in the School of Social Science and Law at Sheffield Hallam University. He edited, with Pete Alcock, *Developments in European Social Policy* (1998). His research interests are in EU social and economic policy, the relationship between globalization and welfare state change in Europe, and the links between socio-economic restructuring and welfare policy in Europe. He is a member of the executive committee of the UK Social Policy Association and convenes its special interest group on comparative social policy.

List of Abbreviations

ACP	African, Caribbean and Pacific countries
AFDC	Aid to Families with Dependent Children
CAP	Common Agricultural Policy (of the EU)
CEE	Central and Eastern Europe
DAC	Development Assistance Committee (of the OECD)
DG	Directorate General (of the EU)
EC	European Community
ELSA	Economic, Labour, Education and Social Affairs Committee (of the OECD)
EMS	European Monetary System (of the EU)
EMU	Economic and Monetary Union (of the EU)
ESRC	Economic and Social Research Council
EU	European Union
FDI	Foreign Direct Investment
G7	Group of Seven (Western economic powers: Canada, France, Germany, Italy, Japan, UK, USA)
GATS	General Agreement on Trade in Services
GATT	General Agreement on Tariffs and Trade
GDP	Gross Domestic Product
ILO	International Labour Organization
IMF	International Monetary Fund
MAI	Multilateral Agreement on Investment
NAFTA	North Atlantic Free Trade Agreement
NATO	North Atlantic Treaty Organization
NGOs	Non-governmental organizations
OECD	Organization for Economic Co-operation and Development
PAYG	Pay As You Go (i.e. pension, etc., schemes where beneficiary makes contributions during (working) lifetime)
PHARE	Poland and Hungary: Aid to Restructuring Economies programme (now extended to all Central and Eastern European countries)
TACIS	Technical Assistance to the Commonwealth of Independent States and Georgia
TEU	Treaty on European Union
TNCs	trans-national corporations

UN	United Nations
UNDP	United Nations Development Programme
UNESCO	United Nations Educational Scientific and Cultural Organization
UNICEF	United Nations Children's Emergency Fund
WHO	World Health Organization
WIDE	Women in Development
WTO	World Trade Organization

1

Challenges and Change: Issues and Perspectives in the Analysis of Globalization and the European Welfare States

BRUNO PALIER AND ROBERT SYKES

Globalization and its effects became key objects of concern in the late 1990s. Politicians, journalists and academics shared this concern, often expressed as a requirement for 'less state and more market' in the new global world. Most failed, however, to support their arguments with evidence. But in recent years, academic social scientists have sought to subject the notion of globalization and consideration of its effects to more balanced and empirically supported analysis. Various studies have also pointed to significant changes in welfare states in the 1980s and 1990s, especially in Europe, some even suggesting the demise of the classic European social model. Whilst there is an ever-growing literature on globalization,[1] matched by a similar, if somewhat less rapidly burgeoning literature on welfare state change,[2] comparatively little has been written on the interaction between the two.[3] The key question with which this book concerns itself brings these two areas of study together and is: *How far, and in what ways, has the process of globalization been implicated in recent changes to European welfare states?* This question is deceptively simple and needs to be unpacked into a number of contributory questions and issues for analysis. What, exactly, *is* the globalization process, and which of its multiple aspects are most likely to affect national welfare states? What have been the most significant changes in European welfare states in recent years? What factors, besides globalization, have been implicated in such changes? Last, and not least, how far do these same welfare state changes affect and, indeed, mould the globalization process?

A central purpose of this book is to challenge the most common approaches to examining the relationship between globalization and welfare state change and to propose an alternative approach. In this introduction, proceeding from an analysis and critique of three of the most common perspectives on globalization and welfare, we shall argue for an approach that:

● deconstructs the 'globalization' discourse, especially the arguments concerning the 'impact' of globalization on welfare states
● analyses and codifies welfare state changes, and
● uses this analysis to 'test' the various globalization and welfare state perspectives.

Why, since we are considering globalization, have we chosen to focus upon *European* welfare states in this book? There are two broad reasons, one substantive, the other methodological. First, the welfare states of Europe, especially those of western Europe, have often been regarded as an identifiable group conforming, indeed, to a 'European social model' (see, for example, Grahl and Teague, 1997). This model has been a reference point for other welfare states around the world in terms of institutional frameworks and the broad political economy upon which this 'European model' is based. In these circumstances, it was considered especially relevant to analyse the role of globalization in European welfare state change, quite apart from the interest that such analysis might command amongst those interested in European developments for their own sake. Secondly, the number of countries, welfare systems and types of policy change in Europe offers a broad range of experience for general conclusions about globalization and welfare to be drawn that can be extrapolated to other regions.

Perspectives on Globalization Welfare: A Review and Critique

The term 'globalization' has become a 'buzz-word' (Scholte, 1996), used to suggest a whole range of phenomena. In the economic field, globalization has been used to designate an increasing internationalization of economic exchanges and production; the abandonment of regulation on financial flows and trade, leading to an increasing mobility of capital, goods, services and labour; a qualitatively different regime of free trade competition at a world-wide scale; new 'dislocation' and 'relocation' of economic activities both and between nations; and increasing tax competition between countries. In the field of politics and political institutions, globalization is said to include several phenomena such as the weakening of nation states and their loss of social and political legitimacy; a decentralization process within national states; and attempts to re-vivify old and/or to create new international political institutions. In the field of cultural analysis, globalization has been associated with the free and instantaneous circulation of information; a threat to traditional cultures and social cohesion coupled with cultural homogenization or 'Macdonaldisation'; a process of individualization, and a tendency towards the marketing of goods and services as 'global products'.

One of the essential features of globalization, it is alleged, is the way in which economic links between nation-states in the world market have become systemic, highly competitive and essentially corrosive of pre-existing political and economic relations. It has been argued that global ization is an inexorable feature of the development of world capitalism, leading inevitably to the demise of autonomous national economies and the power of national governments over their economies and, indeed, to the collapse of nation-states as autonomous and sovereign entities. The 'apocalyptic' version of the globalization thesis found in the work of writers such as Ohmae (1990, 1996), and Reich (1992) is now widely discredited in the academic literature of economics, political science and international relations (see, for example, Boyer and Drache, 1996; Evans, 1997; Hay, 1998; Hirst and Thompson, 1999; Weiss, 1998). Ohmae and similar authors combine an (incomplete) analysis of the increasing linkages between businesses across the globe with an element of (self-fulfilling) prophecy from their neoclassical economics stance, to suggest a 'logic of no alternative' for nation-states and their policies in the face of the globalizing economy. In this scenario, the market would rule supreme: it was pointless for states to attempt to control the world market, and the future for social-democracy as a form of market intervention and general governance would be bleak. Indeed, in the more extreme versions of this argument, the (nation) state itself was either dying, or consigned to a subsidiary role in the globalized political economy of the next millennium.

Somewhat less dramatically, others have argue that globalization has changed the general economic context in which social policies are implemented. Welfare transfers and services must be seen as comprising an element of rigidity, and as a burden for the companies (labour cost) and states (budget deficits) that try to compete in new, global markets. Recognition and response to this new context is said to require a radical adaptation of welfare states. This adaptation implies policies of retrenchment in social policy, and the general change of welfare states in order to render them more market- and employment-friendly.

It now appears to be axiomatic for contemporary social science that *something* has changed in the global economic environment and that welfare states are changing also. Several studies have been undertaken to establish if and how economic globalization is impacting upon welfare state changes, and it is possible to identify three characteristic perspectives on globalization and welfare within these studies.

Perspective 1: Globalization has a Significant Impact on Welfare States through the Increasing Dominance of the (Market) Economy

In this perspective the view of globalization and welfare is closest to the apocalyptic version of the globalization thesis summarized above. Amongst this group are those who argue that globalization has a strong impact because internationalization of the world economy implies the demise of nation-state autonomy, a reduction of national governments' policy options (especially those of social-democratic governments) and a weakening of labour movements. Thus, the main foundations of the national welfare state, it is argued, are fundamentally weakened. Others explain that globalization has an effect on welfare states in the sense that the expansion of trade is responsible for unemployment and rising inequality, which creates (new?) problems for the welfare states. Trade and technological change both create a significant decline in demand for the unskilled, semi-skilled and traditionally skilled workers for whom the traditional welfare states were designed.[4]

Ramesh Mishra (1998, 1999) provides an example of this perspective. He premises his account on the proposition that the socialist alternative to capitalism has collapsed; indeed, this collapse is, for Mishra, the cause of globalization (1999, p. 15). The major effect of globalization is the decline of the nation-state in terms of its autonomy. Mishra makes seven propositions regarding globalization and welfare:

1. Globalization undermines the ability of national governments to pursue full employment and economic growth;
2. Globalization results in increasing inequality in wages and working conditions;

3. Globalization exerts downward pressure on systems of social protection and social expenditure;
4. Globalization weakens the ideological underpinnings of social protection;
5. Globalization weakens the basis of social partnership and tripartism;
6. Globalization virtually excludes the option of left-of-centre policy options for national governments; and
7. The logic of globalization conflicts with the 'logic' of national community and democratic politics. (1999, p. 15)

Mishra argues that globalization has empowered and privileged neo-liberal economics as a transnational force beyond the control of nation states and governments. He suggests that 'Economies have gone global, but societies and communities remain national' (1998, p. 485). Thus globalization 'must be understood as an economic as well as a political and ideological phenomenon', and 'is without doubt now the essential context of the welfare state.' (1999, p. 15).

The problem with this perspective is that accounts of national economic, political and welfare state changes do not, in fact, support such apocalyptic conclusions. At the overall economic and political level, various writers have argued for the continuing autonomy of national economics and national governments (for example, Boyer and Drache, 1996; Hirst and Thompson, 1996; Weiss, 1998; Zysman, 1996). At the level of welfare state change, other writers have challenged the assumption that (economic) globalization represents the sort of direct, debilitating and homogenizing impact outlined by exponents of this perspective.

This study questions Mishra's approach and argues that, globalization's influence in welfare state change should be conceived less in terms of mechanical economic 'impacts' and more in terms of political interventions. This is because globalization is as much a political and ideological phenomenon as an economic one. Welfare state changes should be similarly regarded: they do not happen automatically but are rather the result of policy and other political decisions made, principally, by national governments. In short: policy matters.

Perspective 2: Globalization has Relatively Little Impact on Welfare States

Various writers have argued that globalization has no significant impact upon welfare states. Some claim that there is no such thing as globalization since trade is at the same level as it was at the beginning of this century, and that the changes in the world economy are far less widespread, smaller and more gradual than the full-blown globalization thesis suggests.

Others argue that even if globalization has occurred, welfare states remain compatible with this process, and that it may even be a necessary feature of globalized economies to provide some sort of social welfare and political counterbalance to the effects of economic change (see Leibfried and Rieger, 1998). These writers argue that the erosion of welfare state is due more to the ideological projects of governments seeking to restructure than to the impact of economic globalization processes.

For others in this theoretical camp, the argument is that, whilst welfare states are changing, the cause is not globalization: national welfare states are challenged by domestic factors (demography, technology, changes in family structures, new risks) rather than by globalization. Pierson (1996, 1998, 2000) is probably the most influential proponent of this argument. He asserts that the welfare state, rather than facing fundamental retrenchment and decline, is likely to be sustained in almost all countries in the future. This is not to say that there are not pressures on welfare states. These are likely to lead to renegotiation, restructuring and modernization, but not to dismantling of welfare states. What Pierson calls the 'irresistible forces' playing upon welfare states are *domestic* forces, in particular the changed economies of advanced societies, the consequences of the 'maturation' of welfare states, and demographic change. Globalization as an *exogenous* set of forces is, at best, of secondary significance:

> The available evidence casts doubt on the claim that in the absence of growing economic integration welfare states would be under dramatically less pressure, and national policy-makers markedly more capable of addressing new public demands. (Pierson, 1998, p. 541)

Pierson argues that three processes are largely responsible for the pressures on welfare states and are essentially unrelated to globalization:

1. Advanced economies have witnessed a shift from manufacturing to services as their dominant sector along with slower economic growth. The low productivity associated with service employment means that such economies have a fundamental and growing fiscal problem in paying for welfare.
2. Such economies have, nevertheless, seen a tremendous expansion in the coverage and complexity of welfare state commitments because

welfare states have come to 'maturity'. These present serious budgetary problems, plus a loss of policy flexibility.
3. The changing demographic balance, coupled with the growth of welfare programme commitments, presents two sorts of problems for welfare states. The first is that as the elderly increase as a proportion of the population, there is a corresponding reduction in the proportion in work, and thus in the fiscal base for welfare provision. Secondly, the increasing numbers of elderly people have direct effects in two areas of welfare provision where costs are thus likely to increase significantly: pensions and health care.

In an earlier and more extended discussion, Pierson (1996) provided a compelling argument for seeing change in welfare state provision as something other than a simple reflex to changing economic pressures. His argument there is that the political bargains struck in different welfare states in the past, the existing political alliances in support of current provision, and the need for governments always to consider electoral effects of their policies all tend to support minimal and non-radical change in welfare state provision. In short, whilst there may well be pressures for change, we must also look to the patterns of (political) support for welfare systems in different countries if we are to make sense of what is *actually* happening rather than assuming, for example, that 'globalization changes all'.

Pierson's approach is insightful, but it is focused mainly on the American and British welfare states. The argument that domestic factors in general, and the three factors listed above in particular, are more significant than globalization regarding welfare state change remains to be tested in a broader range of countries. Evidence exists that services are not always associated with low or no productivity growth. As Alan Greenspan himself recognizes, the USA's 'new economy' which is largely composed of services, has recently experienced unprecedented growth. If we are to understand why welfare state are experiencing 'permanent austerity' (Pierson, 1998) then we must look beyond low productivity in services. Pierson's argument that globalization is of very limited significance *vis-à-vis* welfare change is also highly debateable, and seems to overlook the ideological and political dimensions of its role in welfare state change. Governments cite globalization pressures as the external force compelling change, and international organizations such as the World Bank provide both support for this view, and a range of policy 'solutions' to the problems. In this study we argue that it is important to recognize the way in which globalization can have an 'ideological' role in welfare state change even if evidence of direct 'impacts' is difficult to find.

Perspective 3: Globalization is having an Effect upon Welfare States, but these Effects are Mediated through (National) Institutional Structures and Policy Responses

In common with the two previous perspectives, proponents of this perspective focus upon the effect of (exogenous) global forces upon national welfare state changes. They argue, however, that certain types of welfare state (as well as certain types of labour market organization) are more compatible with competitiveness than others, and can adapt better than others to the new environment. Different welfare states are thus differently affected by globalization. Esping-Andersen and his associates (1996a), provide an account of the relationship between the global economy and welfare states that illustrates this approach. Esping-Andersen concludes that a nation's economic growth now appears to require economic openness, involving greater competition and vulnerability to international trade, finance and capital movements. Consequently, national governments are more constrained in their economic and other related policies: 'Keynesianism, let alone social democracy, in one country is accordingly no more an option. It may even be that governments' freedom to design discrete social policies has eroded' (1996a, p. 256). This world-wide competitive economic environment means that high-wage national economies will lose jobs to low(er)-wage countries.

So far there are similarities between this perspective and Perspective 1, but Esping-Andersen's analysis leads to quite different conclusions. First, he argues that Keynesianism in one country was, in any case, something of a myth: 'the most advanced welfare states tended to develop in the most open economies ... the more residualistic welfare states in countries with relatively protected domestic economies' (1996a, p. 257). Secondly, he argues that, in terms of labour costs, the real pressure from globalization for advanced economies is upon their low-skilled and labour-intensive mass-production economic sectors: 'The most acute globalization problem that Europe and North America face may, indeed, be that the market for unskilled labour has become international' (1996a, p. 258).

Esping-Andersen's key point here is that in responding to the dilemmas created by globalization, *different* national systems can and do respond in *different* ways. As an example Esping-Andersen points to different labour supply policies adopted by national governments in response to the pressures of globalization. The continental European states opted mainly for an exit strategy enabling workers to leave the labour market; the US and UK went for a wage deregulation strategy to bring down relative wage costs, and the Nordic countries chose retraining and the provision of welfare state jobs (1996a, p. 258).

Alongside the economic pressures, welfare states also face two other crises, according to Esping-Andersen. The first is the change for advanced welfare states from provision for the working classes to provision for all. The crisis rests in the fact that the principles upon which such universal provision might be made no longer command broad consensus. The other crisis concerns the fact that neither the egalitarianism of the 'Swedish model' nor the targeted approach of the 'US model' seem, for different reasons, to support the sort of human capital improvement which contemporary economies require. In the first case, the system provides disincentives to work and to improve skills and education, whereas the second generates poverty traps and also disincentives to work.

Drawing on these two elements, far from foreseeing a system of 'competitive austerity', as Mishra does, Esping-Andersen concludes that 'the welfare state is here to stay ... The fact of the matter is that the alignment of political forces conspires just about everywhere to maintain the existing principles of the welfare state' (1996a, p. 265). Within the advanced economies, though perhaps less so in the embryonic welfare states, existing political alignments of clients, welfare state workers, trades unions, political parties, etc. imply that welfare state change will be limited and slow, even in the face of global economic changes and challenges. The particular character of the previous political and institutional arrangements in different countries will also heavily affect change. Accordingly, responses to globalization and other pressures on welfare states are also likely to be differentiated.

This perspective is undoubtedly instructive, yet two criticisms may be made of it. The first is that even though such approaches differentiate welfare state changes, they do not differentiate the pressures of globalization. Esping-Andersen (1996a; 1999) and Myles and Quadagno (1997) point to the 'path-dependent' character of welfare state changes, but they assume that globalization and the internationalization of economies occur everywhere with broadly the *same* characteristics. This book argues for a much more differentiated view of globalization. Since globalization has different dimensions it can and does affect different welfare states in different ways, mediated by policy-makers, as is illustrated in Part II of the book. These chapters provide a a complex and nuanced account of the ways in which globalization has in fact had *different* guises and *different* effects in *different* European countries. To use Mary Daly's vocabulary (see Chapter 5 below), different dimensions of globalization create different 'pressure points' on different welfare states, according to their specific institutional features.

The second criticism concerns the view in this perspective that few important changes in welfare states have actually occurred, especially in continental Europe, for whatever reason (Taylor-Gooby, 1996). Esping-Andersen concluded that 'the cards are very much stacked in favour of the welfare state status quo' (1996a, p. 267). This is not to say that he thinks change is not necessary and even overdue because of changing economic circumstances. More recently, he has argued that the nature of new 'risk profiles' in the emerging post-industrial economies requires that welfare states recast themselves to meet the new economic realities. However, despite what he considers to be relatively minor changes in some welfare states, he does not see this sort of fundamental change occurring (1999, pp. 145–69). Although from a different perspective, Pierson has argued along similar lines. Despite the agenda of even the most ardent anti-welfare state governments of Thatcher in the UK and Reagan in the US, welfare state arrangements and funding in these countries remained essentially stable, he has argued (Pierson, 1994).

In contrast to these path-dependency arguments, writers such as Bonoli and Palier have argued that important changes have in fact been introduced in the British and French welfare states by certain 'path-shifting' reforms (Bonoli and Palier, 1998). This book also indicates that welfare state changes of some considerable significance are already in train, and certainly in Europe. The Dutch, French, Irish, Southern and Eastern European cases all provide particularly good examples of such changes.

The 'Impact' of Globalization on Policy Solutions

Instead of thinking of globalization only as a creator of new, mainly economic, problems for the welfare state, it can also be thought of as a provider of specific solutions for the problems met by welfare states, whether caused by globalization or not. Certain international agencies (mainly the IMF, World Bank, OECD) and other international epistemic communities such as economists have proposed 'global solutions' to perceived welfare problems. These proposed (often neo-liberal) 'solutions' illustrate the ideological character of globalization. In this sense globalization is implicated in two ways: (i) the 'ideological globalization' perspective of the OECD etc. provides welfare reformers with a certain repertoire of reforms, and (ii) the threat of globalization provides governments with ideological justification for their welfare state changes.

To promote a specific repertoire of reforms, international agencies have first provided governments with specific diagnoses (or constructions) of the problems confronting welfare states focusing on 'globalization', as was done, for example by the OECD (1981) and the European Commission (1993a, 1993b). They have also promoted specific measures supposedly adequate for adjusting to the new problems: pension reforms following the Chilean model promoted by the World Bank in 1994; diffusion of 'new public management' in welfare administration (e.g. managed competition in health care); promotion of selectivity and conditionality to counter a dependency culture. These global reforms have been promoted by international institutions such as the World Bank, the International Monetary Fund, the OECD and the European Commission (see Deacon, Chapter 4 below). Studying globalization's 'impact' on welfare state reforms thus requires the study of the prescriptions and arguments elaborated by these international organizations and their influence upon national governments, as Deacon's chapter indicates.

Globalization may also be used to legitimate welfare reforms, even where globalization has little or nothing to do with the problems. Reference to globalization *qua* competition and associated economic change is used by national governments as a justification for welfare reform. Similarly, international agencies have sponsored and sustained a discourse around globalization's assumed impacts to legitimate welfare reforms. One version of this in the European Union is the way in which the EMU convergence criteria have been a useful justification for welfare state reforms used by certain EU member states (see Guillén and Alvarez, Chapter 6 below).

To sum up, some globalization processes and actors appear to play a significant role in the legitimation of welfare reforms, namely to legitimate the argument that there is a need for reform, and to legitimate certain kinds (often neo-liberal) of solution adopted. Moreover, some international organizations have contributed to the diffusion, and sometimes indeed the imposition, as in Eastern Europe (see Ferge, Chapter 7), of certain reforms. It is important, therefore, both in a general sense (see

Clarke and Hay in Part I of this volume) and in national senses (see Part II) to unpack and understand globalization's ideological character.

From 'Impact' to Reciprocal Interaction

The unilinear understanding of the relationship between globalization and welfare state change will not be employed in this book. Globalization in our perspective is not regarded as a singular and homogenous process across the globe. The character of globalization (and thus its role in welfare state change) is viewed as being constructed and interpreted differently in different national systems, or types of welfare system. As the chapters in the second part of this book illustrate, different types of welfare state have a different perception of globalization, connected to the ways in which these different types of national welfare system construct and appropriate the processes of globalization. At the national level, there are different globalization processes since there are different welfare state contexts.

National social welfare systems have not only been developed to counter market failure, but are a reflection and a reinforcement of the specific social structural and labour market characteristics of a given country. Social welfare systems constitute specific normative, ideological and cultural legacies in each country. Therefore, welfare states should be seen as important parts of the socio-economic and politico-cultural structures of European and other countries which themselves shape the way that globalization influences these countries.

In a dynamic perspective, welfare state reforms apparently caused by the new globalized context might also be understood as having either anticipated or developed further trends related to globalization. The different moves by national governments to reduce welfare costs as a major part of a rising public debt have themselves realized the so-called 'permanent austerity'. The attempt to improve labour market flexibility as well as to reduce overall labour costs through reforms to the system of financing social policy are also reinforcing international competition between workers. Finally, it should not be forgotten that globalization is partly driven by specific interests linked to social policy, for example international health goods and services producers or international investors of assets of pension funds. The new shape that welfare states are supposed to take as a consequence of a passive adaptation to exogenous economic development, also corresponds to the interests of certain international social policy actors involved in the process of globalization.

To sum up, we have argued in this introduction that:

- policies matter, and analysis should focus upon them in different national contexts;
- globalization should be seen not only as creating new problems for welfare states, but also as providing and promoting certain 'solutions';
- we should expect and look for differentiation both in terms of responses to globalization *and* in terms of the forms that globalization may take; and finally
- we should expect to find that some significant welfare state changes may have occurred.

The Structure and Content of the Book

The book has been structured so as to examine both the theoretical and the empirical issues outlined above. The work focuses upon two dimensions: first, the challenges which globalization in its various guises (arguably) represents for European welfare states and, second, European welfare state changes themselves. Part I focuses on a critical discussion of various aspects of such challenges. Clarke provides the keynote chapter on the problematic character of each of the three main concepts, 'globalization', 'welfare states' and 'Europe'. He argues that we must recognize that each of these terms is contested both in academic and political discourse and in practice. The arguments he makes are echoed time and again in the rest of the book and they set out in general terms the 'informed scepticism' about globalization and welfare which characterizes its approach.

Hay then critically reviews two of the most commonly asserted features of globalization: (a) that globalization causes welfare retrenchment, and (b) that the welfare state is a barrier to economic competitiveness in the global economy. Hay provides a closely argued case for rejecting the simple assumption that globalization 'causes' welfare retrenchment, though it may be referred to be governments and others as if it *was* such a cause. Secondly, he rebuts the argument that welfare provision reduces national economic efficiency and competitiveness, suggesting rather that in the increasingly internationalized marketplace, some form of generalized social welfare provision may well be necessary to support and even improve national social and economic success. Once again, these general points are reinforced in various case studies of the European welfare systems in Part II of the book.

In the final chapter of Part I, Deacon reviews the international politics of globalization and welfare, focusing upon the policies and strategies of the main international organizations and, especially, the European Union. There can be no doubt that these organizations have had, and are likely to continue having, a central role in promoting a particular view of globalization, and, indeed, the economic and social policies that governments should follow in response to globalization. Deacon shows, however, that the neo-liberal position which has dominated in these organizations and their policies in the past may be changing towards a standpoint which is less antagonistic to welfare provision and even towards the advocacy of a more 'socially responsible globalization'. The role of the European Union (EU) as an international organization in all this is becoming more and more significant, yet, Deacon shows, the EU's strategy on globalization and welfare is at best confused and at worst contradictory. The notion introduced above, that globalization does not only create specific problems but also provides solutions and models for reforms, is borne out in Deacon's chapter and the chapters in Part II.

The first four chapters of the book thus raise a number of general questions, debates and issues about the nature of globalization, the challenges it represents for welfare states, and the significance of key international actors in globalization processes. They provide the context for Part II of the book, which focuses upon actual social policy change in European welfare states. In Part II each author has sought to explain how, in the different countries, globalization is (or is not) implicated in the changes outlined and discussed. Each chapter focuses not upon single countries but upon groups or types of similar welfare states. Five different groups of European welfare state are considered: the *Liberal, Nordic, Bismarckian, Southern* and *Central and Eastern European* welfare states. In constituting these five different groups of countries, we have sought to broaden the usual scope of studies on social policy changes. It goes beyond the range of countries usually referred to, and it focuses on welfare changes in a broad sense. Policies analysed include pensions, health care and unemployment insurance reforms, but also social services and broader macroeconomic policies, labour market policies and industrial relations. Intentionally these chapters do not reproduce either the welfare regime approach of Esping-Andersen or any other analyst, although all the authors address the contentious issue of the utility and applicability of such welfare state typologies in their chapters. The aim was more to consider a wide range of the European countries than to illustrate the similarities in evolution of each regime type. Therefore, some regimes are divided into different groups (the cases of Italy and Spain are gathered in a Southern

European group separated from the Bismarckian countries). Our European focus also implied a concern for comparing Central and Eastern European welfare states.

Moreover, within each group of countries, all the countries which might reasonably be included in each group are considered (for example, within the Liberal group, Ginsburg analyses the Irish case alongside the British one; for the Bismarckian countries, Germany, France, the Netherlands, Austria and Belgium are differentiated and analysed; the Nordic chapter does not concentrate merely on Sweden, but presents also the developments of Norway, Denmark and Finland). Such a differentiated approach to national cases within families leads some authors to the conclusion that there is not one single path of change within one group of countries. Our conclusion will be that this is partly due to the differences in politics and political choices made from one country to the other, reinforcing our hypothesis that policy matters.

The central question addressed in each chapters of the second part is: How far, and in what ways, has the process of globalization been implicated in recent changes to European welfare states? In addition a supplementary set of issues and questions are discussed. Do some types of welfare state regime, as identified here, respond differently to, and have different effects on, globalization? Furthermore, are different types of welfare state more or less able to respond to the pressures of globalization?

To address these comparative issues, all chapters follow a common pattern. They first discuss the welfare state characteristics of the countries reviewed in the chapter in order to underline their similarities. The chapters then analyse the possible and specific linkages between specific globalization trends and the welfare states in the group focused upon. Thirdly, they analyse the recent welfare reforms implemented in these countries. Finally, they draw some conclusions on the interaction between globalization and welfare state changes that are particular to the countries analysed. Since this approach starts from actual welfare state changes, the chapters reveal a differentiated picture of the content of globalization across European welfare states.

In concluding this introduction it is worth highlighting the themes that are woven throughout the text:

- Globalization is a contested concept and comprises a contested set of processes – the nature of globalization and its role in welfare state changes differs both between and within different welfare state types.

- The relationship between globalization and welfare state change should be conceptualized and analysed as a two-way or reciprocal process rather than one which is unidirectional – globalization may have effects on welfare state changes, but such changes can and do affect the forms globalization itself takes in specific contexts.
- What constitutes 'Europe' is also a contested conceptually, politically and economically – the particular patterns of institutional and ideological development of different European welfare states are central to any understanding of the role of globalization in European welfare state change.
- Changes have certainly occurred in European welfare states. The fact that these changes differ from one country to another, even in similar international and institutional contexts indicates that there continues to be 'space' within which different policy actors – national governments, international organizations, welfare client groups, political parties – can and do respond in different ways.
- The ideological dimension of globalization and European welfare policy must also be taken into account as an important element in the understanding of the interaction between globalization processes and welfare state changes.

Notes

1. It is not feasible to cite all the references on this subject since so many have been published in the late 1990s. For comprehensive textbooks see, for instance, Held *et al.* (1999) or Baylis and Smith (1999).
2. The list of references for this book alone indicates the number and range of these sources. For other extensive recent bibliographies on aspects of both topics see, for example, Held (1999), Sykes and Alcock (1998) and Esping-Andersen (1999).
3. Martin Rhodes has been amongst the most productive in surveying the topic of globalization and the welfare state (1995, 1996, 1997, 1999). Both authors of this chapter gratefully acknowledge the contribution, both written and personal, that he has made to the development of the arguments and perspective developed here. The views expressed are, nevertheless, the authors' own.
4. For a review of these approaches, see Rhodes (1999).

Part I

Globalization Challenges

2

Globalization and Welfare States: Some Unsettling Thoughts

JOHN CLARKE[1]

Most explorations of the relationship between globalization and welfare states now reject what might be called the simple, or even apocalyptic, version of globalization that has been the dominant approach. That conception had at its core a view of a transformed global economy in which hyper-mobile capital rampaged around the globe, collapsing time and space on its travels, and undercutting both nation-states and their welfare systems. The current refusal to accept this crude economic determinism is to be welcomed. So too is the growing recognition that it is a story told on behalf of narrow economic interests who have a direct stake in their (neo-liberal) version of how the world works being accepted by everyone else (see, for example, Hay, 1998, and below; and Massey, 1999). Despite such progress, however, there seem to be a few difficult issues to resolve in the process of thinking about the relationships between globalization and welfare states, particularly in relation to Europe. In this chapter, I want to explore some of those problems by taking each of the key terms in turn and worrying about them.

The reason for this approach may be simply stated. The 'globalization debate' still seems to me to be dominated by the revival of the claims of economics and political economy to possess superior knowledge about the state of the world. I want to offer some words of caution about the social and cultural complexity of what are usually treated as economic and political institutions, processes and relationships. There are, I will suggest, some difficulties about viewing globalization as an economic process or trend to which nation-states (or welfare states) have to adapt or respond. Of more concern, there are some problems about how welfare states are understood in these debates. Furthermore, there are questions to be asked about this thing called 'Europe'. I will argue that putting three over-simplified terms (globalization, welfare states and Europe) together has not been a sensible or intellectually productive process. I am sure that the position and the procedure adopted in this chapter – which might be parodied as putting all the key terms in 'quotation marks' to indicate their fragile, provisional and contested status – will be a source of irritation to some readers. Nevertheless, if the study of social policy is not to cut itself off from the benefits of other ways of thinking currently available in the social sciences, a small rash of quotation marks may be a risk worth taking.

Which Globalization Is This?

Although there are extensive arguments about the spread, depth, scope and significance of international, transnational and global economic relations and processes and whether these constitute globalization, my discussion starts somewhere else (but see Held *et al.*, 1997; Hirst and Thompson, 1999; Jessop, 1998). I want to look at five issues that shape how globalization is being conceived and used in analyses of changing welfare states.

(1) Should globalization be treated as a distinct process or as an effect of other processes?
The predominant usage seems to be that globalization is a distinctive process: many analyses talk of states, economies, sectors and systems adapting or responding to the 'process of globalization' or the new conditions of 'the global economy' (see, for example, Esping-Andersen, 1996a; Rhodes, 1996). This is, of course, a central structuring conception of political economy – there are economic processes and relationships that are distinct from and establish the (fundamental) conditions for secondary social or political systems and actors. But it is also a view of globalization as an external 'driver' of other changes in social political or cultural formations. In contrast, Jessop (like others) has argued that it is unhelpful to think of globalization as a unique causal process:

Globalization is generally better interpreted as the complex resultant of many different processes than as a distinctive causal process in its own right. It is misleading to explain specific events and phenomena in terms of the process of 'globalization', pointless to subsume anything and everything under the umbrella of 'globalization' and unhelpful to seek to link anything and everything to 'globalization' as if this somehow conveys more insight than alternative rubrics could. (1998, p. 1)

There remain, of course, considerable arguments about what such 'alternative rubrics' might be – changing modes of regulation (Jessop, 2000); new conditions and processes of capital formation (Tickell, 1999); new communicative technologies; new politico-spatial alignments and conflicts (Massey, 1999); new cultural formations and relations (Jameson and Miyoshi, 1998); a renewed and revitalized US imperium and so on. All of those, however, identify more differentiated processes that may have made the world 'a different place'. Globalization, then, can be seen as an effect – rather than a cause. The choice that is made here has significant implications for the analysis that is developed. Let me give one example. Treating globalization as the causal process produces a question that asks 'what is its impact upon' the thing we are looking at. So, what effect has globalization had on (national) welfare states? Or, how have welfare regimes adapted to the new global economy? Alternatively, we might want to explore how the processes producing globalization are both internal and external to the national welfare states that are our object of inquiry. For example, Hudson and Williams (1999) have argued for the importance of seeing processes of globalization as ones of 'linkage and interdependence' connecting 'in here–out there'. They argue that 'globalization is not conceptualized as a process somehow external to a national economy, society and state', not least because 'national states have played a key role in bringing about regulatory and other changes that have facilitated the emergence of processes and agencies of globalization' (1998, pp. 6–7).

I would prefer to work with this more differentiated view of globalization as the effect or consequence of multiple processes, because it allows for the possibility that not all of these processes might be perfectly integrated. It opens up the analytical question of whether they are all moving in the same direction or might involve counter trends or contradictory pressures (see also Jessop, 2000).

(2) Is globalization best understood as a condition or as a dynamic?
There is a temptation, I think, to treat globalization as an 'end state', a condition that has been established: a 'new world order' or a 'new global

economy'. Analysis is then focused on the adaptation of social, political or economic systems or sub-systems to this new environment or set of conditions. The alternative is to view globalization as a set of dynamic processes which are 'unfinished' and which may be uneven or contradictory. For example, in a world of 'free trade', it is clear that different commodities have different mobilities: finance capital moves faster than goods that move faster than factories which move faster than (some) people (see Massey, 1999; Sassen, 1998). There are different regulatory systems and logics that enable and control the movement of different entities in these processes. Indeed, the movement of (some categories of) people is increasingly constrained. If we view globalization as a set of dynamics, we may also be able to see how welfare systems might be facing different demands and pressures, rather than a simple downward pressure to align with the new global economy (for examples of this process, see the chapters in Part II). For example, do we think that the widespread combination of feminization and flexibilization in paid work in Europe is an aspect of globalization? Is it a trend in labour formation or gender relations? Does it represent a change in socio-demographics? Is it the basis for new challenges to welfare states? (For discussions of some of these dynamics, see Perron, 1999; Pillinger, 2000; and Sassen, 1998). Insisting on a view of welfare systems as intimately linked to the structuring of different forms of work (paid and unpaid) highlights both gender divisions and their dynamics. The unfolding of some of the pressures around unpaid/domestic care work may not fit comfortably with the increasing expectation of women's participation in paid employment, unless it is believed that women's labour power is infinitely flexible.

(3) Globalization: homogeneity and difference
Globalization has been understood as producing greater homogeneity in economic, political and cultural terms. Economically, these processes have involved the increasing integration of national economies and other forms of production into capitalist social relationships and transnational processes of investment, distribution and exchange. Politically, there have been claims about the homogenization of political systems and ideologies attributed to globalization, most notably in the work of Francis Fukuyama (1992) but also in more understated claims about the intersection of 'reflexive' modernity and globalization (Giddens, 1994). These homogenizing tendencies, however, seem to co-exist with significant processes of economic, political and cultural differentiation. Writing about these economic dynamics in the European Union, Hudson and Williams (1999)

suggest the need to think how both tendencies may be present. They argue that

> these changes in the character of the EU can also be regarded as bringing about an homogenisation of its space, seeking to establish the hegemony of capitalist social relations over its entirety. At the same time, giving wider and freer play to market forces has led to increasing territorial differentiation within the EU. (Hudson and Williams, 1999, p. 8)

Political homogenization seems to exist alongside both old and new forms of political system and ideological-organizational political differentiation.

At the same time, cultural homogenization (sometimes referred to as either Americanization or MacDonaldization) has been tempered by the proliferation of cultural differences, and by the greater mobility of cultural forms and practices (Jameson, and Myoshi 1998). Differentiation – and the celebration of the 'local' and the 'particular' – seems to be a significant dimension within globalization. We have to think of the production of differentiated collective identities and cultural practices within and against older dominant formations – in new national, ethnic, and communal forms (see, for example, Lowe's work on Asian–American cultural politics, 1996). At the same time, these 'local' identities are less geographically bounded as an effect of the new communications technologies – they can be produced, circulated and consumed well beyond their 'local' setting. Indeed, some authors have suggested that the 'proliferation of cultural difference' is itself a central process for globalizing systems of capital accumulation that work on and through culture. Grossberg, for example, has argued that 'the new consumer market is also defined in part by what I would describe as the fetishization and commodification of difference' (1999, p. 14). Differentiation, then, might be treated as the contradictory combination of this hegemonic commodification and the practice of subordinate refusals of normative identifications.

For our purposes in the analysis of welfare states, it may be important to stress the double significance of difference in relation to globalization. Many studies of welfare state change have stressed the importance of institutional formation and 'path dependency' in explaining resistances or adaptations to the pressures of globalization (see Esping-Andersen, 1996a, and more generally, Skocpol, 1995). This institutionalist approach has been valuable for highlighting the limits to homogenization that 'pre-existing' differences may create. But there is a second dimension that also needs attention: the differentiating implications of the dynamics of globalizing processes. The movements of production, people, profits and problems around and across nations do not, as Hudson and Williams (1999) indicate, result in one undifferentiated outcome: they are spatially distributed and differentiated. Within Europe, Spain, Sweden and Slovakia arrive with their own different 'paths' *and* encounter different forms of 'integration' into the new dynamics (for further articulation of this point see both the introductory and concluding chapters of this volume).

(4) What does it mean to treat globalization as a discourse?
Part of breaking the dominance of the simple or apocalyptic version of globalization has been the development of a view of it as an ideology or discourse. Treating it as a claim about how the world ought to be ordered, rather than as a description of how the world is ordered, has been a significant step. Recognizing that such a discourse is a means by which specific groups and interests might make the world conform to their aspirations is another gain (see, for example, Hay, 1998; Massey, 1999). I would want to add two further twists to this approach to globalization as a discourse. The first concerns whether globalization is 'just a discourse'. The implication here is that the globalization discourse is merely a story, narrative or construction that masks or conceals reality. This is a rather impoverished view of discourse (or ideology). Discourses need to be taken seriously as social practices through which attempts are made to construct reality. This involves not only linguistic constructions, but also making things come true in practice. The dominant globalization narrative about the 'powerlessness' of individual actors, companies, agencies and nations in the face of a global market is an attempt to tell that story in a way that makes all trends seem coherent, uni-directional and inevitable. It is also an effort to make the story come true by installing it in the conventional wisdom and everyday practices of institutions. These institutions may range from the World Bank to managements in 'local' organizations – and through many layers in between (for a discussion of the 'cascading' discourse of change from global to local, see Clarke and Newman, 1997, pp. 46–8). Consequently, I suggest that the formulation of things being 'just' a discourse or 'just' a social construction needs some care.

Social constructions are extremely tangible, solid and unforgiving formations (see Clarke, 1998; Clarke and Cochrane, 1998). For example, poverty is a social construction, which is discursively produced and which constructs subjects (the poor, the non-poor, and those who are empowered to 'work on' the poor, for example). Knowing that this is a social construction does not mean that the effects of being poor are any less dangerous, miserable and painful. But it does mean breaking with naturalizing assumptions about the essential character of poverty or poor people. Similarly, racialized differences are socially constructed (rather than reflecting biological conditions) and they do serious damage to people (see, for example, Brah, 1996; G. Lewis, 1998a and 2000). Secondly, to treat 'neo-liberal globalization' as a discourse should also imply that we recognize the existence – or potential existence – of alternative discourses that may contest the premises, claims and directions of this dominant variant. So, we might reflect on the 'globalization' imagined in, and practised through, ecological and environmental movements, or the conceptions of a global politics that link 'liberation struggles' being fought against authoritarian regimes. We might also see the traces of older imaginings of a global system, such as the view of a world order that was institutionalized in the United Nations. There are both global and local alternatives to the neo-liberal discourse, although assessing their political significance is an extremely difficult issue (see, for example, the discussion in Moreiras, 1999). Discourses (or ideologies or constructions) rarely exist alone and uncontested, and one key element of the neo-liberal project of globalization has been the insistent effort to naturalize itself as the necessary, inevitable and only imaginable globalization.

(5) Is globalization best understood as an economic (even political-economic) phenomenon or a cultural (or socio-cultural) one?
It will, I hope, be clear that I think there are some dangers attached to thinking of globalization in solely – or even primarily – economic terms. Minimally, we might need a view of 'the economy' that grasps how 'culture' is a central element of production and consumption. The extended and intensified 'commodification' of culture has provided a basis for new processes of capital accumulation. Those processes are also enabled by new 'information and communicative technologies' that operate across corporate decision-making, sites of production, processes of distribution and dissemination and the settings of consumption. This articulation of culture and economy is itself the focus of theoretical and political controversies that cannot be pursued here (but see, for example, Gibson-Graham, 1996; Grossberg, 1999; Jameson and Miyoshi, 1998).

However, I would want to take the economy–culture intersection somewhat further than this. For the most part, political economy deals in what might be called 'de-socialized labour' as a factor of production. This is disconcerting given the extensive explorations of the economic and political consequences of the social differentiations of those who labour. For example, we are, or should be, the beneficiaries of twenty years of scholarship examining gendered and racialized divisions in relation to work, welfare, political action, nation formation and so on (e.g., Brah, 1996; Fraser, 1997; Gilroy, 1993; Hall, 1992; Hall *et al.*, 1978; Lewis, 1998b; Morley and Chen, 1996; Taylor, 1996; Williams, 1989; and the overview in Lewis, Gewirtz and Clarke, 2000). With rare exceptions, the political economy of globalization turns its back on such knowledge and opts for 'simple' categories of labour or class. Yet, is it possible to imagine these dynamics of globalization without socially and culturally differentiated labour – groups of people who exist in and are subjected to old and changing forms of national, ethnic, racialized and gendered differences? Even this only poses the questions about processes of differentiation in relation to production. The dynamics may also be thought to be significant for other processes: consumption, domestic economies, household formation, collective action, political organization, and even for relations with welfare states. I will return to this issue in the following section.

I have argued that the move away from the simple and 'inevitabilist' view of neo-liberal globalization has been an important step. But taking this step still leaves questions about what direction to follow thereafter. In this discussion of globalization, I have tried to suggest that keeping to more open-ended, differentiated and non-reductionist views of globalization might be beneficial for analysing the relationship between globalization and welfare states. In particular, I think it is worth resisting the temptations to treat globalization as a basic economic process that is an external condition of other (and by implication secondary) social, cultural and political formations.

Which Welfare State is This?

The second focus of attention is 'welfare states' or, more accurately, the problem of what it is that is discussed when people examine the relationship between globalization and welfare states. I think that many of the current discussions are dogged by a peculiar combination of problems. Conceptions of the welfare state are at one and the same time too loose and too narrowly specified. In the former, it does seem to me to make a difference as to whether we are talking about national welfare *systems* or national welfare *states*, for example. In part, this is because I think the word 'state' carries issues about the formation of political power, public organization and capacities, and the condensation of social relations that makes it a distinctive formation (Clarke, 1996; see also Hay, 1996). Nevertheless, there is an issue about whether it is possible to separate out 'welfare states' from states. Is it appropriate to treat welfare states as corporate actors who 'respond', 'adjust' or 'adapt' to changing environments? Empirically, I suspect, one would be lucky to find a welfare state (as opposed to the welfare functions undertaken by states). 'Welfare states' are convenient and important collective fictions both politically and analytically (see Hughes and Lewis, 1998). It is also clear that, in practice, welfare states (understood as the abbreviated form of 'the welfare functions of states') do things. They pay out benefits, exercise surveillance over problem populations, produce and distribute services, produce, reproduce and revise patterns of social differentiation, repress difficult people and so on. But that is not the same as treating them as 'collective actors' (who respond, adapt and so on) within social policy analysis. To do so misses out the processes of political (and ideological) mobilization and articulation through which the problems of 'the environment' are constructed and solutions to them are proposed and legitimated.

There is also a second problem: social policy analyses often take too limited a view of what constitutes a welfare state. As Sykes (1998) has rightly argued in relation to comparative studies of divergence and convergence, there is 'a question of what policies should be considered and why?' (p.14). For the most part, comparative and 'globalist' studies have tended to ignore this question, preferring to treat welfare states as income transfer programmes. There are plausible methodological, theoretical and political reasons for such a choice (see, for example, the discussion by Daly, 1997, and also Cochrane, 1993), but they are rarely articulated. Because of the intellectual history of social policy, there is a predisposition to focus on these programmes. They are where questions of the scale, cost and scope of 'welfare' can be readily posed. They are the site of traditional inquiries into the existence or extent of redistribution (between socio-economic groups or across the life course). They are where questions about the relation between social policies and economic policies can be most readily sought out. It is not surprising, then, that they are the policies most visible in discussions of the new international political economy and welfare. While I am willing to accept that it is not surprising to find them in this central role, I reserve the right to also be depressed by the discovery.

The first source of my depression is that this is a very narrow conception of welfare states. The funding, provision and coordination of a whole range of benefits and services distributed in more or less differentiated ways to complex social groupings within a national framework, and involving complicated relationships between the public, welfare and the state, is hardly captured by the data on income transfers. As a result, there is a risk of a growing gulf between rich and complex analyses of individual welfare states and an impoverished and predominantly quantified comparative methodology (but see Clasen, 1999). The second reason for being depressed is that such narrow representations of welfare states ignore or even suppress the rather troubling questions that have been raised during the last twenty years about welfare states and forms of inequality and difference. The dominant concern in traditional or conventional analyses is with issues of inequality and redistribution framed within a hierarchy of socio-economic groups (sometimes codified as classes). Issues of how welfare states produce, reproduce or modify inequalities of gendered or racialized divisions (or may produce impoverished dependency for disabled people) are, to put it generously, less than central. Yet, as I will argue, any adequate view of welfare states must treat seriously their role in the reproduction of complexly differentiated populations. The third and final cause of my intellectual depression is that this focus on income transfers is the social policy mirror image of the economic reductionism visible in many contemporary analyses of globalization. They fit together neatly. Socially undifferentiated 'labour' meets socially undifferentiated 'welfare policies'. Jessop (2000), for example, talks about how globalizing tendencies may promote welfare policies adapted to Schumpeterian innovation/workfare regimes. They might, but not all welfare policies are labour-market policies, so there remains a question about how all the other differentiating complexities of social welfare are to be accounted for – rather than ignored. Rhodes, for example, suggests that changes in demography, family and labour market patterns are 'transforming the nature of "needs" and altering the gender/family/work nexus in which western welfare states have traditionally been based' (1996, p. 307). This is tantalizing. Are we to understand these changes as integral to, or separate from, globalization? Is a new nexus being produced at the intersection of global economy and national welfare states? Unfortunately, a political economy perspective rarely pursues such dimensions of social differentiation. Dealing with questions like these will mean more than examining the broad structures and costs of income transfer programmes and requires attention to how different forms of work and gender divisions are articulated in welfare policies and practices (see Lewis, 2000).

I want to suggest that welfare states might usefully be viewed as part of the means by which states produce and reproduce socially differentiated populations. Income transfers, as Daly has argued, are significant because the 'institutional architecture' of benefit systems reveals 'the terms on which individuals can make claims on public resources and the types of solidarity which are fostered by systems of public support' (1997, p. 172). I would argue that welfare states reveal much about how societies are differentiated; about which differences carry or produce material inequalities; and about what the structure of inclusions and exclusions, hierarchizations, marginalizations and subordinations may be (Hughes and Lewis, 1998). In relation to such social differentiations, welfare states may reproduce or reinforce patterns of division and inequality or they may remedy or modify them – but the complex system of differentiation is not likely to be reducible to a simple distributional analysis of socio-economic groups. Conventionally, social policy has dealt with these issues through a rather constraining notion of social structure and social divisions. For example, Esping-Andersen's characteristic argument is that 'welfare states may be equally large or comprehensive, but with entirely different effects on social structure. One may cultivate hierarchy and status, another dualisms, and a third universalism. Each case will produce its own fabric of social solidarity' (1990, p.58). This view of social structure and the forms of solidarity, however, tends to revert to one major axis of differentiation (and that is usually class, in a Marxist or Weberian sense), rather than dealing with the articulation of different axes of differentiation that constitute a society or social formation. I am suggesting instead that social policy analysis needs to be attentive to how social welfare articulates differences into a complex ensemble. For example, the conditions of access to benefits and services embody and enact sets of social distinctions: sometimes about gender positions, sometimes about age statuses or sexuality, sometimes about disability, sometimes about distinctions that are racialized or ethnicized. Citizenship – understood as referring to what Morris (1998) calls 'legitimate membership of the welfare community' – is a complex figure because it condenses (in each national formation) this complexity of relations and because it is traversed by the struggles over them.[2]

Such a view of welfare states suggest that the 'gender/family/work nexus' and how it links to welfare state policy and practice may be significant – and, of course, may vary between national welfare states (Hantrais, 1999; Jane Lewis, 2000; Sainsbury, 1994). Similarly, welfare states vary in their production and reproduction of racialized social differences: for example, in varying strategies of conditional inclusion, assimilation and 'official multi-culturalism' (see, *inter alia*, Lewis, 1998a and 1998b; White, 1999). The specific axes and forms of combination of differentiation clearly vary between nations and their welfare states. This view also suggests that welfare states will be the focus of complex social politics surrounding the forms of difference and the conditions of their relative inclusion, marginalization and subordination. In this role, welfare states can be viewed both as temporary compromises or 'settlements' in which they condense the balance of a particular combination of social relations, and as potentially 'unstable equilibria', vulnerable to new challenges (Clarke and Newman, 1997). The role and place of welfare states in the (complex) reproduction of those combinations could be a central issue for thinking about welfare states and globalization. This significance has something to do with the ways in which the dynamics of globalization processes can both intensify and unsettle such social divisions and the institutional arrangements for their reproduction. Nevertheless, before exploring those dynamics further, there are two qualifying points to make about this view of welfare states.

The first point is that welfare benefits and services are not the only means through which states attempt social reproduction. The management of socially differentiated populations can be accomplished through a range of different means (or, more accurately, through different combinations of the range of possible means). This is most obviously revealed in the case of the USA. As several commentators have noted, its comparatively low male unemployment rate is achieved by virtue of incarcerating a much larger part of its 'surplus' male population than any other Western economy (e.g., Piven, 1997; Hay, this volume). The criminal justice system is also a means of managing socially differentiated populations. Indeed, some analysts have argued that there has been a shift away from 'welfarist' to 'neo-liberal' forms of 'governmentality', one of whose features is the increasing use of modes of policing, surveillance and regulation rather than welfare policies and practices (Rose, 1996; Stenson, 2000). Even in its weakest form, this issue reminds us that states 'do' more than welfare and that we should be careful about what our analytic focus on welfare states may make us forget.

Secondly, there is an ambiguity about the relationship between welfare states and welfare systems. The concept of the welfare state is a convenient one and, as I suggested earlier, it is useful for drawing attention to the place and role of the state in relation to social welfare. However, it is also misleading. It conjures up an over-coherent image of an organizational entity that detracts from consideration of how welfare policies and practices may be distributed within states. It also draws attention away from the place and role of the state in different 'welfare mixes' or 'mixed economies of welfare', featuring changing combinations of, and relationships between, 'sectors'. This is both a general analytic point and an issue in the problems of analysing current tendencies (Clarke, 1996). Despite neo-liberal mythologizing, there were always mixed economies of welfare (rather than monopolistic welfare states). But conjuncturally, many of the attempts to reform or restructure national welfare systems have involved changing sectoral balances. For the remainder of this chapter, I shall carry on using the term 'welfare states' but will do so primarily because I am interested in the ways in which they have been decomposed and recomposed.

Signs of Instability: The Nation-State/Welfare-State Nexus

Social policy has conventionally held the idea of the national welfare state as a central element in its field of analysis. In the main, social policy has explored societies in which welfare has been predominantly organized in and through the nation-state (see Finer, 1999). This may become problematic as we see economic, social and political processes that disturb the apparent unity of the phrase 'nation state'. It has become harder to take for granted what appeared to be a 'natural' fit between the two terms. Nation and state cannot be assumed to be coterminous. Nations have become increasingly unstable entities, most obviously in the post-Soviet-bloc era in Europe. In a variety of ways, the integrity of the Nation has become contested – in terms of citizen-membership, in terms of constitutional arrangements, in terms of geographical, political and cultural boundaries and in terms of the permeability of such boundaries to migration. Nations have been both dismembered and remade (Sassen, 1998). They have been constructed as geographically bounded places, as sets of people, and as inherited, or even repressed but recovered, ways of life or cultures. Even where nations have remained stable geo-political entities, their boundary conditions have changed. Borders have been both weakened and reinforced unevenly in the face of new mobilities and migrations (Hudson and Williams, 1999). At the same time, states – as forms of governance, as representations of collective identities and even as providers of public services to their publics – have undergone challenges and disturbances.

This is not to argue that 'globalization has undermined the nation-state'. As usual, the apocalyptic version of globalization both overstates the case and manages to conceal more complex movements. Rather, this implies tracing the processes or dynamics that produce dislocations or 'unsettlings' in the connection of nation and state (see also Hughes and Lewis, 1998). Such an approach draws attention to the different potential axes of conflict within and beyond the nation and the state. Jessop (1998, 2000) has pointed to the complications of geo-political *scale* associated with globalization. He argues that issues of scale cannot be reduced to the simplifying 'global or local' framework. He argues instead in favour of tracing the differentiated flows of power, resources, capacities and decisions between local, sub-national, national, regional and global levels. In his analysis, the nation-state does not disappear, but is placed within more complex sets of scalar relationships and processes. Indeed, he argues that in some respects the significance of the nation-state may have increased as it plays a central part of managing these 'scalar' relationships.

There are also questions about the changing relationships between 'nation state' and 'welfare state'. These phrases denote central institutional formations in which the nation and the state, and social welfare and the state have been constructed as stable linkages (see also Clarke, Hughes, Lewis and Mooney, 1998). As with 'nation state' the unity of the phrase 'welfare state' can no longer be assumed. The meaning, scope and scale of 'welfare' is being contested and renegotiated in many national contexts, with the USA in the vanguard of the search for the 'end of welfare' (see, *inter alia*, Mink, 1998). 'Welfare' in the US context has been narrowly equated with public assistance (and Aid to Families with Dependent Children (AFDC) in particular) rather than any wider concept of social welfare. However, it is clear that other public programmes are also under threat (e.g., in proposals to 'privatize' social security). At the same time, the role, scope and scale of the state has been under constant challenge, particularly, but not exclusively, from the New Right, since the late 1970s. The effect has been growing uncertainty about what the state can and should do; about what government can be trusted to do; and about what the public-as-taxpayers can (or are willing to) afford. Such efforts to 'reinvent government' have changed the equivalence between the public, public services and the state. 'Public services' can no longer be assumed to refer to both services *to* the public and services located *in* the public sector, given moves towards different mixes in the 'mixed economies of welfare'. Clarke and Newman (1997, pp. 22–33) have argued that it is important to trace both the shift towards other agencies of provision and the new means by which multiple providers are tied by financial and performance management systems into a field of 'dispersed' state power. The difficulty is to grasp how such processes may involve both 'welfare pluralism' and new forms of state power or control 'at a distance' (Hoggett, 1996). Such changes in the mixed economies of welfare disturb the previously established relationship between welfare and the state. It may be helpful to think of each of the terms – Welfare, Nation and State – as being the focus of separate, albeit overlapping, sets of social dynamics and political conflicts. Reforming the welfare state has involved changing welfare and changing the state, as well as changing how the two are articulated.

And ... Which Europe is This?

It will probably be clear by now that my purpose in this chapter is to expose the ways in which the key terms of analysis here are more provisional than they appear. This is not merely a conceptual exercise – a matter of making them more provisional concepts. Rather, my concern is to show how such simple or reified uses of concepts may occlude provisional, contingent and contested social realities. If welfare states are temporary settlements (as I have argued above) then we need a conceptual approach that grasps both sides of that statement. We need to recognize the settlement without excluding its potential instability or susceptibility to challenge. At the same time, we need to recognize its contingent and constructed character without excluding the accomplishment of its 'settlement' – its (temporary) solidity. In a strange way, this approach is easiest to advance in relation to the question of 'Europe'. Europe is more evidently unstable, contingent and contested – yet solidified, institutionalized and (temporarily) settled. It is less 'taken for granted'.

As Sykes has observed, 'Most studies of social policy in Europe focus either explicitly or implicitly on the member states of the EU' (1998, p. 15). As he also suggests, 'there are compelling reasons' for doing so. Yet the European Union has not been, is not and will not be (at least for some time) a stable geo-political entity. Its boundaries (and the patterns of inclusion and exclusion) have changed and will change further. The same might be said about the looser term 'Europe' which oscillates between more or less inclusive conceptions that have their 'core' components in the nation-states of North and West. The 'South' and the 'East' occupy more ambiguous – and intermittent – places in the European imagery (see Williams, 1999). Both the EU and 'Europe' are internally and externally contested formations, subject to challenges about 'membership', the conditions of 'insertion', the nature of collective identity, purpose and direction (see Ferge, 1997; Hudson and Williams, 1999; Mitchell and Russell, 1998; Poole, 2000, for example). But the EU in particular is also an entity – a construct – whose current 'settlements' regulate entry, assign differentiated positions and trajectories to members, and are shaped by internal relations of dominant and subordinate interests.

One of the more difficult questions for such a view of 'Europe' is whether it is part of, or a consequence of, globalization. The geo-political and economic realignments taking place, most obviously but not only in the former Soviet bloc, are both driven by global dynamics and are part of the dynamics of globalization at work within Europe. To make sense of these processes we need to be able to grasp how Europe, and more specifically the EU, are complex rather than simple formations. It is, I think, at least arguable that the EU has been a force of globalization; a defence against globalization and a response to globalization (see Deacon below, Chapter 4). To focus on only one of these would miss both the complexity of 'Europe' and the complexity of globalization. The EU has played a role in developing national economies, coordinating them as a trading bloc and trying to manage the insertion of that bloc into an emerging global economy. At the core of that project has been a concern to establish the trade, fiscal and political arrangements for properly functioning markets, including a reduction in national 'peculiarities' that might block or inhibit 'normal' capital formation and accumulation. As Hudson and Williams suggest, 'the EU was discursively constructed as a model of liberal capitalism' (1999, p. 6). But it was a model of liberal capitalism that also saw the formation of a regional bloc as a means of defending the region and its national economies against the disruptive dynamics of an emergent – neo-liberal – global economy. 'Europe' – as a region, an agglomeration of nations, and a 'civilization' – was viewed as in need of protection against a globalization that was US-centred economically, politically and culturally. Europe, then, might be thought of as hinge – providing both the point of insertion into the 'global' and the point of resistance and accommodation. At the same time, we should not forget that this Europe is internally contested, not least by different 'models' of how its insertion or accommodation to the 'global' should best be accomplished. Here, one might note that the supposed death of social democracy has apparently been overtaken by a proliferation of would-be social democracies (such as the Scandinavian, French, German, Spanish and even that peculiar Anglo-American hybrid 'third way').

Living with Uncertainty: The Benefits of Deconstruction?

This chapter does not claim to offer any distinctively new knowledge about Europe, welfare states or globalization. Rather, it insists on the difficulty of thinking about what we already know. My argument here is an insistence on the importance of not thinking 'one-sidedly'. In particular, I want to emphasize three dimensions along which these issues need complicated thinking. The first concerns the need to think about both the 'solidity' and 'fragility' of institutional formations, whether they be the European Union, a welfare state or social groups, such as 'minority ethnic communities'. They are all 'socially constructed'. While social constructionism has been accused of over-emphasizing the fragile, fluid and plastic nature of social arrangements, it provides a valuable counterweight to social analyses that 'forget' both how institutions are produced and how contingent they may be (this argument is taken further in Clarke, 1999).

The second, and related, issue concerns how to think of social institutions as 'unities in difference'. The tendency of social constructionist or post-structuralist analyses is to decompose unities – to reveal the differences concealed by over-unified or essentializing conceptions of groups, identities or institutions. Whether those unities are 'Europe', the 'German people', or 'women', they are unities that contain, manage and keep quiet about differences within their constituent elements (as well those that are excluded). However, the process of deconstruction – or decomposing – such unities does not mean that they disappear or that they no longer have any social or political purchase. The analytical challenge is to understand how they are produced out of difference (and how they suppress difference in their announcement of their unity) while understanding how they also enable identification, allegiance and action.

The third and final issue concerns how this approach is a necessary counterweight to the role that political economy has played in debates about welfare states and globalization (see also Gibson-Graham, 1996 for a more developed critique). As posed by political economy, questions about the meeting of globalization and welfare states will only be posed in a limited frame of reference. That is because political economy can only form a one-sided view of globalization as economic processes or dynamics. It is also because it can only form a one-sided view of welfare states as political-economic institutions. I do not want to suggest that these questions are irrelevant because they are one-sided. But I do want to insist that they fail to exhaust what is, or ought to be, of interest and import about the relationship between globalization and welfare states. So, let me offer some closing suggestions of questions that might be posed.

We need to think about the intersection between globalization and welfare states as being internal as well as external to nation-states (as this book demonstrates). For example, if the economic dynamics of globalization create new forms of paid work and new groups of labour, then these form integral features of a changing gender/work/family 'nexus' that bears on welfare states. Similarly, if the economic and political dynamics of globalization produce new trajectories and forms of migration into and within Europe, there are vital questions about citizenship, membership and rights to benefits and services within national welfare states and the EU that will be contested and conflictual. In the process, we can expect to see intensified conflict around questions of 'culture', ethnicity and identity, together with the potential racialization of some migrant groups (Clarke, 1999; Ross, 1998; White, 1999).

We also need to recognize the ways in which the alignments of Nation, State and Welfare have been disturbed and their implications for new welfare arrangements. The pressures on welfare may be represented as primarily 'economic' – incarnated as the 'taxpayer revolt' on the one hand and the intemperate hunger of corporate capital on the other. Nevertheless, both domestic and supra-national pressures of other kinds do not simply point to retrenchment of welfare provisions. Some of the 'unsettling' dynamics result from 'local' challenges to the terms of the old welfare settlements – most noticeably in the refusals by significant groups to accept the status of 'second-class citizens'. It might be worth noting that some of those refusals and their challenges to national welfare states are also articulated as international movements, alliances and identifications. In some instances, particularly in equality struggles around gender, disability and sexuality, they have also used supra-national institutions to challenge nation-states. Similarly, the European Court of Human Rights has provided a forum for challenging discriminatory policies and practices of European states.

Most of all, though, we need to be able to insist that none of these dynamics, pressures and changes is ever 'purely economic'. They cannot be thought of as taking place outside of geography – or at least the geopolitical places, boundaries and territories that are fixed and yet can be remade (Massey, 1999). They cannot be thought of as abstract economic forces. Rather, they are embodied in organizations (whether corporate headquarters or the World Bank or the European Union). They are expressed in the institutionalized wisdoms of expert, popular and political discourses. Such discourses – and the organizations through which they are spoken – articulate views about the nature of desirable social orders, as well as desirable economic regimes. Nor are these economic processes and dynamics separate from 'culture' – however much some may wish to attribute to them the irresistible force of Nature. At the very least, the 'economy' has to pass through the socio-cultural realm to realize itself. It has to be someplace; it has to employ somebody; it has to make, do or transmit something; it has to find some other body who wants its something. In its efforts to be, do and sell, the 'economy' is fated to encounter difficult social, cultural and political materials. Our analyses would do well to pay attention to those and not reproduce the illusion of the disembodied economy.

Notes

1. This chapter owes much to conversations with my colleagues at the Open University, particularly Doreen Massey, Gail Lewis and Sharon Gewirtz. An earlier draft has been much improved by thought-provoking comments from the editors and from Larry Grossberg.
2. In my more optimistic moments I think this may be a point at which Marxist and Foucauldian approaches might be forced to meet. Marxist analyses would bring ideas about 'expanded reproduction' (acknowledging the complex and contradictory character of processes of reproduction) while Foucauldians would bring an understanding of the rich complexity of the 'populations' being reproduced. Both might have to give something up in the process, though.

3

Globalization, Economic Change and the Welfare State: The 'Vexatious Inquisition of Taxation'?

COLIN HAY[1]

Introduction

It has become something of a popular truism that globalization spells if not quite the passing of the nation-state itself, then the demise of inclusive social provision and with it the welfare state. The competitive imperatives of a borderless world characterized by the near perfect mobility of the factors of production, it is frequently assumed, reveal the welfare state of the post-war period to be an indulgent luxury of a bygone era. Along with Keynesianism, social democracy and encompassing labour-market institutions it must now be sacrificed, if it has not already been sacrificed, on the altar of the competitive imperative – a further casualty of the 'harsh economic realities' summoned by globalization.

Invariably such portentous accounts take the form of a dualistic history: of 'old times' and 'new times', then and now. Once upon a time, when European economies were closed, macroeconomic policy was Keynesian and capital bore a national stamp, the welfare state provided a series of positive externalities, principally wage restraint in return for investment incentives and a social wage. This, in turn, served to establish and sustain a virtuous cycle of high demand, high productivity, high growth. How times have changed. With open economies, a distinctly post-Keynesian ideational environment and heightened capital mobility, positive externalities have given way to negative externalities. The welfare state is now widely held to represent a burden on competitiveness, a burden manifest in punitive levels of taxation and assorted labour-market (and broader supply-side) rigidities. These can only impede the proper functioning of the market and with it the competitive and comparative advantage of the economy (see, classically, Fisher, 1930, 1935; Gilder, 1981; Okun, 1975; for the contemporary centre-left variant, see, for instance, Cerny, 1997; Kurzer, 1993; Scharpf, 1991). This, at any rate, is the now conventional orthodoxy. It is the wisdom of this view that I question in this chapter.

The near-dominant notion of the corrosive impact of economic global-ization on the welfare state might lead one to expect unequivocal and unambiguous evidence of systematic welfare retrenchment across the advanced capitalist economies. Yet the empirical record could scarcely be more difficult to reconcile with the conventional wisdom. For not only is (aggregate) evidence of welfare retrenchment, far less *systematic* welfare retrenchment, quite difficult to find; the positive correlation between social expenditure and economic openness first observed by Cameron (1978) has only strengthened under conditions of globalization (Garrett, 1998; Rodrik, 1997). These are points to which we return in detail below. Suffice it for now to note that they present something of a paradox: a widely accepted conception not only of welfare retrenchment but of the *necessity* of welfare retrenchment which seems to stand in marked contrast to the available empirical evidence. There are at least four potential solutions to this conundrum:

1. That the conventional wisdom on the subject is indeed correct, that the welfare state represents a drain on competitiveness in an era of global-ization and the competition state (Cerny, 1990, 1997), but that the institutional and cultural architecture of the welfare state has become so entrenched and embedded as to make its reform and retrenchment an iterative and incremental yet cumulative process down which we are now only slowly embarking (Pierson, 1994, 1996);
2. That the conventional wisdom is simply inaccurate and that far from representing a drain on competitiveness, the welfare state (at least in certain institutional and cultural environments) retains and acquires yet further positive externalities (Barr, 1998; Esping-Andersen, 1994; Finegold and Soskice, 1988; Garrett, 1998; Gough, 1996; Pfaller *et al.*, 1991; cf. Polanyi, 1944);
3. That the aggregate empirical evidence in fact masks the actual degree of retrenchment and that once we control for demographic and other

'welfare inflationary' pressures, observed welfare expenditure is in fact substantially below that we would anticipate (Esping-Andersen, 1996b, 1996c; Rhodes, 1996, 1997b);

4. That, once again, the aggregate evidence masks the degree of real retrenchment since the market-conforming nature of that process has served to increase welfare pressures by effectively trading inflation for unemployment. Consequently, although aggregate spending has proved 'sticky', once we control for increased welfare demand we observe both a narrowing of the scope of social provision and retrenchment in terms of the value of benefits to claimants (Ferrera, 1998; A. Martin, 1997; Rhodes, 1997b).

Each of these perspectives, that will be discussed further below, injects a healthy dose of scepticism and some long-overdue theoretical sophistication, analytical clarity and empirical detail into the invariably over-inflated, grossly exaggerated and seldom defended claims of the orthodox view. As we shall see, there is something in each of the arguments briefly sketched above. Moreover, they are by no means incompatible. Whilst one must in the end choose between accounts suggesting that globalization imposes pressures for welfare retrenchment (as in position 1) and those which see a potentially competitiveness-enhancing role for the welfare state (as in position 2), it is important that we acknowledge the attenuating and/or mediating role of institutional factors. Similarly, while authors may differ over the strict composition of welfare inflationary pressures in contemporary societies – with some attributing these to long-term demographic trends (position 3), others to short-term political factors (position 4), and yet others to a combination of the two – it is equally important that we qualify the impression given by the aggregate data of a simple tendency for social expenditure to grow.

In the pages that follow I seek to defend these claims. I argue that:

1. there has indeed been significant welfare retrenchment and reform in recent years in contemporary Europe;
2. such retrenchment has been informed to a considerable extent by impressions of the 'competitiveness-corrosive' qualities of social spending; but
3. such impressions, however paradoxically, have come at a time when evidence of the 'competitiveness-enhancing' qualities of the welfare state have become ever more transparent.

The argument proceeds in four sections. In the first of these I assess the scale of welfare retrenchment in contemporary Europe before moving, in the second, to assess and evaluate the orthodox view in the light of such evidence. In the third section, I attempt to draw up a more balanced assessment of the positive and negative externalities of the welfare state in the competitive environment of the contemporary global political economy. I conclude by considering the prospects for the welfare state in an era of putative globalization. In particular, I focus on the consequences for the form and function of the welfare state of the stark choice currently facing European economies between cost competitive and quality competitive strategies.

The Scope and Scale of Welfare Retrenchment

However intuitively appealing the familiar argument that globalization drives an inexorable process of welfare retrenchment, it is surely tempting to conclude on the basis of the merest glance at the (aggregate) empirical data that there is simply nothing to explain. For, as Table 3.1 demonstrates, the secular tendency of government expenditure to rise does not appear to have been tempered in recent years. Even in the face of consecutive self-professedly radical neo-liberal regimes set on 'rolling back the frontiers of the state' (as, for instance, in Britain), social expenditure has not only held up rather well, but it now accounts for a greater proportion of national resources than ever before (Pierson, 1994, 1996). A certain degree of caution is nonetheless appropriate before we conclude that

TABLE 3.1   *The secular tendency of state expenditure to rise, 1970–95*
             (% of GDP)

	Government expenditure (% of GDP)								
	DK	*G**	*F*	*IRE*	*I*	*NL*	*SW*	*UK*	*EU15*
1970	36.1	32.4	33.9	30.1	28.3	36.2	36.8	31.9	31.4
1975	42.4	43.1	35.4	38.8	34.7	45.4	44.6	37.6	35.4
1980	50.8	42.7	42.8	41.4	37.9	51.1	56.8	40.2	41.8
1985	55.2	43.4	49.4	47.4	45.3	53.5	61.1	41.8	45.8
1990	55.5	42.0	46.5	38.5	48.6	51.5	58.4	36.6	44.4**
1995	58.2	46.3	51.0	37.4	49.2	49.0	64.7	41.0	47.6**

*West Germany (1970–90)   **excluding Luxembourg.
Source: European Commission (1996, pp. 190–1, table 71).

globalization has had and is likely to have no impact upon the welfare state. A number of points might here be made.

First, as noted above, we should be somewhat wary of the aggregate nature of this data, for it can give us no picture of the changing *composition* of social expenditure. It may well be that quantitative continuity masks qualitative discontinuity – the welfare state has certainly grown in size yet this in no way excludes the possibility of a quite fundamental transformation in its very form and function (see, for instance, Jessop, 1994b). Moreover, even were we prepared to accept on the basis of such evidence that the welfare states which came to characterize the post-war period remain essentially intact today, this need not imply an unambiguous rejection of the globalization thesis.

For, as a number of new institutionalists have noted in recent years (see especially Esping-Andersen, 1990, 1994: pp. 23, 267, 1996b, 1996c, 1999; Pierson, 1994, 1996; Skocpol and Amenta, 1988), welfare states once established become embedded and entrenched. Consequently, whilst globalization may bring certain pressures for retrenchment to bear upon contemporary welfare regimes, the process by which such pressures are translated into outcomes is itself likely to prove lengthy and protracted, producing iterative yet cumulative directional change (Pierson, 1996, pp. 178–9). By such a view, the effects of globalization are far from being fully realized.

Yet this does not leave the globalization orthodoxy entirely unscathed. For if, as we are so frequently entreated, inclusive welfare regimes can only be sustained at considerable cost to economic competitiveness, then we would expect to see this secular tendency for social spending to rise to be accompanied by an alarming depreciation in economic performance. Globalization, so the argument goes, unleashes a competitive firestorm fuelled by flows of capital in which only the fittest – and leanest – survive. If global markets clear as instantaneously as casual neoclassicists presume, then we would expect current levels of welfare expenditure within the EU to be unsustainable and to precipitate a haemorrhaging of both investment and portfolio capital. Yet again, however, the empirical evidence simply does not support this abstract and neo-Darwinian logic of downward harmonization and competitive deregulation (for more detailed empirical elaboration, see Hay, 1999a, 1999b).

Despite the tendency for social expenditure to rise, however, there may still be reasons for suggesting that welfare retrenchment is under way. Indeed, if we are prepared to relativize the notion of retrenchment so as to take account of fluctuations in demand, then there is in fact fairly unambiguous evidence of retrenchment across the advanced capitalist economies. Two rather separate issues need to be identified. The first relates to the unemployment–inflation trade-off; the second to demographic and other socio-economic welfare inflationary pressures.

The Unemployment–Inflation Trade-off

Since the late 1970s something of a paradigm shift in economic policy-making has occurred, associated with the widely perceived crisis of Keynesianism and the growing ascendency of monetarism and supply-side economics (see, for instance, Hall, 1993; Scharpf, 1991). This was associated, in turn, with a much greater emphasis upon inflation-targeting, balanced budgets and fiscal austerity with a consequent respecification of the terms of the post-war social compromise with labour. Accordingly, unemployment throughout the advanced capitalist economies has risen, alarmingly in the case of the northern European economies. This has placed a considerable additional burden upon the welfare state – an ironic and perverse consequence of the marketization and liberalization heralded as a solution to the fiscal crisis of the state in the 1970s. Were it not then for a noticeable tightening of eligibility criteria, a greater emphasis upon benefit targeting and means-testing and the more general development of what might be termed a 'conditional welfare state' stressing the obligations and duties of claimants, we would expect far more than a merely secular tendency for social expenditure to rise (Esping-Andersen, 1996d; Ferrera, 1998; Hagen, 1992; Jordan, 1998; Ormerod, 1998; Rhodes, 1997b; Stephens, 1996; Stephens, Huber and Ray, 1999). The difference between expected welfare expenditure (assuming consistent income replacement ratios and eligibility criteria) and that observed provides a rough index of the extent of effective welfare retrenchment (see Figure 3.1).

A further indication of the degree of welfare retrenchment is provided by *income replacement ratios*. These express the value of welfare entitlements (such as unemployment, sickness and disability benefits) as a percentage of the average net (post-tax) working wage. Throughout the advanced capitalist economies they display a common and marked downward trajectory from a range of start dates (earlier in the liberal countries, later in the social democratic countries) and a variety of initial levels (lower in the liberal regimes, higher in the social democratic regimes) (see, for instance, Clark, 1999; Esping-Andersen, 1996d; Hagen, 1992; Stephens *et al.*, 1999).

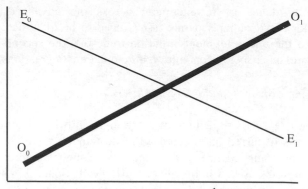

$E_0 - E_1$ expected correlation

$O_0 - O_1$ observed correlation (Cameron, 1978; Rodrik, 1996, 1997)

FIGURE 3.1   *Openness and stateness: rhetoric and reality*

Endogenous Welfare-Inflationary Pressures

The increase in the rate of unemployment in Europe since the post-war period is not, however, the only demand-side factor which might account for mounting pressure on the contemporary welfare state. At least three additional and, for the most part, endogenous variables must be considered if we are adequately to assess the extent to which the welfare state is under threat and the precise nature of the challenge it faces. These are: (i) demographic change; (ii) the escalating cost of state-of-the-art health provision; and (iii) the persistence of low rates of economic growth.

1. The 'demographic timebomb'. If globalization is a largely intangible and hotly contested factor in the causal mêlée out of which we might account for welfare retrenchment, the same is not the case with demographic change. The problem is simply stated: Europe has a rapidly ageing population due to the inauspicious combination of declining birth rates and greater life expectancy. Accordingly, the ratio of net welfare recipi-

ents to net welfare contributors is higher than ever before and rising inex-
orably. This presents an alarming fiscal predicament only likely to be
exacerbated by developments in medical technology and by a projected
further fall in the birth rate (see Figure 3.2).

As Rhodes notes, according to EC data, 'in 1995 around 15 per cent of
the population of the EU were aged 65 or over, [equivalent] to 23 per cent
of the working-age population (15 to 64). By 2005 the over 65s will rise to
26 per cent of the working-age population and to 30 per cent by 2015
[40 per cent in Italy]' (1997b, p. 64; see also Taylor-Gooby, 1999).
Clearly this represents a significant, escalating and potentially crippling
burden on welfare regimes in contemporary Europe.[2]

2. The cost of health provision. A related tendency is that of escalating
health care demand, a consequence again of an ageing population and a
population whose ageing is to a significant extent made possible by expensive and often interventionist medical practices and procedures. According
to OECD statistics (Oxley and Macfarlan, 1995), the share of GDP

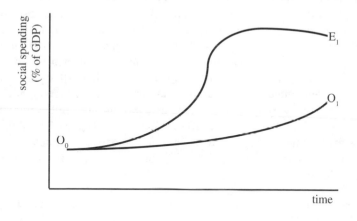

$O_0 - E_1$ expected

$O_0 - O_1$ observed

FIGURE 3.2   *Expected welfare expenditure assuming consistent levels of social
provision and observed rate of unemployment*

accounted for by health expenditure has doubled since the early 1960s and is set to do so again by 2020. Quite apart from new demands, Rhodes is surely right to note that 'the health care sector, broadly defined, contains its own inflationary dynamic' (1997b, p. 64). Yet, were a privatization of health care considered the solution, it should be noted that:

- market provision invariably proves more expensive per capita for a given level of care than public provision (the comparison between Canada and the US is a clear case in point: see Aaron, 1991; Barr, 1998, pp. 277–318); and
- non-mandatory occupational health insurance schemes may impose significant constraints on labour market mobility and hence flexibility.[3]

3. The cost of deflation. A third, and equally significant domestic/ endogenous factor is simply the combination of low economic growth and high unemployment. Since the 1970s, the advanced capitalist economies have failed to secure the conditions for the high and stable rates of economic growth to which they became accustomed in the early post-war period (1945–70). The resulting low growth–high unemployment environment in which inflation has been held down only by shrinking and deflating the domestic economy renders a welfare state premised upon the principle of full employment extremely costly. Moreover, this cost is born disproportionately by capital which, so conventional wisdom goes, pays a high price for the generosity of welfare provision and the institutionalized rigidity of a comprehensive welfare state once established. As Andrew Martin notes, 'the proposition that the viability of the welfare state is contingent on full employment is familiar and presumably generally accepted – it is hard to think of welfare states as anything but "full employment welfare states" or "Keynesian welfare states"' (1997, p. 6). The ability of the welfare state to respond to escalating demands, particularly those associated with an ageing population, is further compounded by low rates of growth. For, as Gøsta Esping-Andersen notes:

> population ageing does not automatically imply crisis ... the cost of ageing depends on long-run productivity growth. The OECD estimates that real earnings growth at an annual average rate of 0.5–1.2 per cent (depending on nation) will suffice to finance the additional pension expenditures. (1996b, p. 7)

This may sound simple enough, yet as he goes on to observe in a footnote:

> the earnings performance of many nations in the past decade suggests that such levels of growth may not be so easily attainable. In the United States, for example,

real manufacturing earnings declined by an annual average of 0.2 per cent during the 1980s. In Europe, where labour shedding has been much more dramatic, productivity and thus wages have grown at higher rates (1.7 per cent in France, 0.9 per cent in Italy, and 2.4 per cent in Germany). (1996b, p. 28, n. 6).

Yet labour-shedding merely compounds the fiscal crisis of the welfare state by increasing the ratio of net welfare recipients to net welfare contributors. In the context of such discussions, the global diffusion of neo-liberalism and with it the global depreciation of growth rates (labour-shedding notwithstanding) is a worrying trend. Identifiable theoretically and observable empirically, such a tendency may serve to translate mounting demographic pressure into a pervasive domestic tide of welfare retrenchment. What this also suggests is that far from being the solution, neo-liberalism may itself be part of the problem. The low growth–escalating demand equation is a difficult one to solve; it may well be that the resuscitation of growth may be a condition for the revivification of the welfare state.

Reassessing the Conventional Wisdom

As the above paragraphs reveal, a quite plausible, compelling and convincing narrative of welfare state retrenchment (or at least of the origins of the pressures for welfare state retrenchment) can be told without reference to exogenous factors so much as to endogenous factors widely experienced (cf. Pierson, 1998). So where does this leave the conventional view so frequently voiced by politicians and academics alike which suggests that it is globalization and the transition from closed to open economies and the flows of capital this has unleashed which have undermined the somewhat indulgent luxuries of the European social model? Is it little more than a convenient alibi, offered as a *post hoc* rationalization for a secular retrenchment already under way and precipitated by rather more immediate and parochial factors?

If we are to assess the impact (if any) of globalization on the viability of the welfare state, it is first essential that we unpack the various logics appealed to and frequently conflated in the claims for incommensurability of inclusive social provision and international competitiveness in an era of deepening economic integration. A series of related, if nonetheless distinct, arguments are frequently invoked, relating to capital mobility, the 'vexatious inquisition of taxation' (Adam Smith) and the need for both flexible labour-markets and a constant supply of cheap malleable labour. It is important that we start by acknowledging what they share. For each exhibits a common analytical-deductive strategy, proceeding on the basis of relatively simple, indeed intuitive, micro-foundations through a process of macro-aggregation and extrapolation, to derive a generic tendency (or series of tendencies) for welfare retrenchment. This is an important point. For, arguably, their common structure reveals a common analytical poverty. Enticing and alluring though the logical deduction of, say, the negative externalities of the welfare state may be, there are dangers in extrapolating so presumptuously from invariably pared-down and institutionally unspecified microfoundations (see also Gough, 1996, p. 224; and, for more general critiques of such 'blackboard economics', Fine, 1998; Sen, 1977). Such microfoundations – those concerning the perfect mobility of the factors of production, for instance – are often difficult to square with the empirical evidence. To generalize and extrapolate from such parsimonious premises in this manner may then merely compound the distorting simplicity of the initial assumptions. The prescriptions derived in this manner (such as the harsh necessity of welfare retrenchment) are only as reliable as the premises on which they are based, and these we know to be dubious. It is crucial then that we: (i) isolate such assumptions, (ii) assess their plausibility, and (iii) consider the sensitivity of orthodox predictions to variations in initial assumptions. This I attempt, albeit briefly, in the following section.

Capital Flight and the 'Vexatious Inquisition of Taxation'

> The ... proprietor of stock is properly a citizen of the world, and is not necessarily attached to any particular country. He would be apt to abandon the country in which he is exposed to a vexatious inquisition, in order to be assessed a burdensome tax, and would remove his stock to some country where he could either carry on his business or enjoy his fortune at his ease. A tax that tended to drive away stock from a particular country, would so far tend to dry up every source of revenue, both to the sovereign and to the society. Not only the profits of stock, but the rent of land and the wages of labour, would necessarily be more or less diminished by its removal. (Smith, [1776] 1976, pp. 848–9)

The mobility of capital, specifically the mobility of (foreign) direct investors, is crucial to orthodox accounts which seek to derive what they see as the inexorable logic of welfare retrenchment from globalization. What passes in the name of the conventional wisdom here is relatively simply stated (and is not so very different from that elaborated by Adam Smith in the above passage). In the (stylized) closed economies of the initial post-war period, capital enjoyed no exit option. Consequently, governments enjoyed the ability to impose punitive taxation regimes upon unwilling and relatively impotent national capitals with little cost to the domestic economy (except for the tendency for capitalists to accumulate rather than to reinvest their profits). With financial liberalization and the elimination of capital controls under open economy conditions, this is no longer the case. Capital may now exit from national economic environments at minimal cost (indeed, in most neoclassical-inspired models, at zero cost).

Accordingly, by playing off the regulatory regimes of different economies against one another, capital can ensure for itself a higher rate of return on its investment. This it does by seeking out the high growth regimes of newly industrialized countries unencumbered by burdensome welfare traditions, rigid labour-market institutions and correspondingly higher rates of taxation. Similarly, mobile ('footloose') foreign direct investors can seek out low taxation regimes and cheap labour whilst securing for themselves attractive relocation packages, tax concessions and other subsidies as competitive national economies (and, indeed, local and regional economies) are effectively forced to compete through a process of 'social dumping' and 'competitive deregulation'. This logic threatens to establish a perverse and pathological 'race to the bottom' (Marquand, 1994, p. 18) lubricated by the 'deregulatory arbitrage' of footloose and fancy-free trans-national corporations. As Duane Swank notes, for both neo-liberal economists and analytical Marxists alike, the structural power of capital has been increased. This generates a 'prisoner's dilemma' for policy-makers. For, 'in the face of inherent impediments to international policy coordination, governments face incentives to engage in competition for investment' (1998, p. 676). The demise of the welfare state is not difficult to derive from such a logic. For, according to such a view, the welfare state represents, quite simply, a cost to capital (in the form of a direct or indirect taxation premium) and hence a drain on national competitiveness. Consequently, centre-left/social democratic administrations, if they are not to precipitate a haemorrhaging of investment and portfolio capital on their election (indeed, in the very anticipation of their election) must convince capital of their fiscal prudence and moderation in advance (Przeworski and Wallerstein, 1988; Wickham-Jones, 1995). It is perhaps chastening at this point to note that, on the basis of such (standard neoclassical) assumptions, the optimal rate of taxation on income from capital in small open economies tends to zero (Razin and Sadka, 1991a, 1991b; Tanzi and Zee, 1997; Tanzi and Schuknecht, 1997).

The policy implications of such an account are painfully clear. As globalization serves to establish competitive selection mechanisms within the international political economy, there is little choice but to cast the welfare state on the bonfire of regulatory controls and labour-market rigidities. Compelling though such an alarming logic may sound, it serves us well to isolate the assumptions which ultimately summon this simple 'logic of no alternative' (see also Hay, 1998; Watson, 1999). They are principally fourfold:

1. That capital invests where it can secure the greatest net return on that investment and is possessed of perfect information of the means by which to maximise this utility;
2. That capital enjoys perfect mobility and that the cost of exit is zero;
3. That capital will invariably secure the greatest return on its investment through minimizing its labour costs by seeking out a captive supply of cheap labour in flexible and deregulated labour markets and by relocating its productive activities in economies with the lowest rates of corporate taxation.

This third assumption leads fairly directly to a fourth and final assumption:

4. That the welfare state (and the taxation receipts out of which it is funded) represent nothing other than lost capital to mobile asset holders and have no positive (or even potentially positive) externalities for the competitiveness and productivity of the national economy.

Each of these foundational premises is at best dubious, at worst demonstrably false. Consider each in turn. Whilst it may seem entirely appropriate to attribute to capital the sole motive of seeking the greatest return on its investment, the history of specific capitals hardly engenders much confidence in the additional assumption that capital is blessed with perfect information of the means by which to realize that objective. Nonetheless, this is perhaps the least problematic of the assumptions considered here and the least consequential for the present analysis.

The second assumption is demonstrably false – or, at least, demonstrably false for certain types of capital. For whilst portfolio capital may indeed exhibit almost perfect mobility – its effectively instantaneous flows conducted in the flickering of a cursor and incurring negligible exit costs –

the same is simply not the case with *invested* as distinct from (potential) *investment* capital. For, once enticed and attracted to a particular locality, formerly mobile foreign direct investment flows 'bed down', acquiring an array of significant sunk costs (however subsidized by their 'hosts') as virtual/immaterial assets are translated into human and physical capital (Watson, 1997). Consequently, once installed, exit options become seriously depleted and incur significant loss (in terms of irredeemable sunk costs). Thus, whilst it may be entirely 'rational' for foreign direct investors to proclaim loudly and exaggerate wildly their mobility and their much-vaunted exit options – especially if they can make these sound credible – it is not surprising that the threat of exit is so rarely acted upon (Hay, 1997). What we do witness, however, is the quite predictable phenomenon of what might be termed an 'exit threat business cycle', indicative perhaps of the hollowness of most exit threats.

What this in turn suggests is that the haemorrhaging of invested capital predicted by standard neoclassical models of open economies in which governments fail to internalize the preferences of capital for minimal social protection are grossly exaggerated. They summon a seemingly inexorable logic of welfare retrenchment which is simply unwarranted and whose logic of compulsion can be attributed and traced directly to the implausibility of the initial assumptions. Once we revise such, frankly false, initial premises, a much higher 'burden' of corporate taxation would appear sustainable, consistent with current levels of social expenditure in Europe (Boix, 1998; Locke and Kochan, 1995; Swank, 1998). As Swank again notes, 'contrary to the claims of the international capital mobility thesis ... the general fiscal capacity of democratic governments to fund a variety of levels and mixes of social protection and services may be relatively resilient in the face of internationalisation of markets' (1999, p. 325). Here it is perhaps instructive to note that despite a marked tendency for direct corporate taxation to fall in recent years in line with the predictions of such neoclassical-inspired models, the overall burden of taxation on firms has in fact remained fairly constant, rising marginally since the mid-1980s (Swank, 1998, 1999).

Yet this does not exhaust the problems of the international capital mobility thesis – not by a long way. For perhaps most problematic of all are assumptions three and four – that capital can only compete in a more intensely competitive environment on the basis of productivity gains secured through tax reductions (whether achieved through domestic political pressure such as the threat of exit, or exit itself) and cost-shedding (through rationalization, downsizing and the proletarianization of labour).

This is a distinctly and peculiarly Anglo-US conception of competitiveness, though one ever more intimately associated with the political discourse of globalization (Watson, 1997).

As we shall see, its considerable limitations are clearly exposed if we seek to draw up a balance sheet of the competitive merits and demerits of the contemporary welfare state.

A Competitive Audit of the Welfare State

Here we can usefully develop, adapt and extend the work of Ian Gough who, in a thorough and perceptive article (1996), assesses the full range of arguments which might be brought to bear upon the complex relationship between the welfare state and international competitiveness (see also Pfaller *et al.*, 1991). Things are considerably more complex than the orthodox globalization thesis would have us believe, for a whole variety of both positive and negative externalities might be identified. At the very least, this suggests that the orthodox account that presents welfare expenditure simply as a drain on competitiveness is a gross and distorting simplification of a far more complex and contingent reality.

Negative Externalities: The 'Competitiveness-Corrosive' Consequences of the Welfare State

As I have been at pains to demonstrate, the conventional orthodoxy tends to posit a simple trade-off between equality and efficiency, such that (redistributive) welfare expenditure comes at a direct cost to economic competitiveness. In addition to the arguments reviewed above, a variety of negative (or 'competitive corrosive') externalities of welfare expenditure – direct and indirect – are identified in this literature. They are summarized in Table 3.2. Due to constraints of space they are not reviewed here (though, for a fuller discussion, see Hay, 1999b). Suffice it to note that the evidence is by no means unequivocal.

At this stage, the economic case for the net competitiveness-corrosive externalities of the welfare state might look impressive. The two most compelling cases are perhaps the first, identifying a tendency for government borrowing to inject inflationary pressures into the economy, and the third, suggesting that the direct and indirect taxation burden associated with social provision increases the cost of labour. Interestingly, however, both of these tendencies are likely to be unevenly distributed amongst

TABLE 3.2   *Negative externalities of welfare expenditure*

	Cost/supply of capital	*Cost/supply of labour*	*Productivity of capital and labour*
Expenditure/ taxation (indirect effects)	1. Borrowing crowds out investment 2. Social costs encourage capital flight	3. Direct taxes increase labour cost and reduce supply	—
Social programmes (direct effects)	4. PAYE (pay-as-you-earn) pensions reduce savings	5. State pensions and unemployment and sickness benefits reduce labour supply	6. Public sector social provision less efficient

Source: Inspired by and adapted from Gough (1996, p. 217).

welfare states. For, arguably, the presence of encompassing labour-market institutions and a social democratic tradition of coordinated national wage bargaining attenuates pressures for wage-push inflation that may be present in more liberal welfare regimes. Moreover, as noted above, tax-induced additional labour costs tend to have a minimal impact on economies which compete in capital-intensive and quality competitive sectors. For labour costs represent a tiny fraction of the overall production costs and it is quality and innovation rather than cost that is most likely to confer a competitive advantage.

What this in turn suggests is that the balance between competitive-enhancing and competitive-corrosive externalities is likely to be mediated by institutional factors. Principal amongst these are the degree of encompassment of the wage-bargaining regime and what might be termed the 'regime of competitiveness' of the economy as a whole. For economies competing solely on the basis of cost in low-skill, labour-intensive industries, the welfare state is a clear burden on competitiveness, whilst for those seeking to pave a high-tech, high-skill route to competitiveness in capital-intensive sectors, any such negative externalities are significantly attenuated. That this is so becomes rather more transparent if we turn from the debit to the credit column of the welfare state's competitiveness audit.

Positive Externalities: The 'Competitiveness-Enhancing' Consequences of the Welfare State

Given the now pervasive orthodoxy, we might expect to find little in the way of hypothesized competitive-enhancing externalities associated with inclusive social provision. Yet what is most striking given the ascendancy of the conventional wisdom, is the sheer range and diversity of factors, even in quite mainstream economic analysis, pointing to the potential contribution of the welfare state to competitiveness in export markets. These are presented schematically in Table 3.3 (for a fuller discussion, see Hay, 1999b).

1. Macroeconomic stabilization effects. High levels of social expenditure will tend to promote economic stability insofar as they have the counter-cyclical economic effects. This is particularly the case with unemployment benefits which (higher underlying rates of structural unemployment notwithstanding) will tend to bolster demand in times of recession. Similarly, transfer payments to the working class are more likely to stimulate consumption (and hence demand) than tax concessions to the middle classes. Consequently, redistributive welfare regimes, particularly those prepared to inject demand into the economy during times of recession, are likely to facilitate macroeconomic stabilization across the economic cycle.

2. Public housing provision boosts consumption. The subsidization or direct provision of housing frees capital for consumption, thereby raising the aggregate level of demand within the economy.

3. Support for women's employment increases supply of labour. Quite simply, the provision of nursery places and pre-school care is likely to facilitate access (particularly that of women) to the labour-market and hence to improve the supply of labour with consequent benefits for the productivity of the economy. Moreover, where access to the labour-market can be facilitated in this way (as, for instance, in Sweden in recent years), the ratio of net welfare contributors to net welfare recipients will increase, easing fiscal pressures generated by demographic change.

4. Human capital is enhanced through education and training. As Gough notes, most contemporary variants of the competitiveness-enhancing view of the welfare state focus on its supply-side contribution (1996, p. 222). Human capital theory is far the most influential current strand of thought

TABLE 3.3 *Positive externalities of welfare expenditure*

	Cost/supply of capital	*Cost/supply of labour*	*Productivity of capital and labour*
Macroeconomic effects		1. Macroeconomic stabilization effects	
Social programmes (direct effects)	2. Public social provision boosts consumption	3. Support for women's employment increases supply of labour	4. Human capital enhanced through education and training
Welfare outcomes (indirect effects)	5. Social inclusion tempers criminality; crime deters investment	6. Reduced costs of ill health	7. Contribution to internal work-place flexibility (trust and reduced transaction costs)

Source: Inspired by and adapted from Gough (1996, p. 217).

in this area (Allmendinger, 1989; Ashton and Green, 1996; Bosworth, Dawkins and Stromback, 1996, pp. 211–52; Finegold and Soskice, 1988; Lucas, 1988; Prais and Wagner, 1987). In an era of heightened competition, it argues, the skill level of the economy is crucial. Here the welfare state has a central role to play, ensuring flexible high-quality training and reskilling programmes oriented directly towards the delivery of the skills required by the economy. The implications of such a theory are that welfare retrenchment, though frequently couched in terms of competitiveness, may come at a considerable price in terms of the ability of the domestic economy to compete on any basis other than cost alone in international markets.

5. *Social inclusion tempers criminality; crime deters investment.* Consequently, a cost–benefit analysis of welfare retrenchment which fails to take account of the likely cost (both substantive and qualitative) of heightened levels of criminality is wholly inadequate. Costs which must be considered include the expense of incarceration and law enforcement, the cost to child development of crime and social dislocation and the cost to capital of excessive insurance premiums in high crime areas. Once such costs are factored in, the suggestion that competitiveness may be enhanced by welfare retrenchment is rendered, at best, equivocal. The US provides a case in point. For, as recent research demonstrates, if the incarcerated are counted among the ranks of the unemployed, the US male jobless rate rises to a level above the European average for most of the period since 1975 (Western, Beckett and Harding, 1998; Western and Beckett, 1998). Moreover, since the job prospects of ex-convicts are significantly eroded such that they invariably leave prison to join the ranks of the long-term unemployed, the impressive employment performance of the US in the 1980s and 1990s has in fact depended in large part on a high and increasing incarceration rate (Western and Beckett, 1999). Moreover, by Bowles and Gintis's calculations, one-quarter of all labour employed in the US is 'guard labour' (1994).

6. *Reduced costs of ill health.* Poor health, arising from under-insurance or non-insurance in a privately financed system, is likely to disrupt production whilst imposing punitive health care costs (however funded). Consequently, health – as a public good – is best provided by the state and is most efficient when it contains a significant preventative component. Moreover, a redistributive welfare state contributes significantly to a

softening of social stratification (itself closely correlated to poor health) (Wilkinson, 1996). An inclusive state-funded national health service may, then, both decrease the volume of health care demand (through preventative medicine) whilst minimizing the cost of satisfying that demand.

7. *Welfare enhances flexibility via greater trust and reduced transaction costs.* Inclusive welfare states, particularly where associated with encompassing labour-market institutions, encourage relations of cooperation and trust. Significantly, this facilitates internal flexibility – in which workers adapt themselves and their working practices to new demands and new technology – as opposed to external flexibility (i.e. recourse to the labour market). This fosters cooperative relations between managers and labour, with consequent reductions in the rate of labour turnover. This, in turn, is rewarded by higher levels of investment in human capital as workers are less likely to depart with their newly-acquired skills (skills acquired at the company's expense) to the competition.

With each of the above observations, the competitiveness balance-sheet of the welfare state moves further into credit.

Conclusion

What the above discussion serves to suggest is that the relationship between competitiveness and the welfare state is far more complex (and perhaps rather more contingent) than the globalization orthodoxy would have us believe. Nonetheless, this cannot and should not serve to hide the fact that significant welfare retrenchment has occurred and continues apace. That this is so is due, in no small part, to the predominance of a view of the competitiveness-corrosive impact of the welfare state which is at odds with the empirical evidence (on the role of international organizations in the propagation of such a view, see Deacon, Chapter 4 below; on the contested discourse of globalization, see Clarke, Chapter 2 above).

As the analysis of this chapter reveals, however, even this is to present an overly simplified picture. The specific consequences of welfare provision will vary on a case-by-case basis, mediated by a range of institutional and cultural factors. Not the least of these are the scope and scale of welfare provision itself and the 'regime of competitiveness' of the economy as a whole. The chapters in Part II of this book illustrate the significance of these factors very well. Low-cost–low-skill competitiveness in labour-intensive industries places a considerable premium upon externally flexible labour markets and a cheap and voluminous supply of docile (for which read de-unionized and/or demoralized) labour. The welfare state in such a scenario is likely to represent little more than an expensive indulgence – though the social and economic cost of its retrenchment (in terms of the criminalization and marginalization of an underclass) should not be underestimated. Whether out-and-out cost competitiveness represents a viable competitive strategy for any contemporary European economy is debatable. What it does suggest, however, is the stark choice that European economies now face and the significance of that choice for the continued viability of the welfare state. Yet one thing should perhaps be made clear. Europe's most open economies (Britain excepted) have, throughout the post-war period, always sought competitiveness on the basis of quality not cost. They have thus sought to promote internal flexibility within the firm rather than external flexibility in the labour-market, permanent innovation in production as opposed to productivity gains on the basis of hire-and-fire and the elimination of supply-side rigidities, high and stable levels of both human *and* physical capital formation, and inclusive and encompassing labour-market institutions. Within such a model, far from representing a supply-side rigidity, the welfare state is not only a competitive advantage it is a competitive necessity.

Notes

1. I would like to acknowledge the support of the ESRC for research on 'Globalization, European Integration and the European Social Model' (L213252043), research which concentrates on globalization, European integration and welfare/labour market reform in Denmark, Germany, France, Hungary, Ireland, Italy, the Netherlands, Sweden and the UK. I would also like to express gratitude to Pete Alcock, Robert Sykes, Matthew Watson and Daniel Wincott for comments on an earlier version of this chapter.
2. This burden is, however, unevenly distributed and has been responded to differently in different national contexts. For a more extended discussion see Hay (1999b).
3. In the US, for instance, occupationally-insured workers are frequently reluctant to move job because of the risk to their eligibility for medical benefits in a context where private provision is likely to prove punitively expensive.

4

International Organizations, the EU and Global Social Policy

BOB DEACON

Much of the discussion about globalization assumes a certain economic logic which suggests there is an inevitability to the process and form of globalization. It is a 'fact' of life to which governments have to adjust. The contribution of this chapter is to draw attention to the politics of globalization and, in particular, the 'hidden' politics of international organizations such as the Bretton Woods organizations, the WTO, the UN social agencies, the OECD and others. Many of them, it will be argued, have been major players in encouraging a particular neo-liberal form of globalization. While encouraging economic globalization they have been engaged in prescribing a set of social policies which they regard as appropriate in a globalizing context. This is not to say that all international organizations have been speaking with one voice. There has been and continues to be a significant international controversy taking place within and between these organizations as to how far the neo-liberal form of globalization should be allowed to continue and what might be appropriate social policies in the context of globalization. The case for a socially responsible globalization has also been articulated within this global discourse. This seeks to reinvent at a global level those mechanisms of redistribution, regulation and empowerment that national states have traditionally used to ensure the meeting of social objectives.

The chapter is structured as follows. First the global social discourse taking place within and between international organizations is reviewed. Second, the emergence of a case for a socially responsible globalization is noted. Finally, the chapter turns to the contribution of the EU to this global discourse. Within the context of a global struggle of ideas regarding the future of social policy this chapter asks whether the EU is on the side of the angels, putting the case wherever it can on the international stage for a reformed globalization which takes social needs seriously, or is it merely an ally of the proponents of global neo-liberalism?

The Global Social Policy Discourse

Earlier (Deacon *et al.*, 1997) I argued that the IMF regarded welfare expenditure as a burden on the economy favouring a USA *workfare* style safety-net approach to social policy and that the World Bank's focus on poverty alleviation led it also to favour a safety-net approach. Within the ILO and some other UN agencies, on the other hand, were to be found supporters of the view that social expenditures were a means of securing social cohesion. The ILO, in particular, supported a conservative-corporatist or Bismarkian type of social protection. The OECD favoured the notion that certain state welfare expenditures should be regarded as a necessary investment. No international organization, save possibly UNICEF, could be said to defend the redistributive approach to social policy characteristic of the Scandinavian countries. In the study of the role played by such international organizations in shaping post-communist social policy, I previously concluded (Deacon, 1997, p. 197) that the

> opportunity created by the collapse of communism for the global actors to shape the future of social policy has been grasped enthusiastically by the dominant social liberal tendency in the World Bank. In alliance with social development NGOs who are being given a part to play especially in zones of instability, a social safety-net future is being constructed. This NGO support combined with the political support of many southern and some East European governments is challenging powerfully those defenders of universalist and social security based welfare states to be found in the EU, the ILO and in smaller number in the Bank.

These conclusions still broadly stand, although there continue to be interesting shifts in the position of particular players within this debate. The IMF has taken the social dimension of globalization more seriously considering whether some degree of equity is beneficial to economic growth. The Bank has articulated more clearly its risk management approach to social protection in the context of globalization. The OECD now warns that globalization may lead to the need for more, not less social expenditure. The ILO has begun to show signs of making concessions to the Bank's views on social security. More recently, the role of the World Trade Organization and its views on the desirability of fostering a global market in health and social service provision is assuming a prominence it did not have in the past. These developments and others are reviewed briefly below.

The Bank Pursues Safety-Nets and Private Sector Risk Management

The intellectual map of the global discourses about social welfare is more complicated than is suggested by the simple *European social market* (ILO) versus *USA liberalism* (World Bank, IMF) dichotomy. The World Bank's encounter with post-communist regimes led, through the employment by the Bank of professionals more attuned to the European tradition, to a heated controversy about desirable social policies within the operations section of the Bank dealing with Eastern Europe and the former Soviet Union. This controversy continues and has now been imported into the heart of the human resources network inside the reorganized Bank.

Internal reorganization of the World Bank in late 1996 gave rise to an extensive Human Development Network which would design sector strategies and offer its services to the country operations units in specific projects. Within this network are three sector families: (a) health, nutrition and population, (b) education and (c) social protection. The first of these sectors produced its strategy paper in 1997 (World Bank, 1997a), and the social protection sector under the headship of Robert Holzmann delivered its paper in the summer of 2000. Many Bank documents on social policy are infuriatingly ambiguous, and the health sector strategy paper is no exception, containing often mutually contradictory sentiments clearly written as a compromise between several positions. Within the health text there is much to suggest that the Bank is leaving behind some of the worst excesses of a faith in free markets and is learning some of the positive lessons from countries that have primarily public health services. It argues that

> this involvement by the public sector is justified on both theoretical and practical grounds to improve equity, by securing access by the population to health, nutrition and reproductive services; and efficiency, by correcting for market failure, especially where there are significant externalities (public goods) or serious information asymmetries (health insurance) ... the experience in devel-

oped and middle income countries is that universal access is one of the most effective ways to provide health care for the poor.
(World Bank 1997a, pp. 5, 6)

However, by a sleight of hand a conclusion is drawn that a mix of private and public services is required, and, because of presumed resource constraints, the public sector would do best to concentrate on those areas where there are large externalities such as preventive public health services. It also argues that targeting is appropriate in lower income countries. This approach has been supported by a fashion in the Bank for *benefit incidence* studies which show what proportion of public expenditure on health or education benefits each quintile of the population. Since these show that the elite and middle class often consume a disproportionate amount of the services, then, on the grounds of equity, a call is made to target the poor. What seems to escape the human resource specialists in the Bank is the taxability and targeting trade-off: once services become services *for* the poor there is a danger that they become poor *quality* services precisely because the middle class is no longer willing to pay taxes for services from which it does not directly benefit.

It is within the social protection section that the continuation of the dispute between supporters of neo-liberal and more universalistic approaches to social policy continues. The debate between European and American perspectives on social protection policy, which had been confined to the operations section dealing with Eastern Europe, is now situated in the heart of the Bank and will influence its emerging social protection strategy. In its own words the section is 'meeting the challenge of social inclusion' laid down by James Wolfensohn when he said that

> our goal must be to reduce these disparities across and within countries, to bring more people into the economic mainstream, to promote equitable access to the benefits of development regardless of nationality, race, or gender. This ... the Challenge of Inclusion ... is the key development challenge of our time. (Wolfensohn, 1997)

The social protection section says it is meeting the challenge of inclusion by focusing on risk management by helping people to manage risks proactively in their households and communities (Holzmann and Jorgensen, 1999). They are concerned to support measures of risk prevention such as job creation, risk mitigation such as insurance against unemployment, and risk coping such as the provision of targeted benefits. Within this remit it is working on labour market reform, pension reform

and social assistance strategies, including supporting NGO and community social funds in many countries. The strategy is one which emphasizes
an individual's responsibility to insure against the increased risks and
uncertainties of globalization, rather than one that puts emphasis on governmental responsibilities to pool risks and to universalize provision and
regulate the economy. Holzmann concentrates on pension policy (1997)
and has lent his support to a multi-pillar approach to pension reform,
which would reduce the state pay-as-you-go (PAYG) schemes to a
minimal role of basic pension provision, supplemented by a compulsory,
fully-funded and individualized second pillar, and a voluntary third pillar.
He claims to see a consensus emerging between the Bank and the ILO
who have hitherto continued to favour only PAYG schemes.

The debate within the Bank between a more neo-liberal tendency and a
more socially responsible tendency burst into the open twice in 2000 with
the early resignations of the then chief economist Joe Stiglitz and Ravi
Kanbur, editor of the World Bank Development Report 2000 on Poverty.
Both reportedly resigned following interventions in the Bank policy-
making process by Larry Summers, the US Treasury Secretary. Stiglitz
had co-authored (Orgsag and Stiglitz, 1999) a trenchant criticism of the
Bank's support for the privatization of pensions. Kanbur had wanted to
give a greater emphasis to the responsibility of international actors to
regulate globalization.

The IMF Catches Up with the Social Policy Debate

It has been the concern of some that as the Bank develops a greater sensitivity to the social dimensions of structural adjustment it will be left to the
IMF to continue to police the economies of the world, with its traditional
style of unrepentant liberalism, inviting public expenditure cuts regardless
of the social consequences. Two considerations suggest that this is an
oversimplification. Firstly, it has always been the case that there have been
views expressed in IMF working papers that are not at one with the dominant orthodoxy of the time (Chand *et al.*, 1990; Mackenzie, 1990).
Secondly, there is evidence to suggest that the financial crisis in Asia,
amongst other things, has prompted a serious reflection within the IMF
upon the adequacy of its current social policy.

The public response of the IMF to criticisms of its handling of the Asian
economic crisis suggests a more thorough review of policy is in train. As a
follow-up to this the Fiscal Affairs department of the IMF convened a conference on the question of equity and economic policy. The conference

background paper reflects upon the traditional trade-off perceived to be between growth and equity and concludes that evidence points both ways:

> Large scale tax and transfer programs may, in fact, slow growth, but poverty alleviation and universal access to basic health care and education can simultaneously improve equity and enhance the human capital upon which growth depends. (IMF, 1998a)

The conference invited participants to reflect upon whether an international consensus could be forged on a minimum set of equity conditions that should be met. Among the scholars invited to reflect upon this issue were Amartya Sen and Anthony Atkinson who have been associated with views concerning the desirability of universal entitlements to livelihood and universal entitlements to a participation income respectively.

On the other hand, there are indications in the first public statements of the new German Director of the IMF appointed in 2000 that the IMF under his guidance might retreat from mission creep into the social policy field and return to its core task of ensuring macroeconomic stability.

The ILO's Universalism is Challenged by Globalization

The relatively reassuring notion that the nature of future globalization is being worked out by the World Bank and the IMF, and that it includes a renewed concern with social protection measures, is challenged as soon as we examine the perspectives of certain Southern governments. Attempts by the governments of the North to argue for common global labour and social standards are often perceived by Southern states to be self-interested attempts to protect the social welfare securities of people in the Northern developed countries from being undercut by competition from the South. This perception bedevilled the discussions of 1996, when attempts were made to establish social clauses in World Trade agreements. These concerns of Southern governments have limited the capacity of UN agencies to put their weight behind social policies of the kind that have ensured a degree of equity in developed welfare states. The impasse within the ILO when initial moves to argue for inserting social clauses into world trade agreements were derailed by a concerted campaign of some Southern governments is illustrative of this. Reviewing the current situation with regard to this debate, Eddy Lee of the ILO notes 'there is a deep fault line of distrust between industrialized and developing countries ... the existing system of international labour standards as it has evolved through the ILO has, willy-nilly, been caught in the cross-fire of this debate' (Lee, 1997, p. 177).

The positive aspect of this debate is the affirmation by all parties of support for what have come to be known as core labour standards. These are generally regarded to be those contained within ILO conventions 29, 87, 98, 100, 105, 111, and 138 concerned with 'the prohibition of forced labour and child labour, freedom of association and the right to organize and bargain collectively, equal remuneration for men and women for work of equal value, and non-discrimination in employment' (Kyloh, 1998).

Within the context of the global debate about pension policy, the ILO has also felt under pressure from the Bank to make concessions to its views. A recent articulation by the ILO of its new pensions policy (Gillion et al., 2000) uses the language of the Bank and suggests the need for a four-tier pension policy. The first tier would be a state welfare pension which could be either universal or means-tested. The second should be a compulsory PAYG pension. The third should be a mandatory capitalized pension. The fourth would be an additional voluntary savings option. The concession that the first tier could be means-tested, and the acknowledgement that there is a role for individualized and capitalized pensions, suggests that the ILO can no longer be regarded as quite the bulwark against Bretton Woods policies that it was a few years ago.

On the other hand, under the new Directorship of Juan Somavir, the ILO established in 1999 a number of In Focus working groups, one of which is focuses on Socio-Economic Security. This group, under the leadership of Guy Standing, is concerned to encourage a new universalism from below by supporting the introduction of child benefits, initially tied to school attendance, in countries such as Mexico and Brazil. (ILO, 2000)

The OECD Calls for More Social Spending in the Context of Globalization

The OECD report on the crisis in welfare (OECD, 1981) was an important document for those seeking to justify cuts in public social expenditures. It concluded that social policy in many countries creates obstacles to growth. The beginnings of a paradigm shift within the OECD's Secretariat of the Education, Employment and Social Affairs could be noted in its subsequent report (OECD, 1994) endorsed by a Ministerial Conference. It argued for a set of new orientations in social policy which included the propositions that welfare expenditure contributed to economic growth and encouraged and facilitated human development. More recently, the

OECD's analysis *A Caring World* asserts in the context of a review of the impact of globalization that 'one of the effects of globalization could be to increase the demand for social protection ... a more useful blueprint for reform would be to recognize that globalization reinforces the need for some social protection' (OECD, 1999, p. 137).

Moreover, at the OECD meeting of Ministers in June 2000 two important policy initiatives related to globalization were endorsed. One of these updated and strengthened OECD guidance to multilateral companies urging them to adopt core labour and environmental standards wherever they operated within the OECD. Failure to do so would be reported within the countries concerned. The other named and shamed numerous tax havens within and outside the OECD with a view to urging their eradication.

The World Trade Organization Emerges as an Important Player

Objection to the attempt to establish the Multi-Lateral Agreement on Investment (MAI) in 1998 was based upon the perceived unfairness of allowing private providers from other countries to challenge national public social provision or national government subsidy to non-profit providers (Clarke and Barlow, 1997; Sanger, 1998). The full range of health and social service, from child-care centres, not-for-profit hospitals and community clinics, to private labs and independent physicians, would have been covered by the MAI investment obligations. The MAI rules governing the treatment of investors applied to a much broader range of health and social service than does the NAFTA investment chapter. Applying the MAI rules to grants and subsidies would have considerably restricted the ability of national and provincial governments and regional authorities to manage and regulate health and social services by attaching conditions to the receipt of public money. The main pillar of the MAI was the prohibition of discriminatory treatment by one country of investors based in another country which is a party to the MAI. For example, it would have entitled a foreign-based health or social services provider operating in, say, Canada to receive public grants and subsidies on the same terms as a similar Canadian health care provider (see Sanger, 1998).

The issue will resurface within the WTO. A background working paper by the Secretariat of the WTO Council for Trade in Services confirms this (Koivusalo, 1999). The document (WTO, 1998) notes that the forthcoming round 'offers members (of the WTO) the opportunity to reconsider the breadth and depth of their commitments on health and social services, which are currently trailing behind other large sectors'. It notes with approval signs of an increased global trade in health care from developing to developed countries 'with better off-people seeking rapid access to high-quality services abroad'. The document is exercised by the fact that under Article 1:3(c) of the General Agreement on Trade in Services (GATS) services which are provided in the exercise of governmental authority, and provided neither on a commercial basis nor in competition, are excluded from free trade obligations. It goes on to note that 'the coexistence of private and public hospitals may raise questions, however, concerning their competitive relationship and the applicability of the GATS'. Indeed it argues that it is unrealistic to argue for the continued application of Article 1:3 to these situations. This seems to confirm the concerns of Sanger noted above. Despite the derailing of the new trade talks in Seattle in 1999 and the failure to reach any agreement, the issue of trade in services will resurface within the ongoing WTO discussions.

Progress Towards a 'Socially Responsible Globalization'

As we see, developments within the global discourse on social policy go in different directions. The IMF, the OECD and the World Bank appear to be more concerned about the negative social impact of globalization, and are revising their remedies accordingly. The ILO, however, appears to be retreating from its earlier commitment to universal public pension provision, and the secretariat of the WTO seems uncritically committed to a global market in private welfare.

Within this fluid context I have argued elsewhere (Deacon, *et al.*, 1997, 1999a) for a *socially responsible globalization* and suggested some of the steps that would be entailed. To recapitulate, what appears to be needed is to envisage at the global level mechanisms of governance in the social sphere that exist at the national and regional level. Governments manage their economies so as to reduce the risk of crisis, they ensure the existence of public goods that markets do not automatically provide, and they raise revenue in order to, among other things, achieve a reasonable degree of equity and social justice. A schematic way of imagining the reforms needed for a socially responsible globalization is therefore to project on to the global level the policies of social redistribution, social regulation and social empowerment that governments do when engaging in social policy nationally.

Inge Kaul, Isabelle Grunberg and Marc Stern (1999) have argued similarly that the world has not yet found a way of ensuring the provision of global public goods because public policy-making has not yet adjusted to three gaps which exist between present practice and present realities. These gaps are identified as *jurisdictional* (the gap between the global boundaries of today's major problems and the national boundaries of policy-making), *participation* (which results from the fact that global issues are influenced by a variety of global actors but policy-making is still intergovernmental) and an *incentive gap* (which results from the fact that moral persuasion is not enough to ensure countries cooperate for the common good). Others have recently begun to think through what their previous criticisms of neo-liberal globalization might mean for global reformist politics. Kapstein (1998), for example, has argued that if public officials wish to pursue deeper integration of the global economy, then they will need to do more than focus on efficiency gains, and will need also to pursue social justice also. In the context of these ways of thinking, a set of global policy measures dealing with redistribution, regulation and empowerment are emerging. The triangulation of Redistribution, Regulation and Empowerment holds the key to global social progress. Global citizens would be enabled to make their claims for social rights as set out by agreed rules because resource redistribution would have made it possible for these rights to be realized in practice. Put differently, the interconnectedness of Trade, Aid and Standards is the key to global social responsibility. Common global social, health and labour rights (the elements of an emerging global social citizenship) cannot be achieved without a policy of intra-regional and inter-regional social redistribution which, in addition to local economic development, is necessary to resource the realization in practice of these rights. Free trade without these two other components will only generate more global inequity and perpetuate the challenge to standards where they already exist.

It is now possible not only to note a set of worthy reform proposals such as these but also to discern concrete steps that are already being taken to usher in a more socially responsible globalization. Among these steps might be noted:

- the move from human rights to social rights and from declaration to implementation
- the trend in international development cooperation towards setting goals and monitoring progress
- the move to secure global minimum labour, social and health standards

- the move to establish codes of practice for socially responsible investment and business
- the calls for global economic regulation and taxation
- the moves to extend constructive regionalism with a social dimension

Each of these steps is problematic in some ways (Deacon, 2000), but taken together they do suggest a shift away from a global politics of liberalism to a global politics of social concern.

The EU as an Actor in the Globalization Debate

Is it possible to characterize the response of the EU as a whole to the pressures of a liberalizing globalization? To what extent has the EU used its position as a global player to push for socially responsible globalization? I have argued elsewhere (Deacon, 1999c) that the response of the EU to neo-liberal globalization in terms of both its internal and external social dimension has been variable over time and between component parts of the EU system. Included within this range of responses are:

- accommodation to the liberalizing global agenda in labour markets and associated social policy
- social protectionist inclinations in some of its trade dealings
- expressions of global social concern for human rights in its common foreign and security policy
- assertiveness at the level of discourse if not in terms of deeds regarding the need for a social dimension to enlargement
- attempts to link trade aid and standards within some of its development policy
- ineffectiveness in terms of World Bank discussions on global financial regulation
- a new assertiveness about the social dimension within the global discourse on social policy

Accommodation to the requirements of a liberalizing globalization certainly characterized much of the discussion about labour markets and social policy during the mid-1990s. Then, a series of Green and White Papers on social policy emanating from the European Commission (1993b, 1994) addressed the need for more flexible working practices; the introduction of new kinds of contract; the reduction of the indirect costs of labour; the shift from passive unemployment benefits to an active labour market policy; and increased retraining and educational opportunities. Here a juggling act was going on with the Commission which wished to support social protection policies, but only insofar as these policies were adapted to the perceived requirements of increased global economic competition. Adaptation to the realities of liberal globalization was the priority at that time.

In the run-up to the establishment of the WTO, and then in relation to the WTO Ministerial meeting in Singapore in 1996, the EU could be said to have been influenced by protectionist concerns. Clearly the need to protect the Common Agricultural Policy, as a kind of minimum income entitlement for a section of the EU population, motivated the restrictions on trade in this sector. At the Singapore meeting the case was put for linking trade to a social clause with a view to protecting the social standards of Europe but also to try to generalize these elsewhere. From the point of view of many in the developing world it was protectionist sentiments which were behind the concerns of Northern countries. In preparation for the 2000 round of trade negotiations the EU seemed to have decided not to raise the issue again. On the matter of increasing the scope for opening the market in services within the existing WTO agreements and of pushing for a new Millennium Round which would encompass investment, competition policy and government procurement, the EU stands alongside the USA. The Commission (European Commission, 1999) seems to see only advantage in the expansion of its role in developing countries. Any potential threat to government public social service provision within the EU from private health and social care providers in the USA or elsewhere is not articulated.

Much was made during this period of the element of the common foreign and security policy of the EU which embraces human rights. The EU clearly sees itself as a player on the global stage concerned to bring about the realization of human rights internationally. This has found reflection in its trade policy with the African, Caribbean and Pacific (ACP) nations; in its foreign policy, even *vis-à-vis* armed conflict associated with NATO; in terms of aspects of its international development policy; and as a consideration in its humanitarian activities. How far these laudable aims have extended to social as distinct from civil and political rights, and how far policy has had a positive impact in practice, is more debatable.

In relation to the enlargement of the European Union, the requirements of membership extend to a limited number of legal requirements in the social sphere. These include the equal treatment of men and women, and the adoption of certain health and safety standards. These legal requirements of membership have however been increasingly talked up by Directorate General 5 (DG5) officials in collaboration with Directorate General 1A (DG1A) officials as they engage in screenings of the applicant countries. It is argued that applicant countries are joining a common 'social space' which has high expectations regarding consensus forms of policy-making and of decent levels of social protection. Paradoxically, the subcontracting methods used by the EU to influence social provision through technical assistance under PHARE and TACIS have programmes led to the Commission losing some control of the policy content of these projects to a diverse army of private consultants.

Some aspects of the trade policy of the EU might be said to be motivated by a concern to use trade for socially beneficial purposes elsewhere in the world. Its system of differential tariff preferences which benefits countries meeting some of the ILO's core labour standards or otherwise improving their social policies, is geared to linking trade to standards, but in a way which is not regarded negatively as a sanction but as a positive incentive. It may be argued that these policies are no more than symbolic, and will be reduced in effectiveness by both WTO negotiations, and the negotiations recently concluded to revise the Lomé agreements between the EU and the ACP (African, Caribbean and Pacific) countries.

In terms of the contribution of the EU to the debate about the social regulation of the global economy, and in particular the EU's contribution to the IMF and the Bank policy, it is difficult to divine a coherent EU contribution. The EU does not exist as an entity in either organization. Countries are grouped within the World Bank voting system in ways which do not conform to the EU as a bloc. Nordic countries vote together for example. The more that issues of global social policy have become the province of the Bretton Woods organizations the less the chance for influence directly by the EU or the Commission. Indirectly, the EU by its attendance in the shape of the Presidency, as well by the full presence of the UK, France, Germany and Italy at G7 meetings of Finance Ministers, has the potential for considerable leverage on global financial policy. However, this only exposes the diversity of government policy on these issues within Europe. On the matter of how the global financial crisis might be managed there is no one single European Union, as distinct from G7, position. In recognition of this the French Prime Minister speaking at the 2000 Annual Bank Conference on Development Economics in Paris reportedly said that the EU punched below its weight in the bank and should organize its interventions more effectively.

The foregoing section has characterized EU policy with regard to the task of injecting a social dimension into globalization as variable both over time and in policy area. It has ranged from the near capitulation to the global liberal economic agenda, to expressions of social protectionism, and to attempts, at least in rhetoric, to inject a social dimension into globalization. One explanation for the confusion in the EU's role as an actor on the global stage is the issue of who has the right to speak on behalf of the EU in different global forums. Who has the power to make external policy? What is the relationship between the Commission and Parliament and the Council of Ministers? How important is the EU Presidency in all of this? Do certain European positions get adopted in global forums without reference to 'official' EU policy? Clarification of these issues and roles is important if we are to discern by what means the EU might become a more effective voice and actor for a socially responsible globalization.

To ask these questions is to enter the terrain of disputes between political scientists and observers of EU affairs, some of whom emphasize the traditional intergovernmentalist approach to EU politics and others of whom emphasize the relative autonomy that the EU through the Commission has won for itself in the making of community policy. Sandholtz and Stone-Sweet (1998) suggest that, at any one time, a snapshot of EU politics might emphasize the role of intergovernmental bargaining. However, on a longer time frame, analysis tends to show the relative power of the supranational institutions of Europe. Their view is a modified neo-functionalist or historical-institutional analysis whereby transnational actors within the EU, the Commission and others who engage transnationally, create space for their autonomy that sets up institutions which limit intergovernmentalism. Even in the case of internal social policy, for example, an area where governments are keen to guard their autonomy under the rubric of subsidiarity, they conclude that 'a historical-institutional perspective highlights the growing significance of European policy, the influence of actors other than member-state governments, and the mounting constraints on the possibilities for initiatives by those governments' (Sandholtz and Stone-Sweet, 1988, p. 56). This echoes the view of Wendon (1998) that the Commission does indeed have the capacity to advance social policy within the EU.

In terms of foreign policy, the EU's standing and role is further complicated. This complexity impacts upon the competence of the EU in relation to dialogue and agreements with other international actors and other countries. The EU does not have a legal status, but the Community *qua* the

Commission can assume legal relations with outsiders. So, too, can member states. This leads to a range of situations from Community agreements in relation to the WTO, through mixed Community and member state agreements in relation to association agreements. The Maastricht Treaty endorsed the competence of member states to negotiate in certain areas with international organizations such as the UN. It is the combination of the role of member states with the emerging role of the Commission that confuses the position. This makes our search for a consistent and overarching thrust by the EU as an actor working for a socially responsible globalization more complicated.

If we focus on the relationship of the EU to other international organizations, we can understand just how messy the situation is. If we then add to that a question about the specific role or competence of the Commission's DG5 in relation to these other actors, we may get a sense of how little might yet be expected of the impact of the EU's social dimension in these global forums. Table 4.1 summarizes the situation.

TABLE 4.1   *The status of the EU in relation to international organizations*

International organization	Status of EU	Role of DG5 or other DGs
WTO	EC legal entity	DG1 leads
OECD	Participant but cannot block country consensus	DG5 in ELSA* committee, DG8in DAC**
G7G8	President of EU attends	DG2 wanting involvement in finance meetings
Council of Europe	EC Observer	DG5 on Social Affairs committees
ILO	EC Observer	DG5 but plays no role
UN	EC Observer	Presidency leads. DG5 with DG1A in Commission on Social Development.
World Bank and IMF	No formal role	DG2 briefs DG8 contact re development DG5 little contact
WHO	EC Observer	DG1A with DG5 (Luxembourg office) consulted

* ELSA OECD = Economic, Labour, Education and Social Affairs Committee.
** DAC = Development Assistance Committee.

Only in the case of the OECD's Economic, Labour, Education and Social Affairs Committee is DG5 able to act on behalf of the European Community as a more or less full member of the committee. In the case of the Council of Europe and the ILO, DG5 is also represented. However, the seat at the Council of Europe is often not taken up and in the case of the ILO the European Union plays no role at all. At the Luxembourg Court the Commission tested its exclusive competence to deal with the ILO on behalf of member states, but the ruling was for a shared competence with countries, and this was perceived by the Commission as a defeat. Subsequently, it has played no real role. At the ILO meetings there is no tradition of EU countries lobbying as a group; rather they work with other industrial countries as a bloc. Relationships between the secretariats of DG5 and the OECD are good, and those with the WHO and the ILO might improve with both organizations being under new leaderships.

The EU has no formal status at the World Bank or at the IMF. The member countries are reluctant to coordinate their positions. Together, the EU countries have more voting power than the US which currently dominates. It has been argued by some (e.g. WIDE, 1997) that if member states were willing to work together they could have a significant impact. There is a memorandum of understanding between the Bank and the EU but it does not appear to touch closely on social policy. The head of the Social Protection Section of the Bank's Human Resources Team has approached DG5 for better liaison, but DG5 remains understandably suspicious of this move.

In the forum of the Commission on Social Development of the UN, and the associated preparatory committee with responsibility for leading the preparation for the Copenhagen plus 5 special session, the practice emerged that the country which has current EU Presidency takes the lead in marshalling an EU position which may or may not rely on DG5 input. In that respect, there is no EU institutional memory and, therefore, not necessarily any consistency in policy adopted. Some attempt has been made by the Council of Europe's new Social Exclusion Committee to coordinate the role of the EU and other European actors.

All this appears to leaves DG5 far removed from direct influence when it comes to the IMF, World Bank, the WTO and, to some extent, the G7/8. Given that global social policy is increasingly being made in these latter forums, either explicitly or by default, it suggests that DG5 has a lot of lobbying to do to get its voice heard as guardian of the EU social dimension. This confusion is compounded by the acrimony between those European governments who see benefits in terms of global economic competition from having low taxes, and those who see the need to harmonize social provision to prevent this competition driving EU countries apart.

Based on the above and the considerations in a more extended discussion of this issue elsewhere (Deacon, 1999c), it may be concluded that in terms of the contribution of the EU to the discourse and policies of globalization:

- the contribution of different elements of the EU institutional structure is different
- the European Parliament has often resolved polices which seem to embody the idea of a socially responsible globalization, but it is not burdened yet with the job of seeing these through
- the Commission, divided as it is along functional lines, speaks with contradictory voices, attempting to juggle the defence of Europe's particular interests with fine words about human rights
- the Economic and Social Committee articulates concerns about globalization, but these are often tinged with a protectionist hue
- the intergovernmental process has led to coherent EU contributions concerning the social dimension of globalization in some forums (such as the Commission on Social Development), but has generated unproductive controversy in others
- the Common Foreign and Security Policy of the EU is fashioned by a dated conception of foreign policy, and has not yet been able to integrate an external dimension of EU social policy as part of its brief

In a number of arenas and policy areas where steps are being taken internationally to fashion a social responsible globalization, the Union is certainly not at the forefront of the debate. The move to fashion a global set of social rights which might be embodied in the proposed global guidelines of best practice in social policy owes little to the EU, despite fine words about the indivisibility of all human rights. Little appears to have been contributed, so far, by the Commission to debates about global taxation policy or moves to socially regulate transnational corporations (TNCs). Nor does the new initiative to reopen MAI-type discussion within the context of the WTO appear to be informed by calculation of the potentially negative impacts of multilateral investment upon European governmental responsibility for health and social services. While exercised by the relationship between free trade and labour and social standards globally, new policy initiatives on this seem to be off the agenda of the EU as a whole. Disagreement between the member states, a fondness for global liberalization on the part of DG1, and an uncertainty about how to proceed in these matters in the wake the Asian economic crisis, have all contributed to this apparent paralysis.

This notwithstanding, there are a number of policy initiatives or existing practices of the EU which could form the basis of a more socially responsible approach. These include the linking of aid to ACP countries with attempts to raise social standards via trade concessions that privilege countries which conform to ILO and other standards. Also, there are European Parliament moves to compel European TNCs to adopt a code of practice with regard to their investments outside Europe. In a similar vein DG5 is concerned to ensure that social policy developments in Eastern Europe reflect European Union standards.

Individual countries within the EU have made significant contributions to the global debate about how to respond to globalization with a social concern. Scandinavian countries remain committed to supporting UN social policies and some have begun to think through what global social democratic social policies might embody. However, because of its special position in relation to both the USA and Europe, the British government seems to be pivotal here. Its recent initiatives on a global social policy code, in ethical trading, in pushing the OECD:DAC targets to the front of the global aid agenda, reflect a global social concern on the part of the UK's Department for International Development. However, this concern is often expressed in a set of safety-net principles for developing countries which fall far short of the more universalistic European commitment to social welfare. For Europe, a key question that remains is whether the UK's apparent accommodation to the neo-liberalism-with-safety-nets agenda is undermining the capacity of the EU to articulate an alternative vision of a socially responsible globalization in keeping with the traditions of universalism.

In conclusion, despite the hopes of some that EU could be a voice on the global stage alongside the other major international organizations – arguing for a socially responsible globalization involving global social redistribution, global social regulation and global social empowerment – its track record so far leaves much to be desired.

Part II

European Welfare State Changes

5

Globalization and the Bismarckian Welfare States

MARY DALY[1]

Neither the character of globalization nor that of the Bismarckian welfare state model is uncontested. In regard to the former, the substance, intensity and effects of globalization are hotly disputed. While some claim that globalization is the main factor shaping current national policies, for others globalization has been used in such a variety of ways that it is in danger of becoming little more than a general term to refer to exogenous economic developments. Nor is it widely accepted that 'Bismarckian' welfare states form an identifiable cluster among European models of social protection. While the German *Sozialstaat* is generally recognized as distinctive, the extent to which countries like Belgium, France and the Netherlands belong to a similar model is questionable. The matter at issue is whether a homology exists among the continental European welfare states to the extent that they could be said to be underpinned by a similar vision of social protection and a similar type of social politics. This chapter sheds insight on both of these issues by considering them together. A further, third, theme underlies it as well. It is the question of welfare state change and transformation and how we study it. At least part of the reason we find globalization interesting is because it is presumed to herald a change in social, economic and cultural arrangements. In fact, it is globalization as an agent of change that clamours for our attention, raising as it does huge questions about how social change is understood and studied. In regard to the study of globalization and the Bismarckian welfare state model, the chapter will seek to be specific about the changes (if any) that have occurred, the differences between globalization and other agents of change as they are played out in particular national settings and what it is that is new about globalization as a harbinger of welfare state transformation.

To be specific about the point of departure, globalization is here taken as a key factor shaping the environment within which decisions around social policy are made. I will adopt a broad view of the welfare state, treating the national social policy configuration as linking intimately with employment and matters of industrial relations. The chapter seeks to make a series of points about likely and actual policy responses to processes of globalization in the context of the characteristics of the Bismarckian welfare state model. The larger argument is that the national *system* (institutional framework, political actors and historical development) embodied in particular welfare state arrangements shapes both the impact of and responses to globalization. The contention is, then, that particular features of welfare state systems render them vulnerable or robust to the pressures that are associated with globalization. Critical features in the Bismarckian model include the funding structure and the strong claims that it grants to some sectors of the population. The time period covered is from the mid-1980s to 1996 (1997 where data allow) and the country cases are Austria, Belgium, France, Germany and the Netherlands. While the first four are generally accepted as being part of the same broad family, the placement of the Netherlands is more problematic. It does not fit so comfortably into the Bismarckian model because it has a number of universal features. Yet the Netherlands is included here partly because it has some Bismarckian affinities and also because it offers one of the most interesting examples of welfare state transformation in Europe and, as we shall see, an insightful contrasting case to some of its neighbours.

The chapter is organized into four parts. Its opens with a brief overview of the Bismarckian welfare state model. It then moves on to juxtapose globalization with the Bismarckian model by identifying how particular features of the model render it vulnerable to globalization. The main policy course followed in the 1990s by the five countries is then analysed in the third part of the chapter. Developments in macroeconomic policy, labour market policy and social policy are each considered in turn. An overview section, drawing out the key insights of the analysis along with their implications, brings the chapter to a close.

Key Characteristics of the Bismarckian Welfare State Model

A hallmark of the Bismarckian model is its embeddedness within a particular institutional framework. As Streeck (1997, p. 35) describes the

German case, it is richly organized and densely regulated by a variety of institutions that have sprung from diverse traditions and interests. Centralized and highly-connected collective bargaining along with bi- or tri-partite administration of the social insurance programmes are key defining features of this type of social protection system. Coverage is high; the link between employment and social insurance is close; the risks covered are selective; the support for a traditional family form is strong (Alber, 1986). These tend to be corporatist welfare states but the degree and form of corporatism varies. In Germany, for example, the corporatist character is limited by the circumscription of the state's capacity for intervention by vertically and horizontally fragmented sovereignty and by strong constitutional limitations on discretionary government action (Streeck, 1997, p. 38).

The Bismarckian model is marked especially by the following five principles:

1. *Performance Principle*: Benefits have to be earned. For men, benefit entitlement is earned through employment, whereas for women entitlement is usually mediated through relations of marriage and family. There are in effect, then, two markets – a labour and a marriage market – through which entitlement to benefits and services is accumulated. Such a 'performance cast' means that social protection systems are predominantly organized along the lines of social insurance. The 'non-performers' are catered for in a general, tax-funded safety-net scheme that is some distance – in status and generosity – from the main social insurance programmes.
2. *Equivalence Principle*: The level of the benefit received depends upon the size of the financial contribution which one has made and indirectly upon one's wage or salary level. The function of cash benefits in this model is to replace male wages – in other words, the set of benefit arrangements serves to compensate people (read: men) for legitimate loss of labour market earnings. The normal *Arbeitsverhältnis* (employment relationship) is the linchpin governing benefit entitlement – full-time, life-long employment secures the strongest claim on social security. With the emphasis on the wage replacement function, this type of welfare state arrangement prioritizes income security (and the maintenance of status differences) over the life course.
3. *Horizontal Equity*: A horizontal conception of equity prevails. This is to be seen in the strong orientation towards the traditional life-cycle and in the fact that the risks covered are those of a typical male life-cycle. This means, among other things, that this welfare state model

has a bias towards the later phases of the life course. However, this kind of social protection system also manifests a concern with another form of horizontal equity: towards families with children. Strong norms exist about supporting the family, integral to which is the belief that families must be compensated for some of the main costs involved in child raising. Overall, social rights in this model are embedded in a hierarchical order that mirrors, rather than alters, the divisions and differentials prevailing in the economy and civil society.

4. *Self-administration*: A hallmark of this type of social insurance system is that it seeks to keep the state at a distance. Hence it is usually financed by payroll taxes and managed and operated by a tri-partite if not bi-partite structure (representatives of employers, employees and the state). Autonomy matters. The self-administration principle is re-inforced by the principle of subsidiarity. In its essence a theory of boundaries, subsidiarity ordains where the line is to be drawn between protection and encroachment on the part of the state. Direct state intervention is a last resort, permissible only to the degree that the natural order of lower units (families and communities for example) is maintained or restored.

5. *Embeddedness*: This welfare state model relates not to individuals in their personal capacity but rather to individuals in terms of their familial and social status. Full-time, highly paid (male) employment is privileged by tax, transfer and social service policies that also encourage married women to be full- or part-time housewives and mothers. This particular social model rests, then, upon a traditional family arrangement of a high-earning father/husband and homemaker wife/mother. These tend to be strong male breadwinner models (Lewis, 1992).[2] Secondly, the corporatist orientation means that social security schemes are tailored to particular social groups, and organizationally fragmented along occupational lines. In other words, this kind of welfare state has a differentiating function and some of its origins lie in the privileging of certain occupational groups over others.

Structured thus, how are the characteristics of the Bismarckian welfare state model likely to interact with globalization?

Globalization and the Bismarckian Welfare State

To be able to understand how globalization might impact upon the Bismarckian welfare state model, one must have a theorization of both the relations between exogenous and endogenous factors and processes in general and how these are relevant to particular welfare state models. In regard to the general processes, I suggest that the relationship between welfare states and globalization is indirect rather than direct. There are two aspects to this indirectness. First, instead of setting in train a straightforward cause- and -effect process, globalization creates general pressure points for policy in national settings. One critical source of pressure is for increased competitiveness among nations, and within them among producers, as markets become more open. As competitiveness or competitive advantage become key concerns, policy attention turns not in the first instance to social policy but to both macroeconomic policy and employment/labour market concerns. This is the second way in which the relationship between globalization and social policy is indirect: much of what happens to the welfare state is filtered through the lens of macroeconomic and labour market developments. These general relationships, as well as some characteristics particular to the Bismarckian welfare state model, are represented graphically in Figure 5.1.

The extent to which these pressure points create problems for particular welfare states depends on the nature and orientation of the national set of welfare arrangements, their history and their economic and political underpinnings. In other words, while globalization may set up pressure points it does not predict outcomes in any one welfare state. What matters in the latter regard are the national institutions, the balance of control over policy and how both facilitate or not the adaptation and manipulation of social programmes and social expenditures.

In relation to macroeconomic policy, the very existence and orientation of such a policy itself comes up for question. Globalization, or the manner in which it is interpreted, appears to force countries to make an anti-inflation/anti-unemployment trade-off (cf. Hay, this volume). In relation to labour market and employment policy, the key pressure points are around wage rates, unit labour costs, and the volume and structure of employment. These set in train issues relating to social policy, especially in regard to the extent to which social protection structures are seen to impinge upon national competitiveness and employment structures. In the Bismarckian model the two aspects that become critical are financing and the structure of claims. I suggest that the most important aspects of the Bismarckian welfare state model as regards the likely impact of globalization on social policy are as follows.

(1) *The funding structure and method of financing.* Financing becomes a pressure point in terms of both expenditure and income, since falling numbers in employment reduce the revenue (from both taxation and social security contributions) available while at the same time

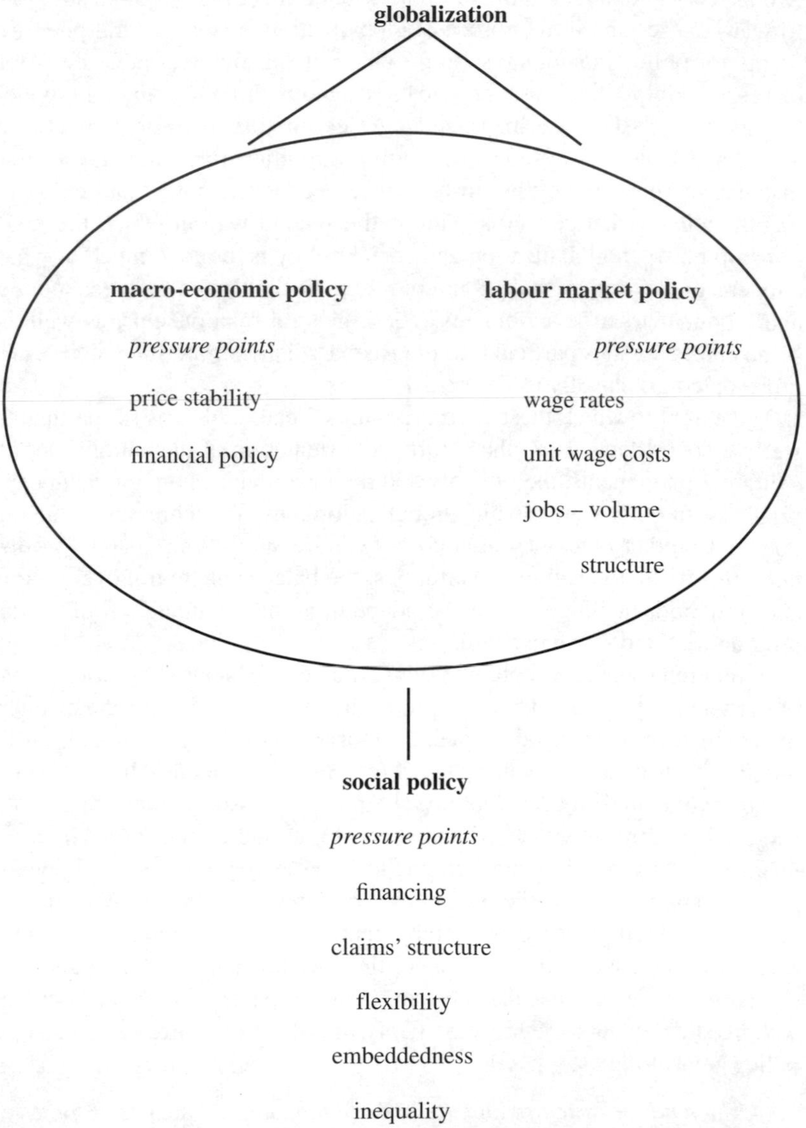

FIGURE 5.1   *Globalization and the Bismarckian welfare state*

increasing the demand for social expenditure. To the degree that it relies on payroll taxes, the Bismarckian model will be vulnerable to pressures arising from globalization. Unemployment will create special problems leading to a loss of revenue and an increased demand on resources. There is, in addition, what we might call the 'dilemma of securing extra resources'. The traditional response of increasing social security contributions will be rendered problematic by concerns about competitiveness (hence labour unit costs will be critical and an increase in contributions unpopular to the extent that it would raise labour costs). One must also factor in the added complication that adjusting the respective contributions of the social partners runs the risk of altering the balance of power relations that underpins the social protection system.

(2) *The nature of the claims system.* Their claims system determines in large part the capacity of states to cope with increased numbers of claimants within existing resources. This is true in terms of the draw on resources but also as regards the extent to which claims or social rights can be altered as adjustment pressures grow. The Bismarckian welfare state model could be said to have a strong claims' system, in that entitlements are constructed as legal rights: particular contributions bring particular entitlements, and lines of hierarchy, differentiation and control are firmly embedded. The individual recipient is constructed as a rights' holder and indeed social security entitlements are akin to a property right in many of these societies. The leeway for policy adjustment is reduced to the extent that strong claims have to be honoured in times of falling resources and increasing numbers of claimants. In addition, the tri-partite system of governance makes for relative stability, protecting especially against the diminution of the claims of rights' holders.

(3) *A further significant aspect of the cash benefit system in the face of globalization concerns its flexibility.* This especially predicts states' capacity to handle new risks and to respond to the breakdown of traditional life-cycle and family patterns. In this regard one would expect that globalization would face the Bismarckian welfare state model with great difficulties, for inflexibility is truly its middle name. Whether one has in mind the very particular risk coverage, the tight link to a traditional family model or the close life-cycle patterning, the Bismarckian welfare state has limited capacity either to respond flexibly to a changed environment or to induce flexibility among its constituent parts.

(4)   *The embedded individual orientation of this type of welfare state should also encumber its reaction to globalization.* The more mobile and flexible people are, the more they must be enabled to act as indi-viduals. Compensating people for their family needs will not only over-burden the state but will render people less mobile and adaptable.

This welfare state model will also be troubled by another, almost inevitable, concomitant of globalization: increases in inequality. Such a development brings a number of challenges. First, the Bismarckian social protection arrangements rest on a precarious balance of insiders (those in high-quality employment) and outsiders (those on the margins of employ-ment). This is a balance that can be maintained only under the condition that the group of outsiders is not too large (or too restive). Such a condi-tion is difficult to fulfil if and when unemployment climbs significantly. A second inequality challenge concerns the stratification focus of the social protection system. To the extent that the Bismarckian model orients itself towards horizontal redistribution, it has limited means to correct the type of vertical inequalities which globalization exacerbates.

What particular forms have the responses to globalization and other pressures taken? Developments in macroeconomic and taxation policy, labour market policy and social protection policy in the five countries will each be considered in turn.

Policy Responses and Recent Developments

Macroeconomic and Taxation Policy

The run-up to European Union Economic and Monetary Union (EMU) altered the state of public finances in all member states of the European Union. This was true also in our five countries.

To summarize the macroeconomic situation, there has recently been an emphasis on monetary discipline in all five countries. The overall story is one of convergence in macroeconomic policy among nations that were in earlier times tending towards expansionary policies. In some cases this has involved reducing or maintaining debt levels (the Netherlands and Austria), but in others the debt has continued to climb (Germany and France) (see Figure 5.2). Belgium has had overall levels of indebtedness that were and are much higher than the other nations, although declining from 1992. In Figure 5.3, the convergence effects of EMU upon levels of public deficit are quite identifiable; what remains unclear is the extent to

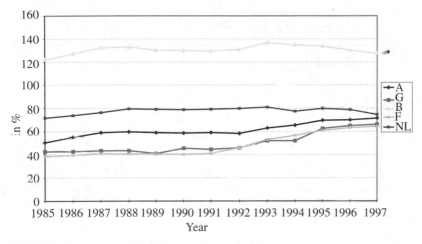

FIGURE 5.2 *Gross public debt as a share of GDP*

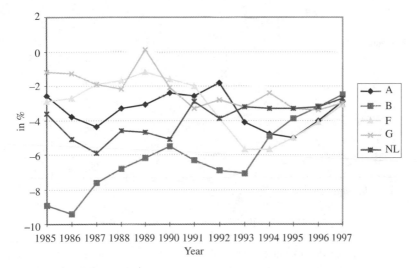

FIGURE 5.3 *Public deficit as a share of GDP*

which globalization is the push factor behind these developments in general and EMU in particular.

When it comes to taxation, these countries have generally similar policy preferences (Table 5.1). What they all have in common is a very high

TABLE 5.1   *The composition of total tax revenue in Austria, Belgium, France,*
Germany and the Netherlands, 1985, 1990, 1995

	Goods and services	Corporate	Personal income	Payroll	Property
Austria					
1985	32.6	3.5	22.9	37.5	2.4
1990	31.5	3.6	21.0	38.9	2.7
1995	27.7	3.7	20.9	42.9	1.5
Belgium					
1985	25.2	5.4	35.0	32.4	1.8
1990	26.1	5.4	31.8	33.8	2.6
1995	26.0	6.6	31.5	33.1	2.4
France					
1985	29.7	4.5	12.8	45.4	4.4
1990	28.4	5.3	11.8	46.0	5.1
1995	27.3	3.7	13.9	45.7	5.2
Germany					
1985	25.7	6.1	28.7	36.5	3.0
1990	26.7	4.8	27.6	37.5	3.4
1995	27.8	2.8	27.3	39.4	2.7
Netherlands					
1985	25.6	7.0	19.4	44.3	3.5
1990	26.4	7.5	24.7	37.4	3.7
1995	27.4	7.5	18.9	41.8	4.1

Source: *Revenue Statistics*, OECD, 1997.

reliance on payroll taxes (defined to include social security contributions).
This is true especially of the Netherlands and France but in all of these
continental European nations payroll taxes are the single most important
source of tax revenue. The significance of personal income tax varies considerably – in France it accounts for only about 13 per cent of total tax
revenue compared with around a third in Belgium and over a quarter in
Germany. Corporation tax is rather insignificant in all these nations,
accounting for between 4 and 8 per cent of total tax revenue. When one
examines changes in the composition of tax revenues in the 1980s–1990s
some policy alterations are indicated for most of these countries (see

Table 5.1). In all except the Netherlands, payroll taxes have grown as a proportion of total tax revenue. This growth has been in the order of 10 per cent in Germany and Austria whereas it was much more modest in Belgium and France. In France, the changes have been relatively slight, similar to the Netherlands which has seen a lot of movement from time to time but relative stability 1985–95.

It is clear that there has been some activity around taxation in these five countries. There is no uniformity amongst them, however, either in the structure of their tax revenue or in how this has (been) altered in recent years. In Germany more than anywhere else, there has been a marked reduction in corporate taxation – a policy stance which has been legitimated with reference to globalization and increasing competitiveness. To some extent, payroll taxes have taken up the slack – contrary to what one might expect given expressed concern about unit labour costs and the dilemma of securing extra resources. In fact, the height of payroll taxes is on the increase in four out of the five countries – with the Netherlands as the exception – although in Belgium and France these increases have been of a relatively modest nature. Overall, it is interesting to observe that there has been no dramatic change in taxation policy and that, with the exception of the Netherlands, the continental European countries continue to operate a strategy that levies very high social costs on labour.

Labour-Market-Related Policy

Employment levels tend to be problematic in Bismarckian welfare states. Two main factors are responsible. The first is that the incentive structure embodied in the social protection system can encourage 'welfare before work'. A second factor is that this welfare state model generates less public employment than other models since social services tend to be provided by private or community organizations rather than by the state. In all five countries except the Netherlands, employment ratios have been on the decline. Germany has suffered the most – with a four percentage point fall in employment between 1990 (West Germany) and 1997. France and Austria have also had poor employment performance in the 1990s. The Netherlands is the big exception in this grouping. In little more than a decade it engineered a spectacular turnaround in its employment levels, securing a growth of nine percentage points between 1990 and 1997. Table 5.2 shows some other features of labour markets in the 1980s and 1990s, covering part-time employment, fixed-term contracts and unemployment.

TABLE 5.2   *Selected labour market indicators in Austria, Belgium, France, Germany and the Netherlands, 1985, 1990 and 1997*

Proportion of labour force unemployed

Country	1985	1990	1997
Austria	3.6	3.2	4.5
Belgium	10.3	6.7	9.0
France	10.1	9.0	12.4
Germany	7.2	4.8	10.0
Netherlands	8.2	6.2	5.2

Part-time employment as a % of all employment

Country	1985	1990	1996
Austria	7.0	8.4	14.9
Belgium	8.6	10.9	14.0
France	10.9	11.9	16.0
Germany	12.8	15.2	16.5
Netherlands	22.7	31.7	38.1

Proportion of employed with fixed-term contracts

Country	1985	1990	1996
Austria	Na	na	6.0
Belgium	6.9	5.3	5.9
France	4.7	10.5	12.6
Germany	10.0	10.5	11.1
Netherlands	7.5	7.6	12.0

Source: *Europäische Union* (1997, pp. 118. 120, 123, 127, 128).

Taking an overview, one can identify a clear trend towards flexibilization of the labour market (although some aspects of employment structures have been transformed more than others). The growth of part-time employment has been a steady trend, touching all countries but especially the Netherlands. A second element of flexibilization is fixed-term contracts. While their expansion has been less rapid than that of part-time employment, up to 12 per cent of workers in the five countries are employed on a fixed-term contract basis. Unemployment is on the high side and tends to be quite volatile, except in Austria. The general trend over the last decade in these five countries is of increasing unemployment. There is great variation though. Austria, nowadays as in the past, has the least problem with unemployment, followed closely by the Netherlands. France and Germany are at the other end with at least 10 per cent of the labour force unemployed. Germany saw the doubling of its unemployment rate between 1990 and 1997. The Netherlands forms the opposite pole to Germany, having reduced its unemployment rate by almost 40 per cent between 1985 and 1997.

With the exception of the Netherlands, labour market policy and that on unemployment in particular has been similar in these countries. Governments and social partners have preferred passive transfer payments over active labour market policies, have maintained high wage rates, and reduced labour supply by relying on early retirement (Ebbinghaus, 1998, p. 20). In essence, they followed the route that had become traditional for them. It was these kinds of policies, leading to high unemployment and unfavourable pensioner/wage earner dependency ratios, that occasioned the higher payroll tax contributions which we saw above. The emphasis of labour market policies can be discerned from the expenditure statistics (see Table 5.3). The Dutch and the Belgians have been the highest spenders on measures for the unemployed in the 1980s and 1990s, targeting their pro-grammes especially at the core of long-term unemployed. France is in comparison to these two countries a relatively low spender on unemploy-ment (3 per cent of GDP) considering that about 12 per cent of its labour force is unemployed. In terms of changes over time, the countries divide into two groups: those with falling expenditure on unemployment (Belgium and the Netherlands) and those where it has been increasing (Germany and Austria and to a much more moderate degree France). In Germany the increase dates from the early 1990s and is largely a function of reunification which occasioned a huge increase in unemployment.

One can also read the active/passive bias in expenditure from Table 5.3. These countries have had a strong preference for cash transfers (as against active labour market measures) as a way of dealing with unemployment and they continue to favour such an approach. The average active/passive ratio of expenditure is one-third/two-thirds with only France electing for an active labour market approach. For France, this represents a significant change in unemployment policy, since in the mid-1980s it was very much in line with its neighbours in favouring a passive (transfer) response to unemployment. France and, to a lesser extent, the Netherlands are the only countries manifesting a significant change in the composition of expendi-

TABLE 5.3 Expenditure related to unemployment as a share of GDP in Austria, Belgium, France, Germany and the Netherlands in 1985, 1990 and 1995

Country	1985	1990	1995
Austria	1.22	1.27	1.80
of which:			
active	0.28	0.31	0.37
passive	0.94	0.97	1.43
Belgium	4.74	3.83	4.17
of which:			
active	1.33	1.22	1.40
passive	3.41	2.61	2.77
France	3.08	2.68	3.09
of which:			
active	0.67	0.81	1.30
passive	2.41	1.87	1.79
Germany	2.22	2.14	3.73
of which:			
active	0.80	1.04	1.36
passive	1.42	1.10	2.37
Netherlands	4.24	3.56	4.12
of which:			
active	0.80	1.01	1.06
passive	3.44	2.55	3.06

Source: Employment Outlook, OECD, various years.

ture on the unemployed over the period studied. Turning their back on earlier policies, the Dutch directed their attention towards maximizing the rate of labour force participation (Hemerijck et al., 2000). Wage moderation, labour market flexibility and measures to redistribute employment formed the heart of the new policy approach. This package of policies has occasioned a return to an employment-intensive growth pattern, securing an extraordinary increase in part-time jobs, a huge entry of women to the labour force and the replacement of older workers by younger, cheaper and possibly more flexible and skilled workers (Visser and Hemerijck, 1997, p. 17). In all the other country cases, increased (or reduced) numbers of transfer claimants appear to account for the growth (or reduction) in expenditure on unemployment. Hence there has been no significant change in emphasis in this domain of policy.

Social Protection

As outlined earlier, two aspects of social security are of especial relevance: financing and the structure of claims. Each will be considered in turn. Table 5.1 hinted at an important aspect of the context of social security funding by showing the developments in payroll taxes. It confirmed a general trend towards higher payroll tax revenue in all these countries except the Netherlands. By comparison, the internal composition of social security funding has not been altered as much but there were some significant changes within and across nations in the 1980s and 1990s (see Table 5.4). To the extent that there has been an identifiable trend, it is towards a greater contribution on the part of employees. This is to be seen in all the five countries and is at its most marked in Belgium and the Netherlands. A second trend is towards greater state funding (with Belgium as the exception, experiencing a sharp and consistent trend downwards in state funding). The rise in the state's contribution was steepest in the Netherlands. This, together with the increase in the proportion of revenue paid by employees, suggests a policy of unburdening employers. Belgium pursued a somewhat different strategy – a virtual swapping of funding shares by the state and employees (with the proportion contributed by the latter increasing as that of the former fell). In Germany and France the most significant change has been a fall-off in the social security contributions of employers. There are important nuances in the developments in these two countries though. In Germany any exemptions of or reductions in employers' contribution are primarily intended to boost job creation. Such an objective is also adverted to in France but a general move is under way in that country towards tax financing of social security. This is part of a larger contest about control of the social protection system. The recent introduction of two new taxes specifically for social security funding[3] and the amendment made to the Constitution in 1996 so as to allow the parliament from now on to decide on the general orientations and political objectives of the social security system can be interpreted as a move in the direction of the empowerment of the state (Bonoli and Palier, 1997). Even though as yet modest, the significance of these developments is great in a

TABLE 5.4   *The financing of expenditure on social security in Belgium, France,*
Germany and the Netherlands, 1986, 1990 and 1993

	Employer	Employee	State	Other
Belgium				
1986	40.8	19.4	30.3	9.5
1990	40.6	26.1	24.2	9.1
1993	41.5	27.4	21.0	10.1
France				
1986	52.8	26.0	18.3	2.9
1990	52.1	28.7	16.7	2.5
1993	49.8	28.1	19.6	2.5
Germany				
1986	41.2	30.3	25.1	3.4
1990	41.5	30.6	24.3	2.6
1993	38.4	31.0	27.3	3.3
Netherlands				
1986	33.3	34.5	15.6	16.6
1990	20.1	38.7	25.0	15.9
1993	20.1	42.2	21.9	15.8

Source: *Statistisches Jahrbuch für das Ausland*, 1991, 1995, 1996.

system where autonomy of the state was a founding principle of social insurance.

To summarize, the five countries are similar to the extent that they have seen considerable change in the respective contributions of the state, labour and capital to social security revenues and programme administration. Only in Germany have these developments been confined to the last years. The most general trend is for a lessening of the burden on employers and a corresponding increase in the contributions from employees and the state.

Examining the composition of expenditure on social security does not tell us anything about the level of expenditure. Information on this as a share of GDP is presented in Table 5.5. The trend is upward (in all countries except the Netherlands) but moderately so everywhere except France and Germany. In the latter case, the year-to-year patterns reveal that the increase is closely associated with the reunification. The individual social

TABLE 5.5   *Total social expenditure as a share of GDP in Austria, Belgium, France, Germany and the Netherlands in 1985, 1990 and 1995*

Country	1985	1990	1995
Austria	25.4	25.2	27.1
Belgium	28.2	26.6	28.8
France	27.0	26.7	30.1
Germany	26.3	24.8	29.6
Netherlands	28.9	29.7	28.0

Source: *Social Expenditures*, OECD, 1996.

security funds show not only a considerable increase but that these increases are accounted for by payments (and deficits in) and services to residents in the former German Democratic Republic (Deutsches Institut für Wirtschaftsforschung, 1995). In effect the German authorities relied to an increasing degree on social insurance to fund the necessary adaptations in the eastern half of the country. Both by extending existing entitlements to residents in the east (who had never paid any contributions) and by allowing uncompetitive labour there to be sidelined into unemployment and early retirement programmes (both of which are financed largely by employers and employees), the Kohl government succeeded in loading up to a third of the costs of the reunification project on the social insurance funds (Manow and Seils, 2000).

Turning to the structure of claims and the basis of entitlement, these social protection systems grant relatively strong claims. Although the entitlement conditions are by no means easy to fulfil – hingeing as they do in most cases on sustained labour market performance – once one meets them one has a legally protected set of claims. These are welfare states that make a relatively strong distinction between insiders and outsiders – the insiders are the well-paid male workers who receive relatively generous social protection benefits and the outsiders are those who have to resort to the catch-all, social assistance benefits. As regards reform over the last years, while there has been some change, no transformation has taken place. That is, the principles of the Bismarckian model as outlined earlier remain firmly in place in the welfare states of continental Europe (with the exception of the Netherlands). Hence these welfare states continue for the most part to adhere to principles like performance, equivalence and self-administration.

However this picture only holds at the most general level of analysis. A more penetrating look at developments in each of the countries reveals differences that are too strong to be ignored. The grouping of five countries actually displays three patterns. At one end of the continuum of change are those countries that have seen little or no change in their principles (Austria and Germany); at the other end is the Netherlands which arguably has effected if not a transformation then a significant change in its social policy model by the 1990s. In between are Belgium, towards the German and Austrian side, and France which, in the last number of years especially, has seen significant change. A brief overview of the comparative situation is instructive.

Germany and Austria have reacted to significant change in their external (and in the case of Germany internal also) environments by adhering closely to long-standing organizational forms and principles. There have, of course, been changes in the conditions of entitlement in both of the national benefit systems. However, of the two the change has been less extensive in Austria. In a climate where the welfare state has not been the subject of opprobrium, only the pension system has seen large cut-backs. In Germany, where the welfare state has been made a culprit for many of the country's economic ills, practically every programme has seen some change. The value of benefits such as sickness pay and unemployment benefit has been frozen or lowered; waiting periods for some benefits have been introduced or lengthened; there has been a general tightening of the rules governing searching for and accepting offers of employment; the required periods of labour market participation have been lengthened (Daly, 1997). However significant the changes may be for individual well-being, they do not amount to a fundamental alteration of the structure of the German and Austrian social protection systems overall. These are still social insurance welfare states, prioritizing horizontal over vertical equity and the maintenance of both traditional family arrangements and differences of status. If anything there has been a tendency to adhere even more closely to existing principles when carrying out reform. There is no threat to the hegemony of the male breadwinner model for example – extra tax privileging and better benefits (such as parental leaves and improved pension entitlements) for women who are caring for their families have acted to reinforce traditional patterns. Moreover, the introduction of *Pflegegeld* (carer's benefit) in Austria in 1993 and care insurance in Germany in 1995 represents a continuation of the traditional emphasis on cash benefits rather than services.

France and Belgium have seen somewhat more change although caution should be exercised in assuming durability for recently proposed or enacted measures. Of the two it is France that is witnessing the more far-reaching reforms. Plan Juppé, which was enacted in November of 1995, set out to effect significant changes in the French system of organizing social protection. Among the legislative changes was a move to a principle of universalism in access to health care, which introduced a universal health insurance scheme that makes health a right of citizenship. A second significant aspect of Plan Juppé was its proposals for funding of social insurance. As mentioned earlier, it took significant steps in moving the financing of health care and family benefits from a contribution-financed to a tax-financed system through the introduction of a number of general taxes (Bouget, 1998, p. 162). While the Jospin government has yet to make a decisive mark on social security, Bonoli and Palier (1997, p. 241) suggest that the overall direction of recent changes in France represents a shift away from the Bismarckian model towards a Beveridgean approach, especially in health, family and social insertion policies.

The Netherlands deserves attention for its social protection system that is in the process of being profoundly reformed, if not transformed. Of all of our countries the Netherlands has seen the most sustained and radical attack on problems perceived to be associated with the welfare state. Such problems include the condition of the public finances, the low volume of employment, dependency ratios, unemployment and income levels. The welfare state was not only central to reform efforts but was blamed for occasioning a crisis of inactivity. Social policy reform has set in train a trend towards privatization, selectivity, the dilution of the social insurance principle and individualization. Disability and sickness payments were the first to be targeted since in the Netherlands they had served as the main exit channel from the labour market. In an effort to control perceived abuse, a new incentive structure was introduced including shifting (partly at any rate) the responsibility for these programmes to employers and allowing them to opt out of the public disability programme. A second form of privatization also loomed large. Independent supervisory institutions have been introduced for many social insurance programmes. (Hemerijck *et al.*, 2000). All this is intended to increase public control over social security and limit the involvement of the trade unions and employers in its administration. An increasingly selective orientation has been realized by the intro-duction of means-testing for old-age and survivors' pensions and in the generally increased role of social assistance (Van Oorshot, 1998, p. 199). These measures also had the effect of undermining the significance of social insurance as did the 'modernization' of gender relations. Moving towards a more equal treatment of women and men and reconstructing women as workers (rather than family carers as in the past) have helped to dilute the male breadwinner orientation. In these and other ways, the Dutch have been moving away from the passive type of social protection that characterizes the Bismarckian model. Theirs is no longer a system gov-erned by principles of self-administration and embeddedness.

Overview

In deciphering the relationship between globalization and the Bismarckian welfare state, two aspects are central: the financing and management of social security and the structuring of claims. To conceptualize how these and other aspects of social policy are affected by globalization, this chapter has argued that one must also take into account the proficiency and content of macroeconomic policy and the working of labour markets. Within this general framework, it has sought to answer two questions: (a) what happened to the Bismarckian welfare states in the 1990s (b) how has the make-up of this welfare state model fashioned responses in a climate of globalization?

In regard to the first question, each of the three spheres of policy has seen considerable attention. Moreover, much of the policy change has been in a similar direction. This is especially true in the macroeconomic domain where a monetarist orientation prevails in all five countries. No doubt the hand of Maastricht and EMU is at work here, having led in the recent past to a degree of convergence that is remarkable in the context of past divergence in monetary policy of these five countries. While the five nations are characterized by considerable similarity also in their social and labour market policies, the Netherlands and to a lesser extent France and Belgium are the countries that fit least comfortably into a Bismarckian pattern. For one, they have seen a much greater degree of change in the 1980s and 1990s than either Austria or Germany. For another, they have diverged in how they have reformed their social expenditure, taxation and labour market policies. The path taken by the Netherlands has been espe-cially noteworthy – it has 'flexibilized' its labour market to a remarkable degree (and in a very short time); it has secured a return to a job-intensive growth pattern and dealt successfully with unemployment; it has managed to significantly lighten the burden of payroll taxes on employers while at the same time effecting a reduction in overall levels of social expenditure. In comparison with the Netherlands, developments in the other four countries appear sluggish if not uneventful. Within their own context they are nevertheless significant. Germany, for example, greatly increased its unemployment-related expenditure (although the bulk of this is on passive rather than active measures), reduced the generosity of its benefits and managed to more than halve the contribution of corporation taxes to the overall tax revenue. In France, important developments have taken place in labour market and anti-unemployment policies as well as in the rights- and funding basis of health care. Belgium has also been concerned about labour market policies and has taken steps to alter the funding and scale of its social security expenditure. Austria has been the country that has, apart from a significant increase in payroll taxes, seen the least change.

The second question guiding the chapter was whether particular features of the welfare states of a Bismarckian provenance render them vulnerable to pressures associated with globalization. In this regard, the Bismarckian model has three weak points. First, resting as it does on a very rigid model of employment – lifelong male employment interrupted only by one of a number of relatively predictable risks – the model has difficulty in dealing with most forms of flexibilization of the life course. It clings determindedly to 'old' risks – illness, accident, child-bearing and old age/survivorship. Second, since Bismarckian social policy over-relies on a form of social insurance that is largely funded by payroll taxes and differentiates between status groups, unemployment and trends towards flexibilization of the labour market render it vulnerable to a loss of contributions at the same time as it is experiencing a growth in claims. Third, this model is one that grants strong and enduring claims on public resources, with benefits that are viewed almost as property rights and social programmes that are governed in such a manner as to render them resistant to change. In hard times such strong claims make it difficult for this type of welfare state to cope with funding pressures without resorting to expansionary policies.

Globalization is, though, only one of a number of factors providing the impetus for social policy and other reforms. The push towards EMU (which itself is related to globalization, of course), and, in the case of Germany, the reunification process, have been very significant sources of pressure on national policy-makers. One must also emphasize that the actual adjustment path taken depends to a considerable extent on the institutional framework in place in national settings and what political and economic interests make of it and of the pressures for change. When considered from this perspective, the 'Bismarckian cluster' begins to look less like a secure whole and one can see how politics makes a difference. The Netherlands and, to some extent, France and Belgium seem to have moved some way from the Bismarckian model already. Austria and Germany are quite similar and remain closer to the model, however, showing a marked preference for a set of 'holding policies'. Such a policy package has been characterized by passive transfer payments (instead of active labour market policies), the maintenance of high wage levels, and the reduction of labour supply through early retirement routes.

The view of globalization that emerges from this chapter is that it is, above all, a process that is difficult to pin down in a concrete relationship to welfare states, either in a descriptive or explanatory sense. To be able to make a strong argument about it in relation to contemporary welfare states, one has to interrogate the changes which it invokes as against those from other sources. But this is difficult if not impossible to do. In fact, what is remarkable about studying globalization is that far from focusing exclusively on exogenous factors, it (once again) turns the spotlight on the mechanisms that shape the policy choices and responses at the national level. The interaction between economic and political factors is drawn to the fore. Looking at the divergence within just one 'cluster' indicates the limitations involved in positing globalization as some kind of all-powerful force for change. What seems to have made the difference between the countries in the present comparison is a combination of factors: not just an exogenous economic impetus for change but political and social factors as well. In the French case for example, a financial crisis of the social insurance funds led to change only when strong political leadership committed to reform emerged. Although the details are different in the Dutch case, there too one can see the importance of a combination of political leadership, economic crisis and a loss of legitimacy in the existing sets of arrangements. The other side of this explanatory coin is that this 'precious combination' of push and pull factors was not present to a significant degree in either Austria or Germany. These latter cases suggest a hypothesis to the effect that the more closely a country adheres to the Bismarckian model the more resistant (or powerless) it is to pressures created by globalization.

The study of globalization raises important issues in regard to the study of welfare states. A focus on globalization not only turns the spotlight on exogenous factors but helps to elaborate how these operate together with endogenous factors to affect the welfare state. What is clear also is that the study of globalization can lead to a broader conceptualization of the welfare state. One cannot consider social policy in isolation from economic policy, labour market policy and industrial relations. A further challenge associated with globalization is that it directs attention to the future. In this regard it compels and at the same time entices thought about the form that a 'globalized social policy' might take. Thinking along these lines, and in particular about how the Bismarckian welfare state model may be further challenged by developments, suggests the following conclusions.

- To the extent that a cash transfer-oriented social policy model would be more consonant with a globalized environment than one oriented to service provision, the Bismarckian model is well-placed in the face of increasing globalization.
- However, in that globalization encourages flexibility and discourages welfare state arrangements from supporting people on a long-term basis, the Bismarckian welfare state is out of line with the swing towards globalization. A globalized social protection system would offer primarily weak, rather than strong, claims and people would be encouraged to find their main sources of income support outside of the state system and would therefore enter and leave the 'benefit express' in as short a time as possible. These, as we have seen, are opposing emphases to those of the Bismarckian welfare state model.
- The Bismarckian model is also out of step to the extent that it engages with people as members of families (rather than individuals) and recognizes the need to compensate people for their family responsibilities. A globalized social policy model would tend to treat people as individuals and family responsibilities and burdens as private matters.
- Finally, the Bismarckian social policy model is also outdated by virtue of its strongly differentiated coverage of risks. In times of globalization social protection would be relatively undifferentiated, consisting mainly of general programmes that sought to 'tide people over' until they could organize an alternative source of livelihood.

It will be interesting to observe the extent to which the Bismarckian model can and does adjust further to pressures associated with globalization.

Notes

1. The assistance of Torsten Denkmann in the preparation of this paper is gratefully acknowledged.
2. One needs to exercise caution here, however, since the form of family arrangement that is favoured by public policies varies considerably among the five
countries. Germany and Austria represent one pole, adhering most closely to a
traditional male breadwinner model, whereas France, encouraging employed
motherhood, makes up the other pole. The arrangements in Belgium and the
Netherlands, making it easier for women to be employed than it is in Germany
but being less supportive of female employment than France, place these countries in the middle.
3. The CSG (*Contribution Sociale Généralisée*) is a tax levied on all kinds of
income earmarked for non-contributory social protection programmes. The
RDS (*Remboursement de la Dette Sociale*) is another new tax that has been
introduced specifically for the purpose of paying off the accumulated debts of
the social insurance system. See Bonoli and Palier (1997).

6

Globalization and the Southern Welfare States

ANA M. GUILLÉN AND SANTIAGO ÁLVAREZ

Introduction

This chapter is devoted to the analysis of the relationship between social policy reform and globalization in Italy and Spain, both southern European countries and members of the European Union. Reference will also be made to Portugal and Greece, which share similar conditions. A caveat should be introduced here regarding the use of the term 'southern', since confusion is possible between the usages of 'southern' denoting a geographical area, *and* also as a theoretical construct or model. For clarity, we therefore use 'southern' (i.e. small 's') when using the term generally/geographically, and 'Southern' (i.e. capital 'S') when referring to the family of welfare states in a model or regime-like sense.

The chapter is divided into three sections. The first one considers the potential existence of a distinct Southern welfare regime, that is, it discusses whether southern European welfare states present differentiating characteristics that allow us to speak about a 'family of nations' and/or a 'welfare regime'. In our view, southern welfare states show enough differentiating characteristics to consider them a 'family of nations', but it is hard to defend the position that they constitute an independent 'welfare regime'. The second section is devoted to the analysis of policy reform. It includes a consideration of how globalization is defined in southern countries, an analysis of actual reforms undertaken, and changes in the policy process. The questions to be answered here are related to the appearance

103

of new actors, to changes in the relationship between them and to the construction of the political discourse regarding globalization. Globalization has been tightly linked to European integration in southern Europe. In other words, the political rhetoric is that national competitiveness and adaptation to global pressures would be achieved by macroeconomic adjustment in order to meet the economic convergence criteria for membership of the EU's Economic and Monetary Union. However, macroeconomic austerity policies did not lead to indiscriminate cutbacks in social policy, but rather to the rationalization of some social protection areas, and expansion in other areas which were underdeveloped in comparison with other EU welfare states.

The relationship between globalization, understood as European integration, and social policy change in the Southern welfare states is discussed in the third section. This will take into account both directions of the influence, i.e. of globalization, on social policy developments, and the role of pre-existing institutional social policy arrangements in defining what 'globalization' meant, and how reforms in 'response' to it were designed.

Is There a *Southern* Welfare State System?

Southern European countries have either been considered as examples of the conservative, Bismarckian model of welfare state, or as constituting a distinctive *Southern* model, a welfare system distinct from the liberal, conservative, and social-democratic sytems. Esping-Andersen (1990) considers that the Italian and Spanish welfare states show the same characteristics as the Conservative systems such as Germany, their origin and development being essentially based on the Bismarckian tradition. In this sense southern welfare states show a strong commitment to the male breadwinner/female carer model. This is a stronger commitment even than that of their Conservative northern European counterparts, so that pensions substitute for the family wage in an even more intense way. In this sense, Esping-Andersen's interpretation is also in line with that of Castles (1994 and 1995) and van Kersbergen (1995) who argue for the importance of cultural and religious traditions in the development of welfare states in connection with how family and gender roles are assigned. Katrougalos (1996) also considers Southern welfare states as a less developed version of the Conservative model. Leibfried's approach (1993), which considers Southern welfare states as belonging to a distinct 'rudimentary' model, consisting of little more than an institutional promise of welfare, is now largely discarded, as it considers only social assistance.

However, Ferrera (1996) has defended the existence of a separate model of welfare state in southern European countries on very different grounds. There are three basic characteristics of this *Southern* model as defined by Ferrera. Firstly, the main principles of access to welfare provision, funding arrangements, and welfare ideology combine welfare services based on the social-democratic tradition with income transfers that have remained occupational. This feature apparently combines elements of two of Esping-Andersen's regime types, a sort of 'dual welfare state'. Where there has been universalization of welfare services, primarily in health and education, this was a consequence of old aspirations of many social actors, such as unions, left-wing parties, and the population in general. Income-maintenance policies have remained occupational in response to the wishes of these same actors. Thus, in the income maintenance domain (disability and retirement pensions, sickness cash benefits, unemployment benefits), welfare has remained directed mainly (but not only) at workers and their dependants, managed by semi-public bodies, and financed largely out of social contributions. Conversely, welfare services have been based on direct public provision for all citizens and increasingly financed out of state revenues (above all, for health care and educational services). Thus, different areas of social policy in southern European welfare states follow quite different principles in relation to redistribution.

Secondly, Ferrera argues that Southern welfare states over-privilege labour market insiders in an even more intense way than Conservative welfare states. In addition, Southern welfare states over-privilege the elderly against people of working age. Pensions have the biggest share of social expenditure in these countries, much more than unemployment subsidies, activation policies, family allowances, tax exemptions and minimum wages and salaries. Public social and caring services show lower levels of development than in other welfare states, either in terms of expenditure or in the number of services provided.

Thirdly, Ferrera argues that Southern welfare states show a particularistic–clientelistic profile, meaning that public welfare institutions are 'highly vulnerable to partisan pressures and manipulations' (1996, p. 25). In his view, 'welfare manipulation takes the form of political clientelism, i.e. favours exchanged for support to a public organization, such as (preference) votes for a given party'. While the two first characteristics of Ferrera's Southern model (1996) are generally accepted, there is no agreement on the third, i.e., clientelism and patronage practices. In our view, clientelistic practices are not so widespread in Southern welfare states as to consider them a regime-differentiating feature. Furthermore, the clientelistic practices existing in the 1980s were largely corrected in the 1990s (for example, the ending of the concession of invalidity pensions to those who were not, in fact, invalids). Furthermore, clientelistic practices have not been researched systematically, so that a conclusive comparison cannot be reached on whether Southern welfare states show a larger share of clientelistic behaviours than in other systems. As Ferrera himself acknowledges, it is a phenomenon more related to the working of income maintenance systems in some specific geographical (often rural) areas than to the whole range of activities in southern European welfare states. Esping-Andersen, when revising his typology of welfare regimes, notes that 'a perverted use of welfare programmes and public bureaucracies may define the character of a polity, but it is difficult to see how it defines a welfare regime unless the entire system was from the very beginning specifically designed for the purpose of clientelism rather than social protection' (1999, p. 90). In sum, in our view, clientelism is not a basic characteristic of southern European welfare states.

Interestingly, Ferrera does not refer to the particular features of social assistance and personal social services in southern Europe, which we do consider a differentiating feature. They are distinctive in the sense that such services have been much less developed in Southern Europe in the past than elsewhere in Europe. Even though they have undergone clear expansion for the last twenty years, they still show a lower level of development than in other European welfare states.

Nonetheless, it may be easily deduced from Ferrera's analysis that there are significant deviations in Southern welfare states from the Conservative/Bismarckian model . Consequently, it is possible to speak about a distinct Southern welfare *pattern* or *family* of welfare states. This is so, above all, because welfare services (notably health care and education) have become more like the Social Democratic welfare systems, in that they are directed at the whole population, as citizenship rights, and financed out of state revenues (especially in Italy and Spain in this latter case). This evolutionary pattern has resulted in a mixture of the Bismarckian (income maintenance policies) and Social Democratic (health care, education policies) traditions, which may be established as the basic characteristic of the Southern model of welfare: to repeat we thus have a dual model in the Esping–Andersen sense.

Welfare System or Welfare Regime?

However, can we talk about a Southern welfare *regime*? Welfare regimes are constructed on different basic principles that differentiate them from one another. Thus, one could argue that liberal welfare states show a clear preference for the market as a superior method of distribution *vis-à-vis* the state. They are also aimed at enhancing or securing freedom of choice for individuals, who are considered capable of facing risks. Conservative/ Corporatist regimes, in turn, are based on the breadwinner/carer model. Finally, Social Democratic regimes are predicated on individual public entitlements as citizenship rights. Is there such a distinctive principle in Southern welfare states, or is it just a mixture of existing principles?

One possible basic differentiating principle of Southern welfare states could be what has been termed the 'familialism' of south European countries, meaning that families (rather than the state or the market) provide for a broad range of welfare services. Extended family networks (not necessarily living in the same household) share economic and caring resources. Families also tend to function as loan agencies and as employment agencies for their members, by using their relational capital. In the face of high rates of unemployment and high rents for housing, young people remain in the parental home until remarkably late ages in comparison with other European countries: around 40 per cent of people aged 25–29 in Spain and 57 per cent in Italy, as compared with around 18 per cent in the United Kingdom or 13 per cent in West Germany. Although decreasing, the number of elderly people living with their families is also higher than in other EU member states (see OECD, 1997a). Put in this way, Southern 'familialism' seems to be a clear differentiating feature of Southern welfare states. This is especially so when a broader view of welfare policies is taken, meaning not only publicly provided services, but also those delivered by markets and families. However, one could also ask whether familialism is a principle adopted by southern European welfare states by choice – do people think that family provision is superior to that of the state or the market, or is it simply a way of filling the gaps left by other welfare providers? If the latter is the case, familialism could not be considered as the basic principle informing policy design in southern Europe. Rather, it would be a contingent characteristic that would eventually wither away once public provision closed all the gaps in provision.

Some studies show that size of family correlates with levels of economic development. The largest families in Europe are probably still to be found in southern countries, despite the fall in fecundity rates. In fact, the average size of families was 3.3 persons in Spain, 3.1 in Portugal, 3.0 in Greece and 2.8 in Italy in 1991, while the average for the EU 15 was 2.6 for the same year (Durán, 1999, p. 19). This may constitute an argument for familialism as a constraint, rather than a choice, as people are forced to share households because they cannot afford to become established independently.

Several scholars (Castles, 1994, 1995; van Kersbergen, 1995) have related familialism with cultural traditions, tied more or less intensely to Catholicism (or the Orthodox Church in Greece) and Christian democracy. Other scholars (Bettio and Villa, 1998; Garrido and Requena, 1996) have argued that it is not a matter of religious tradition in increasingly secularized societies, but of the will of families to preserve the living standards of their offspring in the face of unemployment. The existence of older housewives who still feel it is their duty to care for the elderly and the disabled may be pointed to as another reason explaining familialism in the South of Europe.

Whether one should refer to one of these reasons or to all of them in explaining social behaviour in relation to welfare in southern European countries is still a matter for investigation and debate. When assessing the dimension of familialism in southern Europe, Esping-Andersen (1999, pp. 93–4) finds no crucial differences from other continental welfare states. Thus, current discourse does appears to argue against both familialism and clientelism as distinctive characteristics of a *Southern* welfare regime.

Moreover, differences within the region have also been developing in recent decades, as far as institutional arrangements and patterns of provision are concerned. Between Italy and Spain, on the one hand, and Portugal and Greece on the other, these differences seem to be deepening in recent times, in the area of health care, for instance (see Guillén, 1999a, for a comparative analysis of southern health care systems), and decentralization. Italy and Spain have undergone a radical decentralization process in the recent past, whereas Portugal and Greece have not. Decentralization in Italy and Spain has brought about a considerable number of innovative undertakings in social policy, together with an expansionary trend in coverage and expenditure terms.

In conclusion, then, it may be argued that southern European welfare states have some characteristics in common that differentiate them from other European welfare states, but it is hard to talk about a Southern *welfare regime* predicated on a basic guiding principle. Therefore, it is in this rather restricted sense that the term *Southern welfare states* is henceforward used in this chapter. Let us now turn to the analysis of policy reform in Spain and Italy in the past few years, and to the consideration of emerging patterns of decision-making and new developments in the construction of their political discourses around welfare.

The New Politics of Social Policy in Southern Welfare States

In southern Europe, recent arguments for policy reform have revolved around the issue of European integration rather than around globalization in general. This was so especially during the 1990s, after the European Union's (EU) Maastricht Treaty was signed. In particular, the political discourse in southern welfare states has pointed to European integration as the main objective to be achieved both in macroeconomic and in social policy terms. However, in order to understand the developments of the 1990s, it is necessary to go back a little in history.

In Spain and Italy, public policies have undergone a dramatic process of transformation during the last twenty-five years. Such a process has been fostered, to a large extent, by external factors. The internationalization of markets, the opening to external competition and European integration can be considered as crucial factors in the transformation of southern political economies. They went from a clearly problematic situation in the 1970s, to macroeconomic adjustment in the 1990s which allowed for integration into the EU's system of Economic and Monetary Union (EMU) (C. Martín, 1997; Neal and Barberat, 1998). In many senses, the changes introduced by Spain and Italy were similar. Furthermore, they also share several problems, especially with regard to the labour market. Both countries underwent strong economic growth after the Second World War. In the case of Italy, growth took place between 1950 and 1970. In the Spanish case, growth began later but it was even more intense, taking place from the early 1960s to the mid-1970s. In both countries, these developments were closely linked to the opening up of the economies to international competition. In Italy, economic growth was produced by the industrialization of the North and the penetration by the new industries of the international market. Economic development in Spain was related to the liberalization of the economy, industrialization and the development of the service sector for tourism. In addition, industrialization in both countries was based on the development of public enterprises (Fuentes, 1993; Salvati, 1984).

However, from the point of view of social policy, the evolution did not show the same parallels. Italian governments were able to develop a much more powerful welfare state than the authoritarian government in Spain. As Tables 6.1 and 6.2 show, while Italy was close to other EU members with regard to expenditure on social protection and tax receipts as a percentage of GDP, Spain clearly lagged behind during the 1960s and 1970s. In 1975, social expenditure amounted to 10.26 per cent of GDP in Spain, while it reached 22.6 per cent in Italy. Tax receipts for the same year were 19.5 per cent of GDP in Spain, and 26.2 per cent in Italy.

From the mid-1970s to the mid-1980s, southern economies had to face the same economic crises as other countries in the western world. The oil crises implied severe problems for the economies of southern Europe, creating numerous difficulties for them in competing in international markets. Spain also had to face the simultaneous process of transition to democracy (a problem for Portugal and Greece too). The need to concentrate on the reform of political institutions meant that the reform of social policy was ignored. Consequently, the welfare system inherited from the authoritarian regime remained untouched in its basic institutional arrangements until the mid-1980s in Spain (Guillén, 1992). However, the new social needs generated by the economic crises had to be met, and social expenditure and state intervention grew considerably. As Tables 6.1 and 6.2 show, social expenditure grew by 150 per cent in Spain from 1975 to 1980, while taxation

TABLE 6.1   *Evolution of expenditure on social protection (%GDP) (1970–94)*

Country	1970	1975	1980	1985	1990	1994
Belgium	18.70	24.2	26.1	29.0	26.7	27.0
Denmark	19.60	26.9	29.7	27.8	29.7	33.7
Germany	21.50	29.7	28.6	28.1	26.9	30.7
Greece			13.3		20.5	16.0
Spain	*7.69*	*10.26*	*15.6*	*18.0*	*20.7*	*23.6*
France	19.20	22.9	25.9	28.8	27.8	30.5
Ireland	13.20	19.7	20.6	24.0	20.3	21.1
Italy	*17.40*	*22.6*	*22.8*	*22.5*	*24.0*	*25.3*
Luxembourg	15.90	22.4	26.4	25.4	25.9	24.9
Netherlands	20.80	26.7	30.4	31.1	32.2	32.3
Portugal			14.6	16.1	17.0	19.5
UK	15.90	20.1	21.7	24.5	23.0	28.1

Sources: Eurostat, several years; and González *et al.* (1985).

TABLE 6.2   *Tax receipts as percentage of GDP (1970–94)*

Country	1970	1975	1980	1985	1990	1994
Belgium	35.7	41.8	44.4	47.7	44.8	46.6
Denmark	40.4	41.4	45.5	49.0	48.7	51.6
Germany	32.9	36.0	38.2	38.1	36.7	39.2
Greece	25.3	25.5	29.4	35.1	37.5	42.5
Spain	*16.9*	*19.5*	*24.1*	*28.8*	*34.4*	*34.0*
France	35.1	36.9	41.7	44.5	43.7	44.5
Ireland	31.0	31.3	33.8	36.4	35.2	37.5
Italy	*26.1*	*26.2*	*30.2*	*34.5*	*39.2*	*41.3*
Luxembourg	30.9	42.8	46.3	46.7	43.6	45.0
Netherlands	37.0	42.9	45.0	44.1	44.6	44.0
Portugal	20.3	21.7	25.2	28.4	30.8	33.0
UK	36.9	35.5	35.3	37.9	36.4	35.3

Source: Messere (1997, pp. 298–314)

increased from 19.5 per cent of GDP to 26.1 per cent. Social expenditure grew slightly in Italy in the same period (from 22.6 per cent to 22.8 per cent). In Italy, however, the first universalist reforms had already taken place in the late 1970s, with, for example, the creation of the Italian national health service in 1979. This sweeping reform involved the suppression of all the pre-existing health funds and the inclusion of all citizens in the new national health service (Ferrera, 1989).

Spain and Italy used very similar devices to fight economic crises: industrial restructuring, restrictive monetary policies to fight inflation, currency devaluations, and expansionary fiscal policies. Social agreements were also reached in both countries: the EUR ('Accordo dell' EUR', named after one of Rome's neighbourhoods) in Italy in 1978, and the Pactos de la Moncloa in Spain in 1977. These pacts sought to establish the conditions to make the modernization of industry possible, alongside the fight against unemployment and the moderation of wage growth. Fiscal policy reforms were aimed at reducing labour costs and at increasing competitiveness (Cella and Treu, 1989: De la Villa, 1985). Both reform trends were largely successful, although Spain had to pay a much higher price in terms of unemployment, which grew from 4.4 per cent in 1975 to a peak of 21.7 per cent in 1985. In Italy, unemployment almost doubled from 4.8 per cent to 8.4 per cent (see Table 6.3)

TABLE 6.3   *Unemployment rates (%) (1975–95)*

Country	1975	1985	1990	1995
Belgium	3.8	10.3	6.7	9.9
Denmark	3.9	7.1	7.7	7.2
Germany	3.5	7.2	4.8	8.2
Greece	1.5	7.0	6.4	9.2
Spain	*4.4*	*21.7*	*16.2*	*22.9*
France	3.9	10.1	9.0	11.7
Ireland	7.3	16.9	13.4	12.3
Italy	*4.8*	*8.4*	*9.1*	*11.9*
Luxembourg	1.1	2.9	1.7	2.9
Netherlands	4.3	8.3	6.2	6.9
Portugal	4.4	8.7	4.6	7.3
UK	3.2	11.5	7.1	8.8

Source: European Commission, *Employment in Europe* (1997).

Social concertation continued until the mid-1980s, when it started to wither away. In Spain, social pacts were signed in 1981 and 1984 (in particular, the Acuerdo Nacional de Empleo – ANE – and the Acuerdo Económico y Social – AES), which secured the participation of representatives of interest groups in the national institutes of social security and increased the state intervention in the financing of social protection. However, wage control was the main achievement of these social concertation episodes, such that real wages decreased significantly before 1986, after which there was an upward trend until the economic recession of the early 1990s (Ministerio de Trabajo, various years; De la Villa, 1985). In Italy, salaries were indexed to inflation since 1975, so that the 1978 EUR and 1983 social pacts (the latter known as the 'Lodo Scotti', i.e. the Scotti Agreement, after the name of the Labour Minister in office at the time) aimed at the moderation of wage increases. It was not until the early 1990s that this indexation was abolished by the Amato and Ciampi agreements (Cella and Treu, 1989).

Spain in the 1970s and 1980s

In Spain, the motto 'becoming Europeans' was commonplace in the political discourse and declarations of pressure groups during the late 1970s and early 1980s. This implied economic growth, and an improvement of social policy along the lines of the social democratic, Scandinavian systems. The emphasis on the need to cover all citizens through individual entitlements continued through the 1980s under the Socialist governments, especially regarding health care and education policies (Maravall, 1995). Catching-up and gains in equitable access were the driving and legitimating forces behind welfare reforms. Entry into the European Community in 1986 reinforced these ideas. In this way, health care and educational policies were universalized during the 1980s, with finance coming increasingly from state revenues. Social services also grew in extent of coverage and in the amount of resources devoted (Barrada, 1999). Income maintenance policies were reinforced in a number of ways by the Spanish regions during this period: establishment of minimum income policies between 1989 and 1993, development of family policies in 1990, and non-contributory cash benefits for the disabled and the elderly in 1991 (Cruz Roche, 1994; Moreno and Arriba, 1998; Rodríguez Cabrero, 1994).

However, the Spanish contributory pension system underwent its first restrictive reform in 1985. This reform was in line with the policy of economic adjustment, based on the control of public deficit and inflation. The 1985 reform changed the formula for calculating the initial amount of the pension received by including more salaried years (up from two to eight) and also lengthened the period (from eight to fifteen years) of minimum contributions needed for entitlement to a public pension (Guillén, 1999b).

Overall, and despite the latter restrictive reform, expenditure on social protection grew from 15.6 per cent of GDP in 1980, to 18.0 per cent in 1985, and to 20.7 per cent in 1990. Also, state revenues increased by ten percentage points, from 24.1 per cent of GDP in 1980 to 34.4 per cent in 1990 (see Tables 6.1 and 6.2 above).

Labour market reform, in the direction of flexibilization, also started in Spain in the mid-1980s. The 1983–4 reform had the effect of increasing the number of temporary contracts. Such contracts grew to the extent that they came to constitute over one-third of all jobs by the end of the decade. This posed increasing problems for the financial viability of unemployment protection due to the continuous movement in and out of the labour market by large numbers of workers. Unemployment protection grew steadily during the 1980s, covering around 80 per cent of all the unemployed by the end of the decade. Such levels of protection were also possible because of the change of focus in the unemployment protection system, so that the proportion of contributory benefits decreased in favour of non-contributory benefits. The latter are lower and are aimed at older people and the long-term unemployed with family dependants (Gutiérrez and Guillén, 1998). In 1990, due to an upturn in the economy, the unemployment rate fell to 16.2 per cent from a high of 21.7 per cent in 1985, and even long-term unemployment, as a proportion of total unemployment, decreased slightly from 58.5 per cent in 1985 to 54.7 per cent in 1990 (see Table 6.3 above and Table 6.4 below).

Italy in the 1970s and 1980s

In Italy, the Christian Democratic Party was not successful in effectively opposing the expansionary thrust of the social protection system produced in the late 1970s. Left-wing parties and unions managed to create a stable and strong coalition in favour of expansionary reform. Nonetheless, awareness of the necessity to reform social protection in the direction of efficiency gains was already emerging during the 1980s. One reason for this was a broad acknowledgement of the Italian macroeconomic imbalances. The blame for such imbalances was partially placed on a social protection system that was perceived as unequal and inefficient. However, political conflict slowed the introduction of the rationalizing reforms during the 1980s (Ferrera and Gualmini, 2000). As Tables 6.1 and 6.2 show, expenditure on social protection in Italy suffered a slight decrease from 1980 to 1985 (from 22.8 per cent to 22.5 per cent of GDP). It increased again during the second half of the decade, reaching 24.0 per cent in 1990. Conversely, taxation increased from 30.2 per cent of GDP in 1980 to 39.2 per cent in 1990, a move that would have significant implications for the restrictive reforms undertaken in the 1990s.

Growth in unemployment caused by industrial restructuring led to important social agreements in Italy in the period 1983/1984. These included the passing of several legal measures aimed at increasing labour market flexibilization. Training programmes and part-time contracts were fostered, together with job opportunities for young people and women. From 1986 onwards, the establishment of cooperatives by young people and regional employment agencies were also promoted (Cella and Treu, 1989). However, overall unemployment continued to grow during the second half of the 1980s, from 8.4 per cent in 1985 to 9.1 per cent in 1990. Moreover, long-term unemployment swept upwards, from 65 per cent of total unemployment in 1985 to 70.8 per cent in 1990 (see Tables 6. 3 and 6.4).

TABLE 6.4   *Long-term unemployment rate (% unemployment) (1985–95)*

Country	1985	1990	1995
Belgium	69.2	68.2	62.4
Denmark	38.6	32.5	27.7
Germany	53.7	46.0	48.7
Greece	46.2	51.8	51.3
Spain	58.5	54.7	54.6
France	46.8	44.8	40.2
Ireland	64.0	66.7	61.3
Italy	65.8	70.8	63.6
Netherlands	58.8	47.1	46.7
Portugal	56.2	47.5	50.8
UK	48.1	35.5	43.5

Source: European Commission, *Employment in Europe* (1997).

Towards European Integration: The 1990s

A different phase of public policy reform was initiated with the implementation of EMU, starting on the 1st of July 1990. From this date, convergence among European economies has marked the development of public policies of all European Union members, impinging on reductions and/or rationalization of public expenditure (including social expenditure) and public deficit and inflation control. The economic recession of 1993–6 challenged the whole European Monetary Union process. The crisis struck hard in southern Europe. In Italy, the lira was withdrawn from the European Monetary System (EMS), and Spain devalued the peseta on several occasions. Unemployment rose dramatically in Spain and in Italy, reaching overall levels of 22.9 per cent in Spain and 11.9 per cent in Italy in 1995 (see Table 6.3).

These crises led national governments to become more aware of the need to apply new economic adjustment remedies. Radical reform of public policies was necessary to balance the economy in the medium term, if Spain and Italy wanted to comply with the conditions for membership of EMU. Accordingly, the strategy of reform of economic and social policy clearly changed direction.

In Spain, by the end of the 1980s, attention to equity in social policy had lost ground in favour of a search for efficiency and equity. In this context, the recommendations of the European Commission's White Paper *Growth, Competitiveness and Employment* (1994) were seriously considered. Also, the British government's White Paper on the reform of the National Health Service was scrutinized. Nevertheless, strong resistance to a reduction in achieved levels of equity and, even more so, to privatization moves, were witnessed during the 1990s in Spain. This was probably due to the concentration of historical events, as the austerity period and the conditions for European monetary integration came very soon after the universalist reforms of health care and education had been introduced.

The need for adjustment was felt most keenly in Italy. This did not necessarily mean a less pronounced emphasis on equity, as reforms sought an internal re-balancing of social protection by decreasing existing inequalities while at the same time gaining in economic efficiency. Moreover, macroeconomic imbalances, as compared with the conditions required by the Maastricht treaty, were higher in Italy than in Spain. As Table 6.5 shows, budget deficit was of 9.5 per cent of GDP in Italy as compared with 6.9 per cent in Spain in 1993. However, both countries were able to reduce it to 2.5 per cent and 2.2 per cent respectively by 1998.

Spain in the 1990s

In Spain, reforms were focused on the protection of the unemployed (enacted through legislation in 1992). The continual moving into and out of the labour market associated with the increase in temporary jobs, together with the intensification of unemployment protection during the second half of the 1980s, took the National Institute for Unemployment close to bankruptcy in the early 1990s. Restrictive reform was imposed by the Socialist Party in 1992, which meant a drastic reduction of the replacement rates of unemployment benefits and in the time-span during which benefits can be claimed. In addition, the minimum period of contributions required for access to benefits was extended. By the late 1990s, only half the unemployed received benefits in Spain, as opposed to coverage rates in excess of 80 per cent of the unemployed in the late 1980s (Gutiérrez and Guillén, 1998). Also, in 1993–4, several laws were passed enabling further flexibilization of the labour market. This time, part-time jobs were heavily subsidized and the establishment of private non-profit employment agencies was allowed.

In contrast to income maintenance programmes, cost control measures have proved much harder to apply to welfare services in Spain, especially in the domain of health care. The proposals aimed at slowing down the growth of public expenditure on health care made by a parliamentary commission in 1991 – Comisión Abril – were a complete failure, because of the frontal opposition they aroused among the unions and the population in general. These proposals for cost control arrived only five years after the date on which the health system was reformed (General Health Law of 1986) and three years after full universalization of benefits was attained (State Budget Law of 1989). Ever since the Conservative Party gained office in 1996, the opposition, headed by the Socialist Party, has turned into a sort of 'guardian' of existing levels of provision. Thus, cost control measures have been introduced in a piecemeal and quiet way into the health care system, and have consisted mainly of measures affecting the supply side (as in, for example, prospective budgeting, contract agreements with hospitals, and several managed competition devices). No cost-sharing measures have been introduced so far in the Spanish NHS (Guillén, 1999a; Guillén and Cabiedes, 1997).

Italy in the 1990s

In Italy, despite the lack of success in the rationalization of public policy during the 1980s, the debate resulted in broad changes in public discourse and political action during the 1990s. The push towards managerialism and efficient administration characterized political endeavours during the 1990s, eased by some change in the political elites and reform of the electoral system. Strong emphasis was placed on the view that public administration should adopt the principles of managerialism, and reform was undertaken energetically. This led to radical change in Italy during the 1990s. Reform of the pension system took place in 1992, under the Amato government. It increased the age of retirement from 55 to 60 years for women and from 60 to 65 for men who were workers in the private sector. Moreover, the minimum contributory period for being entitled to a contributory pension was extended from ten to twenty years, the longest in the EU. The income replacement rate was reduced by virtue of including the last ten salaried years (instead of five) in the formula to calculate the initial amount of the pension. The reform of the health care system involved the extension of the decentralization process, the implementation of strict measures of cost control, and a change in the administration of health institutions in the direction of managed competition (Ferrera and Gualmini, 2000; Guillén, 1999a).

TABLE 6.5   *Evolution of budget deficit (%GDP)*

Country	1993	1994	1995	1996	1997	1998
Belgium	7.1	4.9	3.9	3.2	2.1	1.7
Denmark	2.8	2.8	2.4	0.7	(0.7)	(1.1)
Germany	3.2	2.4	3.3	3.4	2.7	2.5
Greece	13.8	10.0	10.3	7.5	4.0	2.2
Spain	6.9	6.3	7.3	4.6	2.6	2.2
France	5.8	5.8	4.9	4.1	3.0	2.9
Ireland	2.7	1.7	2.2	0.4	(0.9)	(1.1)
Italy	9.5	9.2	7.7	6.7	2.7	2.5
Luxembourg	(1.7)	(2.8)	(1.9)	(2.5)	(1.7)	(1.0)
Netherlands	3.2	3.8	4.0	2.3	1.4	1.6
Portugal	6.1	6.0	5.7	3.2	2.5	2.2
UK	7.9	6.8	5.5	4.8	1.9	0.6

Note: Figures in brackets indicate estimates.
Source: European Commission, *Euro 1999: Informe sobre la Convergencia* (Brussels, 1998).

Overview and Comparison

The impact of the reforms of the 1990s, on Spanish and Italian social protection systems, can be seen in Tables 6.1, 6.2, 6.5 and 6.6. Table 6.1 shows how total expenditure on social protection has continued to grow in Spain (from 20.7 per cent in 1990 to 23.6 per cent of GDP in 1994) at a similar pace to that of the 1980s, while it has grown to a lesser extent in Italy (from 24.0 per cent in 1990 to 25.3 per cent in 1994). Fiscal pressure has decreased slightly in Spain (34.4 per cent in 1990 to 34.0 per cent) and it is certain to decrease again after the restrictive reform enacted in 1998. In Italy, the data show a slight increase: 39.2 per cent in 1990 to 41.3 per cent in 1994. However, in the latter, taxation has grown much less than in the 1980s (see Table 6.2). Table 6.5 shows the impact of rationalization measures on public deficit control. Both Spain and Italy have been able to reach the Maastricht criteria, although the effort has been much more intense in the case of Italy.

In Table 6.6, the growth of social expenditure by function is summarized. Spain shows moderate increases in expenditure in almost all areas of social policy (with the exception of housing) for the period 1990–5. Conversely, in Italy decreases have taken place in sickness benefits, health

TABLE 6.6   *Growth of social expenditure by function in purchasing power parities (1990–95)*

Function	Spain	Italy	Europe 13
Sickness cash benefits			
1990–93	8.2	–5.1	0.3
1993–95	–0.9	–9.5	0.3
1990–95	4.5	–6.9	0.3
Health			
1990–93	5.8	0.0	4.1
1993–95	0.4	–4.9	1.8
1990–95	3.6	–2.0	3.2
Disability			
1990–93	4.6	1.6	5.6
1993–95	0.1	–1.5	2.8
1990–95	2.8	0.3	4.5
Old-age and survivors			
1990–93	5.2	4.8	4.1
1993–95	2.7	2.0	2.4
1990–95	4.2	3.7	3.4
Family and children			
1990–93	6.2	–5.8	3.3
1993–95	1.8	–3.3	0.5
1990–95	4.4	–4.8	2.2
Unemployment			
1990–93	14.0	14.3	10.4
1993–95	–14.5	–4.1	–5.3
1990–95	1.6	6.5	3.9
Housing			
1990–93	–0.7	–3.1	8.9
1993–95	–10.5	–5.3	2.7
1990–95	–4.8	–4.0	6.4
Social exclusion			
1990–93	18.3	10.9	7.2
1993–95	–1.3	12.4	6.4
1990–95	10.0	11.5	6.9

Source: European Commission, *Social Protection in Europe 1997* (Luxembourg, 1998).

care, family and children policies and housing. Increases in the remaining categories are only moderate. The highest expansion in both countries has taken place in expenditure on policies to fight social exclusion. On balance, nothing seems to indicate that either globalization or European integration directly imposed severe cutbacks in either of the welfare states considered here. What happened was a slowdown in social expenditure growth, which was in line with the need for macroeconomic adjustment in both countries.

New Actors in the Policy Process?

In Spain and Italy, one cannot really talk about the appearance of new actors in the policy-making process, with the important exception of the European Union. The EU gained prominence because (a) globalization has meant, above all, European integration in both countries, and (b) because experts and government officials in the European institutions and pressure groups have introduced and spread new ideas for policy reform.

Though not really 'new' actors, autonomous regions have developed their roles in both countries since the process of transition to democracy started. This is unrelated to the impact of globalization and is more a matter of internal politics and historical aspirations. Nevertheless, regional bodies have played a crucial role in both countries. Firstly, decentralization has often had a sort of 'domino effect', such that initiatives undertaken in one region have quickly spread to other regions which wanted to prove to their citizens that they could do as much for them. Also, and no less important, a number of innovative measures in social policy were introduced first within regional settings, the central state later adopting them at a national level. This has resulted in an expansionary trend in areas of social policy in those countries that decentralized – Greece and Portugal have not witnessed this expansion because of the absence of similar devolutionary trends. Not all the consequences of devolution have been positive in Spain and Italy. Comparative grievances, increased territorial inequalities, and difficulties in implementing cost control have increased, together with highly complicated processes of negotiations in relation to the funding of regional welfare provision.

In southern Europe, rather than to focus on new actors it would be more appropriate to speak about the birth of different patterns of action undertaken by traditional actors. For example, organized labour and employers' organizations have continued to play a role, and have agreed, since the mid-1990s, to reach important pacts with governments regarding the reform of social policy, public administration, labour market flexibilization and macroeconomic adjustment. This constitutes what Rhodes (1998) has labelled 'competitive corporatism'.

In Spain, such 'competitive corporatism' appeared especially after the Conservative Party (PP) gained office in 1996, but other important agreements had been achieved under the previous Socialist government. The Toledo Pact (Pacto de Toledo) was reached in 1995 between all political parties with parliamentary representation, and later confirmed by the unions and employers' organizations. It was an agreement to rationalize the pension system by formulating a set of proposals aimed at cost control and ensuring the future viability of the public system. In 1996, another social pact was signed between the Conservative government and the unions regarding the application of the Toledo Pact. This agreement became law in 1997, when pensions were further reformed. In particular, income replacement rates were decreased again by including more salaried years (one year to be added to the formula from 1997 to 2002). Finally, in 1997, a social agreement was reached between the Conservative Party and the unions, enabling further flexibilization of the labour market by decreasing redundancy payments. In exchange, by decreasing the social contributions of employers, the conversion of temporary jobs into permanent ones was fostered by the government. In 1999, the conditions for part-time, marginal and work-experience contracts in relation to social security benefits were harmonized with those of full-time workers. This is a crucial measure, as one of the most prominent traditional features of southern welfare regimes was that of overprotecting core workers. This reform indicates a significant change of strategy. Also in 1999, the reform of public administrations in line with the principles of the 'new public management' was agreed with the unions.

In Italy, important social pacts were also reached in the 1990s. In particular, in 1992 and 1993, two significant social agreements were signed under the Amato and Ciampi governments. The indexation of salaries to inflation was abolished, so that wage policies underwent dramatic change. It was decided that wages would be linked to expected inflation in a flexible way. These measures were complemented in 1996 with a Pact for Employment, promoted by Ciampi, in order to stimulate activation measures. Temporary contracts were introduced and, in 1997, private employment agencies were set up throughout the country (Ferrera and Gualmini, 2000).

An Overview of Changes

In order to assess whether the features of the welfare regime changed in response to any one factor, in this case globalization, one has to choose a point in time to do the comparison. If one compares the Southern welfare states of the 1970s with the present, then the change is from a Bismarckian/Conservative model to a dual one, in which different principles are adopted for the provision of income transfers and welfare services. This change was due to such a long list of factors that it is difficult to isolate from the impact of globalization *per se*. (It is difficult, if not impossible, to assess change with reference the 'Southern model of welfare' as defined by Ferrera, because this model was defined in 1996, by taking into account the characteristics of Southern welfare states at that point in time.)

Even so, some significant developments can be pinpointed for the period 1996–9. Among these are the financing of health care services out of state revenues introduced in Italy in 1998, and in Spain by the State Budget Law of 1999, and the improvement of non-contributory transfers and the rationalization of contributory transfers that had the effect of reducing inequalities between the protection levels of labour market insiders and outsiders. A minimum income scheme was introduced in Italy in 1998, the Spanish regional minimum income programmes have experienced expansion, and legislative action has taken place in Catalonia and the Basque Country in order to improve protection. Finally, as Table 6.6 shows, expenditure on the fight against social exclusion increased significantly during the 1990s, producing evidence that Southern welfare systems are not 'rudimentary' in the social assistance domain.

To sum up, one could say that an intense expansion of Southern social protection systems was combined in the 1970s and 1980s with the introduction of some rationalizing reforms, whereas efficiency became one of the main target of the 1990s. It seems that external pressures due to globalization and European integration affected Southern welfare states more intensely in the 1990s than ever before. Let us now turn to consider such pressures in more detail.

Globalization and Social Policy Change

Globalization, rather than constituting a disembodied exogenous force, has affected southern Europe through the process of European integration in at least two senses which have influenced the attitudes and perceptions of policy-makers. In the first place, the need for macroeconomic restructuring was seen as essential for joining the EU's Economic and Monetary Union. This would allow southern European countries to be part of a strong economic area, leading to a higher degree of competitiveness as a result. In the second place, becoming 'Europeans' in its full sense also meant that the achieved levels of social protection could not be put at risk, but rather rationalized in order to close the gaps and correct past inequalities. We are talking here about conscious, strong political choices made by internal political actors, not merely the passive acceptance of a strategy imposed by abstract, external globalization pressures.

Have Southern welfare states shown a high level of vulnerability to the influences of globalization? In our view, Southern governments have lost some autonomy, as have other European governments, when faced with European integration and economic globalization. However, this has not led to a drastic reduction of social protection in order to gain national economic competitiveness. Social policy arrangements changed significantly in the 1970s, 1980s and 1990s due to a combination of a clear political will to catch up with the more advanced EU welfare states (mainly in the 1970s and 1980s) and the pursuit of rationalizing strategies and the reduction of past inequalities (mainly in the 1990s). They have clearly avoided becoming basic safety net systems, and few indiscriminate cut backs have occurred.

It appears that the basic features of Southern welfare states stayed the same in the 1980s and 1990s. None of the challenges to the universality of social policies that were discussed actually occurred. Furthermore, there is no clear evidence of privatization, severe cut-backs or of a social-dumping strategy. As a result, Southern welfare states have continued to be based on Bismarckian principles (albeit with significant redistributory revisions) in the income maintenance domain, and based upon the social citizenship principles in the health care area. Social services have been redirected to citizens instead of to workers and their dependants only, although they have also become means-tested. Two parallel developments appear to have occurred. On the one hand, cost-control devices have been introduced and more efficiency has been sought, especially during the 1990s. On the other hand, a thrust towards increased redistribution of benefits to previously excluded social groups is evident in the expansion of non-contributory transfers, non-contributory services, the development of policies aimed at combating social exclusion and by the universalization of some areas of social protection. Moreover, past inequalities embedded in traditional areas of social protection, such as contributory pensions, have been reduced.

It would appear that Southern welfare states have shown moderate vulnerability to globalization trends, with a greater impact on macroeconomic policy than on social protection policies. Reaction to globalization, understood here as economic adjustment and social policy rationalization aimed at European integration, has resulted mainly in *positive* results in both fields. By 'positive results' we mean:

- the achievement of the Maastricht criteria for convergence, as regards inflation and public deficit control, a goal that presented more challenges to Southern economies than to the other EU members;
- in the social policy domain, a gain in efficiency and an increased focus on previously excluded groups of the population.

The loss of government autonomy has occurred to no greater or lesser extent than in any other EU member-state in terms of macroeconomic policies related to European economic integration. This may be more challenging in the future for southern countries in the event of deeper economic recession since their economies are not so strong, and they are no longer able to use monetary devaluation strategies. The pressures of globalization, mediated through European economic integration, have helped to bring to the fore past inequalities, reinforce some policy areas with more redistributive devices, and apply rationalizing measures. Integration within the EU has borne positive effects in the social policy area, where EU recommendations have drawn the attention of Southern welfare states to the needs of the elderly and the disabled, the reconciliation of family and working life, gender equality, and social inclusion.

As regards the labour market, governments have lost autonomy, especially in terms of their regulatory powers (for example, in regulating salaries), and mediation mechanisms. This is mainly due to the globalization of the markets for several products. However, governments have to play a more important part in dealing with the consequences of flexibilization of labour markets, such as increased unemployment and the growth of new inequalities. They have had to redirect public protection to cover new needs and design innovative activation policies.

Anticipation of the consequences of globalization has had the effect of pushing southern governments into action related to increased labour market flexibility, facilitating the creation of firms, supporting the production of competitive export products, backing up national companies abroad and so on. Southern labour markets were especially rigid in comparison with those of other EU members, so that flexibilization measures adopted in the 1980s were further intensified in the 1990s. Globalization (*qua* European integration) has also been used as a convenient ideological distraction and excuse for making changes that were actually determined internally (see, for example, the reform of passive unemployment protection in 1992 in Spain, that was presented by the government as a necessary move in order to meet EU recommendations). Blame-avoidance strategies (Weaver, 1986) have been used on many of these occasions, to put the blame on Brussels rather than on national governments, especially when restrictive reforms were introduced.

Conclusions

The relationship between globalization and social policy change may be considered as highly significant in southern European countries, but not in a negative 'rush to the bottom' strategy. This has been due to the perception in these countries of globalization as being about the need to attain European integration. Integration into the Union was associated not only with macroeconomic reform, but also with the respect of social protection standards and a move to reduce past inequalities within the social protection distribution and allocation mechanisms. Growth in social protection expenditure did decelerate during the 1990s in order to balance the economy, but this was coupled with an reform of management, a search for efficacy and efficiency, and increased attention to previously excluded or weakly protected social groups.

The desire for integration in the European Union was due to the perceived challenges that a global economy poses for competition, which, it was argued, could be resolved by belonging to a powerful economic area. The need to adjust local economies fostered a new consciousness of existing inequalities in social policy. It pushed governments and other political actors into thinking about their welfare states in a new light, to pose different reform questions such as who was benefiting from public provision, and how best to provide for the excluded. Also, efficiency seeking has had positive results in relation to problems revealed by the crisis of the welfare state, such as bureaucratic managerial practices, solidarity issues, employment patterns, and so forth.

In southern Europe, one can see a clear pattern of interaction between social policy change and globalization effective in both directions, constituting a two-way road. It is not only that southern countries have adopted a specific approach to globalization, but also that pre-existing social policy structures have moulded their policy responses. Thus, the pre-existing institutional arrangements have influenced policy reform. As far as cash transfers are concerned, Spain and Italy have changed their income maintenance policies like other Bismarckian systems – by reducing the level of protection of future contributing pensioners and by increasing non-contributory benefits. In reforming their health care systems that are directed to all citizens and financed out of public revenues, however, they have emulated the British strategy of reform of the national health service. Managed competition devices have been adopted in both countries. Finally, activation policies have come to gain importance *vis-à-vis* unemployment subsidies, but this constitutes a general trend, which is probably due to the fact that all European economies face a severe problem of unemployment.

7

Welfare and 'Ill-Fare' Systems in Central-Eastern Europe

ZSUZSA FERGE

There are huge variations in the political structure and in the public policies of the post-state-socialist countries, called hereafter 'transition' countries. The view widely shared in the early 1990s that all of them would
pass from dictatorship to democracy and from state planning to a market
system in a relatively short time, proved to be oversimplified for all, and
widely off the mark for quite a few. The countries in the 'western belt' of
Eastern Europe, in the region called (for varied historical reasons) Central-
Eastern Europe (CEE) have come closest to this model. This chapter considers the whole Eastern European region, but focuses particularly on the
following Central-Eastern European countries: the Czech Republic,
Hungary, Poland, Slovenia, and Slovakia.

The aim of this chapter is to describe the forces that have shaped the
social policy of the 'transition countries'. It starts by looking for general
characteristics of the welfare regimes of the region. It suggests that the
new global ideology, conservative and populist endeavours, historical
inertia and path-dependency, all play a part, resulting in producing faceless or mixed systems, some of them close to what is called 'ill-fare'.
Secondly, it describes the welfare reform agendas of the countries in the
region. Out of the various projects, those of the IMF and the World Bank
are chosen for particular consideration, since they have been the most
elaborated. They were meant to serve the economic competitiveness of the
transition countries in a globalizing world, simultaneously pushing them
towards a residualized social policy. Thirdly, it gives an overview of the

127

main changes in the welfare arrangements of the CEE countries in which, despite path-dependency and institutional inertia, these pressures were rather successful. The final part attempts to explain why the resistance to the globalizing pressures for state retrenchment was weaker in Central-Eastern Europe than in most of Western Europe. It suggests that the impact of 'globalization' as a powerful ideology rooted in transnational economic interests is strongly mitigated by the economic vulnerability of the given country, by the political orientation of its government, and by the strength of its civil society.

East-European Welfare Regimes

Gøsta Esping-Andersen's work on welfare state regimes created a new intellectual fashion. The classification into 'ideal types' of modern welfare regimes becomes relevant only, though, when the logic behind it is made clear (as it is in the original work). Thus before labelling, one has to analyse the political or economic factors shaping the welfare regime; the way a regime impacts on social stratification, on ethnic and gender issues; on the strength of social rights; on the emancipatory potential of the welfare system; and also on its outcome, whether it assures a basic minimum income preventing poverty, or an adequate standard promoting social integration for all. Notwithstanding the limitations of using labels, this chapter will also start by characterizing the 'transition' countries, discussing former labels, and will turn to some of the 'real' questions later.

An understanding of current welfare structures is helped by some reference to their immediate past. Interestingly enough, the social policy of the 'second world', or communist states, attracted hardly any interest in the West while the former political regimes were in place. Also, within the countries themselves, the political and ideological climate was not conducive to any critical analysis of national social policies for a very long time.

When the discourse of welfare regimes first emerged in the early 1990s, some authors characterized the former system as relatively close to a social democratic model. Deacon (1992) described it as a 'state bureaucratic collectivist system', while in Götting's view it was 'state-paternalistic' (Götting, 1998, p. 84). My own approach in those early days was less clear-cut. I thought that the understanding of the past and the future might best be served by acknowledging the lack of uniformity between the countries, and the mixed character of 'state socialist' social policy within each of them.

(D)espite formal similarities, the liberal and emancipating dimensions of the Scandinavian model were entirely absent from the state-socialist model of welfare. It had even less in common with the other regime types in Europe. If one wants to label it, it could be described as an anti-liberal, statist, hierarchical, socialist mix, with conservative elements thrown in. (Ferge, 1992, p. 207)

In the early years of the transition, it seemed as if the liberated countries could choose a future for themselves depending on their pre-socialist and socialist past. Deacon could muse that

Czechoslovakia is the best bet for a type of social democratic welfare regime, and Hungary is set to develop liberal welfare policies ... In Bulgaria, Albania and Serbia ... more of the old regime looks likely to remain in place ... A new type of post-communist conservative corporatism might emerge here with the old state continuing to play a major role ... A Latin-American authoritarian populism may be the only solution in Poland and elsewhere. (Deacon, 1992, pp. 12–13)

At that time, I thought that the welfare regime of the coming years would consist of a minimal safety-net – along with corporatist, private, and semi-private solutions, some kind of mixture of conservative and liberal elements (Ferge, 1992, p. 220). In a later book (1997) Deacon distinguished in the region

the existing welfare model of Bismarckian conservative corporatism and the new post-communist conservatism, which is always in danger of giving way to welfare collapse. A new social liberalism (liberalism with safety nets) is also evident. (Deacon *et al.*, 1997, p. 52)

These assessments are all fragile because all the countries are continuously in flux. Lelkes (1999) takes this into account when she concludes that the Hungarian welfare state is rather 'faceless' at the moment. She also suggests that it may still be regarded in terms of Esping-Andersen's model as being closest to the social democratic ideal type, due to its inherited structures.

Ten years after the government changes, one can talk, hypothetically at least, about four trends in the welfare politics of the region. The dominant one is a practically ubiquitous *neo-liberal* tendency that seems to be dictated by concerns allegedly related to the globalization process. Its hallmarks are the will to deregulate all markets, the labour market included; the drive to lower direct and indirect labour costs; and the privatization and marketization of former public goods and services resulting in a smaller state. These endeavours are underpinned by a forceful rhetoric about the need to end 'state paternalism', and to strengthen self-reliance and self-provision.

Neo-liberalism is often combined with a more country-specific and government-specific *conservative trend*, with the Church, the family, and the nation as central values. The corollaries include the revival of nationalism (with fatal consequences); hidden or open ethnic prejudices; the emphasis on protecting 'healthy' families and on boosting fertility (occasionally by banning abortion); and some privileges assured for the middle and upper strata.

The *third* tendency may be termed *path-dependency*. Some of the former schemes represent state commitments that are hard to restructure quickly and in a legitimate way. Therefore a genuine residual, neo-liberal model is unlikely to appear quickly even if the neo-liberal rhetoric is extremely strong.

The *fourth* trend is the most tragic one. It is related to a *near-collapse of the state*. If the state is losing its power of taxation (income generation), then most public expenditure, welfare outlays included, will undoubtedly evaporate. On the basis of available data on budget revenues, this seems to be the case in Russia, Albania, and some of the countries of the former Soviet Union, for example Armenia. The IMF statistics show that in Russia the government revenues dropped to about 10 per cent of the GDP from the mid-1990s. This was in contrast to most other European countries where revenues were between 30 to 50 per cent of GDP (World Bank, 1999a, pp. 286–8; IMF, 1998c). Public social expenditures, which are between 20 and 30 percent of GDP across Europe, dropped to 7.7 per cent of GDP in 1995 in Russia.

The countries close to becoming '*ill-fare states*' are apparently losing the potential to become modern welfare states in the foreseeable future. This may be due partly to the collapse of a repressive and ineffective system. However, the question is whether the collapse of the state was an inevitable outcome of the transition in those countries (Holmes, 1997). It is possible that the supranational agencies were promoting the recipes of the 'Washington consensus' too relentlessly. This consensus defined an economic policy which, as Stiglitz (1998) argues, seems to have been agreed upon in the 1980s by US economic officials, the International Monetary Fund, and the World Bank. This consensus emphasized liberalized trade, macroeconomic stability, and getting price levels right. Government should keep out of the market to allow economic growth. This policy position was uniform but its impact was not. Due to the specific history of the Soviet Union, and of some other countries of the region, it was particularly ill-adapted to them. I would suggest that the implementation of such policy probably precipitated the collapse of the state. The examples of China and, perhaps, Vietnam suggest that there may be alternatives to the rigid adaptation of these monetarist recipes.

Of the other countries in the region, some have hardly started on the road towards market and political democracy, and try to maintain the former welfare system (Belarus is an example). Among the countries of CEE, the post-Klaus Czech social democratic government and, perhaps, some Baltic state close to Scandinavia, seem to look for a compromise between the pressures of globalization and concern for the 'public good'. Others are open to the neo-liberal reforms promoted by the Washington consensus, though the speed of the reforms may be slowed down by the 'inertia' of former arrangements. Hungary, for example, has become a curious mix of policies that bear the marks of three successive governments. The first tried to avoid change. The second introduced a type of neo-liberal shock therapy. The third, without giving up neo-liberal endeavours, uses social policy for the promotion of highly conservative policies.

One has to conclude that there is no unique label to describe these countries, and none of the relatively clear-cut ideal-typical labels applies to them. They differ from each other, and they are all changing constantly, influenced by internal and external social forces. Most of them seem to share just one feature: the *absence* of a project for a welfare system which would significantly mitigate the costs of the transition in the short run, and would promote the emancipatory dimension of social policy as well as the formation of an integrated society in the long term.

The Agenda and Ideology of the Welfare Reforms

At the time of the collapse of the former system, the citizens expected that the new governments would produce a combination of a market economy, a free society, and improved social security. The political programmes and the politicians responded to this expectation by promising a 'social market economy'. Vaclav Klaus was the noted exception to this – he committed himself to a market economy 'without adjectives'. The meaning of the 'social market economy' was never made clear and the slogan slowly disappeared.

In the early years of the transition, 'reforms in social programs and services were minor parts of the adjustment agenda' (Nelson, 1998, p. 7).

Inasmuch as the diagnosis is correct, it should not be explained mainly, as is often done, by reference to the vested interests of former bureaucracies or 'stake-holders', and by institutional inertia. Many social policy arrangements of the former system were, formally at least, similar to the western models so that their reform looked less urgent than that of politics or of the economy. More importantly, in contrast to the other subsystems, these arrangements had relatively strong legitimacy. For instance, even the World Bank realized, when criticizing Hungary for the postponement of public finance reforms, that the government was slow because it hesitated 'to implement *unpopular* measures'. Indeed, despite grave economic difficulties, no democratically elected government that came to power directly after the regime change dared to increase the burden of the transition by a radical cutback of social benefits.

Meanwhile fundamental reforms may have been absent, but lots of small-scale reforms were undertaken. They may have been *ad hoc* reforms, incremental changes, or efforts to manage imminent crises without a coherent reform pattern. After a decade it appears, however, that in most countries the sum of the reforms amounts – intentionally or not, and with due variation between the countries – to the 'reform agenda' formulated by the IMF and World Bank.

Both these agencies saw privatization and liberalization as a first priority in the economy. They were also concerned, though, with some social issues (World Bank, 1991; IMF, 1990). The IMF and, more particularly, the World Bank were advocating the rapid introduction of provisions for the unemployed whose number was increasing. The World Bank also recommended the regular indexation of benefits, a correct system of social assistance, and in the early days (1991) it also looked for ways to assure that 'no household is put at risk of poverty and undue hardship' (1991, p. iv). This concern did not appear in later reports.

The recommendations about a benefit system for the unemployed were implemented in most countries. (In some countries the creation of the necessary institutions preceded the external advice.) The handling of poverty remained extremely inadequate, though, with the exception of the Czech Republic (OECD, 1998). The reason was not merely the lack of resources. Rather, in many of these countries there remained a deep-seated aversion to assistance based on rights (instead of discretion) together with strong prejudices against the 'undeserving poor'. It should be said that the recommendations for a European-style assistance or for the prevention of poverty never figured among the loan conditions. In other words, their neglect was never considered a serious failure inviting sanction.

The documents of the supranational agencies in this period also outline a broader reform framework. The most important elements may be divided into short-term and medium-term priorities. In the short term, the emphasis was on savings. Recommendations included keeping labour costs low – 'the total cost of labour should be distinctly lower if Hungary is to compete effectively with other middle-income countries' (World Bank, 1991, p. iii); making short-term economies by reducing the number on disability pension, by introducing users' fees, or by shifting the first 30 days of sick-pay to the employer instead of the health fund. (The IMF suggested six weeks: IMF, 1990, p. 9). A more far-reaching measure that was included in the recommendations was the rapid withdrawal of price subsidies without compensation. According to the terms of the first Hungarian Structural Adjustment Loan (SAL1) signed in 1990, 'Consumer and housing subsidies will be reduced from about 8.2 of GDP in 1989 to no more than 6 per cent of GDP in 1990, 5 per cent in 1991 and 3.5 per cent of GDP by 1992.' According to UNICEF (1997, p. 138), the ratio of consumer price subsidies actually did go down in Hungary from 7 to 1.5 per cent, and in Poland from 8.2 to 0.7 per cent in the period between 1989 and 1993.

The medium or long-term overall priorities in the social sphere consisted of the withdrawal of the state from the existing services, and the improvement of efficiency by the privatization and marketization of these services. These steps were to be completed by the reduction of the coverage and standards of all social benefits except social assistance, which is a well-targeted safety-net for the poor. According to the Hungarian loan agreement of SAL1 signed in 1990: 'The development of a market economy is not possible without a significant reduction in the role of the state budget in redistributing resources within the economy through taxes and subsidies.' According to the World Bank, in a report on Hungary published in 1994:

> Social cash transfers in a market economy need to have the right incentive structure to encourage individuals to work, save, pay taxes, take risks, and fend for themselves as much as possible, turning to the state only as a last resort. This underlying philosophy differs from the past where the state was an integral part of the income security of the family. (World Bank, 1994a, p. 4)

The 1996 World Development Report prescribed the 'minimal state' not just for one country, but in a more general sense:

> State intervention is justified only where market fails – in such areas as defence, primary education, rural roads, and some special insurance – and then only to the extent it improves upon the market. (World Bank, 1996, p. 110)

The post-Washington consensus seemed to offer a radical alternative to the 'Washington Consensus' by redefining the role of the nation-state and of civil society.

The rhetoric in relation to both empowerment and participation and to the independence and the growing functions of the nation-states is really new and welcome. It is supported by such democratizing initiatives of the Bank as its Speakers' Corner on the Internet. However, there are some catches. It is difficult to assess increased participation of the citizens. It is also the case that while citizens may have a public voice, they might not necessarily have the institutional means to control the impact of their voice. Moreover, the redefinition of the role of the state seems to be more apparent than real. The details of the new outlook reveal that the building of human capital is restricted to financing primary education and to some preventive health measures excluding all curative care (World Bank, 1997a). All in all, the concrete and measurable targets of social policy in the new agenda do not differ radically from the old.

A recent World Bank document on the Bank's web page (1999b) is evidence of this allegation. While recognizing that there may be several reform agendas in the social protection field, it declares that 'they have two shared aims'. First, they have to empower the population to make informed choices about the handling of social risks. Second, they have to operate in '*a common fiscal context of sharply reduced real public expenditures*'. Common objectives can be reached by common instruments within the reform agenda. These include a 'fundamental systemic pension reform, mainly through the introduction of mandatory and voluntary funded pension schemes'; 'moving social assistance from universal coverage to more targeted protection'; 'promoting more efficient labour markets including less rigid wage determination processes', as well as the strengthening of the safety-net and community participation (World Bank, 1999b).

The similarity of aims and means allows for a common yardstick in the measurement of the progress of the reforms. The four dimensions of the overall assessment are 'liberalization, property rights and private ownership, institutions, and social policies' (World Bank, 1996, p. 13). Each dimension is represented by several indicators combined to form one index of social policy. 'The social policy index measures progress in pension reform, reduction of subsidies, streamlining and targeting of income transfers, and divestiture of social assets' (World Bank, 1999b, p. 17). The social assets may refer to the social infrastructure of firms, such as workers' hostels or holiday homes, but also to state-owned large public utilities such as infrastructure, energy or water, or even to the collectively owned funds of public social insurance. Based on such measurements, the World Bank distinguishes four groups of countries. The group most 'advanced' in terms of these reforms comprises Poland, Slovenia, Hungary, Croatia, FYR Macedonia, Czech Republic, and Slovakia: the countries of Central-Eastern Europe.

The dimensions of empowerment and democratization have not yet been included in the measurement of progress. 'Extensive progress' or 'substantial reform' do not take into account the social outcomes of the reforms such as the failure of the original aim to assure that 'no household is put at risk of poverty and undue hardship'. Also, some traditional components of social policy never crop up in any of the IMF or World Bank documents. Social integration, social exclusion, the containment or reduction of income inequalities, labour rights, a living wage and such like do not form part of the reform agendas. These are more characteristic of the outlook of the International Labour Organization (ILO). However, the ILO – despite its long presence in the region – had only a very sporadic and weak impact after the transition. The efforts of the OECD – often wavering between the 'European' and the 'monetarist' outlook – were similarly weak (Deacon *et al.*, 1997).

The multifaceted impact of the above agendas on Central-Eastern and Eastern Europe is difficult to assess empirically. Things are in flux, data are controversial, and value-laden preconceptions colour the answers. Even if it is shown that one of the agendas had an impact on the region, a caveat must be added. The region has become politically free. Therefore, *no outside agency could force any reform on the countries without the cooperation and agreement of local political actors or, more precisely, of the governments*. Thus the responsibility for any decision ultimately rests with national governments.

The Welfare Reforms – an Overview

One of the basic aims of the transition was to change the role of the state and of the market fundamentally, notably in social provision. This aim has been quite successfully realized.

The state as owner, as financing agent, and as service provider is withdrawing from the welfare sector – sometimes slowly and sometimes more rapidly. There are positive aspects of this withdrawal, such as the abolition of top-heavy monopolies; the pluralization of service providers; an increase in freedom of choice; and, most importantly, administrative decentralization. Meanwhile, the unreflective nature of the change is disquieting. The future role of the state has never been thought through. This results in erratic, inconsistent and frequently arbitrary state policies. The lack of accountability and transparency of public administration breeds corruption all over the region. A further difficulty is the ongoing ambiguous situation of local authorities in almost all of the countries. Their new independence is mobilizing local resources, and this often produces local renewal. However, their power and responsibility were enlarged without adequate funds, administrative capacity, or professional know-how to fulfil their role.

One indicator of state retrenchment is the changing role of redistribution through the state. The data of the OECD (OECD, various years) on social and total state expenditures of western countries do not point to dramatic changes. The ratio of social expenditures to GDP has remained relatively stable. It decreased with the biggest spenders (e.g. the Netherlands), and increased in the case of some former laggards (e.g. Greece), producing some convergence. However, since GDP has increased almost continuously everywhere in the West, even decreasing ratios do not necessarily mean decreases in public expenditure in real terms.

The situation is very different in the transition countries. Ratios of social expenditure to GDP that have decreased significantly are more common than those which have increased. Even when the ratios have increased, the expenditure in real terms has usually declined because of the huge reductions in GDP (see Tables 7.1 and 7.2.). The per capita GDP in Central-Eastern Europe is about five to eight times lower than in Western Europe. In other words, similar percentages mean significantly lower actual social expenditures and provisions.

Detailed data on social expenditure were available only for Hungary which is used as an example. Table 7.3a shows the continuous decrease in the real value of social expenditure even when the ratio within the GDP increased. Table 7.3b presents some details. Unemployment benefits and social assistance were the only items that increased, in real terms, although their overall value was still low. The real value of all the other benefits and services declined. Price and housing subsidies, sick pay and family benefits lost most, but health and education also fared badly. On the face of it, pensions did not deteriorate too much. However, the number of pensioners increased so rapidly (because of disability pensions and early retirement) that the real value of *individual* pensions declined by about 30 per cent – a greater decline than in real wages.

TABLE 7.1 *Government revenue and expenditure in percentage of GDP in some Central-Eastern and Eastern European Countries, 1991–7*

	% of revenues	% of expenditures
Bulgaria		
1991	37	40
1993	33	45
1997	33	33
Czech Rep		
1993	35	35
1996	31 (35*)	31 (36*)
1997	30	31
Estonia		
1991	24	22
1993	29	28
1996	34 (33*)	33(34*)
Hungary		
1991	51	55
1993	48	56
1996	42 (40*)	45 (43*)
Latvia		
1995	15	19
1996	31(30*)	32(31*)
1997	37	36
Poland		
1994	42	44
1997	39	41
Romania		
1991	36	34
1993	34	31
1996	28	31
Russia		
1995	14	17
1996	13 (19*)	20 (25*)
1997	12	17
Slovenia		
1993	43	42
1997	40	42

Sources: IMF (1998c); own calculations; data in () and marked by an *: World Bank (1999a) pp. 234–6. The data are in the majority of cases identical, but in some cases there are discrepancies I am unable to explain.

TABLE 7.2   *Per capita GNP and the change of real GDP in some Central-Eastern and Eastern European countries; projected real GDP in 1999 (1989 = 100)*

	GNP per capita in USD, 1994	Index of real GDP 1989–99 1989= 100 data for 1999 = projection
Albania	380	91
Bulgaria	1250	66
Croatia	2560	79
Czech Republic	*3200*	*95*
Estonia	2820	79
Hungary	*3840*	*99*
Latvia	2320	60
Lithuania	1350	65
FYR Macedonia	820	60
Poland	*2410*	*121*
Romania	1270	74
Slovakia	*2250*	*101*
Slovenia	*7040*	*107*

Note: Countries close to or above their pretransition levels in italic.
Sources: GNP: World Bank (1996, pp. 188–9). Indices: European Bank for Reconstruction and Development (1999, table 1.1, quoted in Barr, 1999).

One area in which there has been a great deal of progress is in the *pluralization* of welfare. The rebirth of 'civil society', of the voluntary sector and non-governmental organizations (the 'third sector') is a major gain. New opportunities are being grasped everywhere. In Hungary in 1997, 48,000 foundations and associations existed, and almost a quarter were active in the area of social provision. The 'third sector' is making an important contribution in completing the statutory services, and in introducing flexible and innovative welfare practices. Difficulties arise when the state expects the 'third sector' to replace it, without guaranteeing the necessary funds and professional standards.

One of the consequences of state retrenchment and a poorly funded 'third sector' is the serious and harmful overburdening of families, particularly women. The problem is compounded by the conservative and pro-natalist emphasis to be found in many countries. The socially accepted

TABLE 7.3a *Total state expenditures on social welfare–social policy in Hungary. 1989–96, in real value by year*

Year	Consumer price index	Real GDP index	Social expenditures		
	(1989 = 100)		in % of GDP	In real value 1996/1989	1996/1991
1989	100	100.0	33,4	100	
1991	174	85.0	33.8	86	100
1993	262	81.9	31.2	77	89
1995	399	85.6	26.7	68	80
1996	494	86.7	24.3	63	73

TABLE 7.3b Detailed state social expenditures in Hungary, 1989–96, in % of the GDP and in real value (1989=100)

	In % of GDP				
	1989	1991	1993	1995	1996
Consumer price subsidies	2.6	1.8	0.6	0.6	0.7
Health care	5.7	5.3	5.1	4.3	4.5
Education	7.0	5.5	5.2	4.3	4.1
Housing subsidies	3.5	2.5	1.1	1.2	0.9
Unemployment	0.0	0.7	1.7	0.9	0.7
Pensions	9.1	11.5	11.4	10.4	9.9
Social assistance	0.3	0.6	1.0	0.9	0.8
Family support	4.0	4.6	4.1	2.7	2.2
Sick-pay	1.2	1.3	1.1	0.8	0.5
Total	33.4	33.8	31.3	26.1	24.3

Sources: Lelkes (1999); CSO yearbooks; own calculations.

dual role of women as workers and mothers was often criticized in the old days as 'gendered citizenship' created by a patriarchal state. There is now a shift to a new model in which the most legitimate female role is that of the mother and housewife (Funk and Mueller, 1993).

The void created by state retrenchment and a weak 'third sector' is supposed to be filled by the market. The revival of the market in transition countries is an obvious gain. The question, however, is its proper domain. As in the case of the state, this issue was never reflected upon: 'spontaneity', or the free play of interests, led the changes. At present, privatization and marketization invade fields in which economic efficiency was usually a secondary consideration to social equity or the 'public interests'. The market has made some more or less significant inroads in health and education. The privatization of social insurance (pensions, sick pay, unemployment) has begun, as has that of all public services, and housing has been almost completely absorbed by the market. No doubt similar trends may be observed in Western Europe. However (with the exception of the Netherlands) they seem to be less rapid, more attention is being paid to the failures of the market, and the neo-liberal trends seem to encounter more resistance than in the eastern parts of the continent.

The Specifics of the Welfare Reform

After this general overview on welfare reforms, a more detailed description concerning universal benefits, social insurance, and means-tested social assistance follows.

Universal Benefits

All universal benefits, including price subsidies, the health service, and family benefits were curtailed across the region. They were either simply withdrawn or transformed into public or private insurance, or into means-tested benefits. A further, less conspicuous, strategy was to let the value of the benefits erode. The consequences of these changes are, to say the least, controversial. Child care services are shrinking or their costs increasing (UNICEF, 1997). The withdrawal of universal subsidies combined with the privatization of all public works (public transport, energy, water, sewage, garbage collection) is leading to the exclusion of large segments of the population from the market. Households are increasingly prone to the accumulation of debts, which could lead not only to cuts in energy or water provision, but also to eviction. These changes are illustrated by the data relating to family benefits. Means-testing and benefit erosion have reduced their value significantly, in some cases leaving them as of sym-

TABLE 7.4   *Public expenditure on family and maternity benefits in some Central-Eastern and Eastern European countries, 1989–95*

	GDP in 1995 (1989 = 100)	Family benefits		
		1989	1995	In real terms (1989 = 100)
		(in % of GDP)		
Bulgaria	76.5			
Family allowances		1.6	0.9	43
Maternity and child care		1.1	0.3	21
Czech republic	85.3			
Family allowances		1.2	1.0	71
Maternity and child care		0.3 (1990)	0.6	171
Hungary	83.0			
Family and maternity		4.0	2.7	56
Latvia	50.0			
Family and maternity		0.4	1.6	200
Romania	82.2			
Family allowances		2.9	0.7	20
Maternity and child care		0.3	–	–
Slovakia	86.9			
Family allowances		2.9	1.5 (1994)	45
Maternity and child care		1.0	0.9 (1994)	78

Sources: UNICEF (1997); p. 95 plus own calculations.

bolic relevance only (see Table 7.4). One of the consequences is a marked increase in child poverty.

Social Insurance

Throughout the countries of Central-Eastern Europe social insurance schemes are undergoing various alterations. The reforms have political, social and economic implications. From a political perspective, it is noticeable that although 'empowerment' and 'community participation' now form part of the World Bank discourse, the democratic control of the public insurance schemes has never become an issue. Hungary was (as far as I know) the only country where the tradition of elected independent boards was revived in 1992. However, the conservative government elected in 1998 abolished this 'corporatist' institution, and simply included the pension fund in the budget, following the practice of 'state socialism'. Vaclav Klaus did not allow the creation of any independent boards (Rys, 1995). Civil or participatory control over public funds is missing, leaving ample room for illiberal practices in the reforms of the public insurance scheme.

In terms of the economy, the greatest concern was sustainability. While the concern was fully justified, the measures taken were, to say the least, haphazard, and they have created undue hardship for many people. The standards of most benefits (pensions, sick pay, health services, and unemployment insurance) have been continuously lowered in all the countries, and the conditions of access or eligibility have been toughened. Alongside these benefits cuts there are health service restrictions: public health funds, operating now mostly as public insurance schemes, severely limit the services they pay for. Many preventative health services, as well as screening, medical interventions, dentistry, and a long list of pharmaceuticals, have been excluded from public funding.

The privatization of the pension system is the most advanced programme in a number of the countries in this region. The influence of the World Bank is the most visible in this case. The 'new pension orthodoxy' (Müller *et al.*, 1999) was introduced by the Bank in the region in about 1992 and has been promoted relentlessly ever since. The original proposal was the three- or four-pillar scheme of the World Bank (1994b). It consists of a remodelled 'first' public, pay as you go (PAYG) pillar, with higher age limits and lower benefits. The 'second' pillar is the mandatory privately-funded pension, no more and no less than a compulsory individual money-saving scheme. The third pillar consists of voluntary funds accompanied, usually, by substantial tax incentives. The fourth pillar, or rather a 'zero' pillar, is a means-tested assistance scheme for those who do not manage to accumulate enough pension rights through other channels. Some variant or other of this multi-pillar model is widely found. The changing pensions legislation is shown in Table 7.5. The Bank is continuing its efforts: Estonia seems to be the next one to join the 'mainstream'.

The alleged advantage of private pension schemes is increased savings, benefiting the economy; the development of a private banking sector; and the gains for the future pensioners who are promised safer and higher benefits. However, all of these advantages are strongly questioned by an increasing number of experts (Müller *et al.*, 1999; Barr, 1999). The Chilean experience, a reference point for these schemes in the CEE countries, also suggests that the private pillar is sure to increase inequality

TABLE 7.5 Pension reforms in the transition countries

Country	Comprehensive reform programme			Second (mandatory, private, funded) pillar introduction			Major first (public, PAYG) pillar reform			Major third (private, voluntary) pillar introduction		
	In preparation	Approved	Legislated	In preparation	Approved	Legislated	In preparation	Approved	Legislated	In preparation	Approved	Legislated
Hungary			X			X			X			X
Latvia		X			X				X	X		
Kazakhstan			X			X			X			
Poland		X				X		X				X
Croatia		X				X			X		X	
Romania	X			X			X			X		
FYR Mac.	X			X			X					
Russia	X			X			X				X	
Slovenia	X			X			X					
Bulgaria	X			X			X			X		
Cz. Rep.	X								X		X	
Slovak Rep.								X			X	
Ukraine	X			X			X			X	X	
Armenia	X								X		X	
Georgia	X								X		X	
Lithuania	X								X		X	
Estonia									X			X
Albania					X				X		X	

TABLE 7.5 (Continued)

Country	Comprehensive reform programme			Second (mandatory, private, funded) pillar introduction			Major first (public, PAYG) pillar reform			Major third (private, voluntary) pillar introduction		
	In prep-aration	Approved	Legis-lated	In prep-aration	Approved	Legis-lated	In prep-aration	Approved	Legis-lated	In prep-aration	Approved	Legis-lated
Kyrgyz Rep.		X	X					X				
Uzbekistan	X						X			X		
Azerbaijan	X						X			X		
Moldova	X						X				X	
Belarus							X					
Bosnia & Herc.							X			X		
Tajikistan							X					

Source: Rutkowski (1998), completed with assistance of Merita Xhumari for Albania, and Sandor Sipos for Croatia (Second pillar legislated in May 1999, first reading, September second reading).

among pensioners, and to add to female poverty in particular. The first negative consequence in the transition countries is that the contributions accruing now to the funded pillar are largely missing from the public, pay-as-you-go pillar. This is leading to an increase in state debts, and a decrease in existing pensions.

The new uncertainties surrounding public health schemes and pensions and their worsening standards undermine the legitimacy of public insurance schemes. They stimulate the better-off to opt out of the public schemes altogether, and private insurers, most of them international or foreign firms, are extremely active in seeking potential clients.

Means-Tested Social Assistance

Means-tested social assistance, or 'targeting the truly needy', is rapidly gaining ground everywhere in the CEE countries. It can be used to replace part of the universal or the insurance-based benefits. It can also be used as a new instrument to deal with new needs, such as long-term unemployment or the escalation of housing or medical costs. The rapid increase in the numbers of people claiming regular or occasional assistance as a percentage of the population, and the variations between CEE countries, are shown in Table 7.6.

Few countries have adopted the 'good' (European) practices of social assistance, despite the efforts of local experts since before the transition and the recommendations of the IMF (1990), the World Bank (World Bank, 1991), or the OECD (1995a) from the early years of the transition. With very few exceptions (probably the Czech Republic is the only one), there is no attempt to define an adequate subsistence minimum. This objective seems to have been deliberately ignored, largely because the statutory minimum wage and the minimum pension are usually below the subsistence minimum. If a poverty line approaching the subsistence minimum were adopted, it would be seen as a strong disincentive to work. For the same reason, the right to assistance is usually weak. In most CEE countries, local discretion, combined sometimes with humiliating practices such as home visits, plays a significant role. The levels of assistance are inadequate, not only in Russia or in poor countries in the Balkans, but also in Hungary and Slovakia. The sums are so low that they do not represent any significant assistance. In Poland, the rules of eligibility are so strict that they exclude the majority of the poor (Barr, 1999).

TABLE 7.6   *Reported number of regular and occasional social assistance per 10,000 population in some Central-Eastern and Eastern European countries*

	1989	1993	1995
	Regular social assistance		
Bulgaria	915	1089	999
Czech Rep.	95	691	1041*
Hungary	116	355	623
Latvia	–	1572	2509
Poland	273	410	469*
Slovakia	41	1026	930
Slovenia	41	155	179
	Occasional social assistance		
Bulgaria	388	982	896*
Czech Rep.	241	541	513*
Hungary	793	2115	2382
Latvia	–	368	5567
Poland	262	738	770*
Slovakia	83	219	229*
Slovenia	203	80	237

*1994.
Source: UNICEF (1997; p. 152).

However, one must acknowledge that local authorities face a very difficult task when administering social assistance. The central state has devolved benefit responsibilities to them without adequate resources, and allowed them a large margin of freedom in applying the law when they adapt the rules of assistance to the local conditions.

The expansion of social assistance has resulted (as in the West) in an increasingly vigorous attack on the able-bodied poor. The argument is that they should not get 'something for nothing' but should reciprocate, at least, by taking up low-paid compulsory public work. This argument is increasingly popular. The difficulties involved are almost insurmountable. There is never enough public money for public works. Even when public works are funded, wages are so low that they produce large numbers of working poor. This attack on the able-bodied poor is disproportionately harming ethnic minorities, particularly the Roma (Gypsies) in the Czech Republic, Hungary, Romania, and Slovakia.

Despite the expansion of social assistance, poverty and social exclusion are seldom on the political agenda in the countries of Central-Eastern Europe. Many governments are unwilling to face what seems to be an intractable problem. Also, in the context of the new globalizing ideology, poverty is no longer seen as a scandal. The lack of concern is, to some extent, portrayed in Table 7.7. Most countries have signed the Copenhagen commitment in 1995 to eradicate or, at least, to reduce poverty. Yet, most of them have neglected this commitment and have not worked out or implemented the necessary measures. The majority did not even reflect on possible steps – only Moldova, one of the countries facing the greatest difficulties, seems to have a fully-fledged 'plan'. The politics of the Hungarian government, elected in 1998, openly favours the middle and upper strata. Its measures may neglect the alleviation of poverty and may even increase the burden on the poor (for instance, by new discriminatory assistance schemes).

In summary, as a consequence of economic scarcity, bad administrative practices and an anti-poor perspective in some cases, poverty, including absolute poverty, is only partially alleviated in the transition countries

The Meaning of the Welfare Reforms

I now attempt to draw some preliminary conclusions. A debate has unfolded in recent years about the present and possible future of the transition countries. In a recent paper, Deacon expresses doubts about the dominance of the neo-liberal model. He reiterates that most of the 'eastern' part of the region still tries to conserve the old benefit schemes, even at the price of possible collapse. The CEE countries and some others are 'developing into one or another variant of a West European Welfare state, combining a mix of Bismarckian style insurance and Scandinavian style state financing' (1999a, p. 40). Yet he perceives a tension 'between the aspiration towards a European-style social-market economy (or conservative corporatism) and a budget-induced and IMF-World Bank backed residualism' within the 'reforming' countries (p. 45). He also thinks, not without reservations, that more recently 'the influence of the Bank is countermanded for those countries who are candidates to join the [European] Union by the Social Democratic and Christian Democratic ideals within the EU' (p. 48).

I wish Deacon were right in his last assessment but I do not think that he is. The evidence does not support his argument that 'there was remark-

TABLE 7.7 *Implementing World Summit for Social Development Commitment in Central-Eastern and Eastern European countries*

	Poverty planning			Poverty estimate		Poverty targets	
	Explicit national poverty plan in place	*Explicit national poverty plan in preparation*	*Poverty reduction only in national planning*	*Extreme poverty estimate*	*Overall poverty estimate*	*Target for extreme poverty reduction*	*Target for overall poverty reduction*
Albania			●	●	●		
Bulgaria			●	●			
Croatia			None				
Czech Rep.			None				
Estonia		●		●			
Hungary			None			+	+
Latvia		●		●	●		
Lithuania		●		●			
Moldova	●				●	●	●
Poland		●		●	●		
Romania		●		●	●	+	+
Slovakia			None				
Slovenia			●		●		

Legend:
● = in place.
+ = in preparation.
Source: UNDP (1998, table 2.A.1).

able continuity and stability in the provision of state social-security, health and education services although in some countries some private provision was appearing on the margins' (1999a, p. 45). The stability is, at best, apparent. Standards have deteriorated practically everywhere, at least in line with the economic downturn. There are no mechanisms in place and (as far as I know) no political will to bring them even close to the former low levels if the economy recovers. Deacon sees the *structural changes* – privatization, marketization, weaker social insurance and the attraction of a safety-net – as marginal. According to my reading of the situation, they are not. Rather, they signal a trend rooted in increasing income and wealth inequalities as well as in the global pressure to reduce both payroll and income taxes. Inequalities are likely to widen further in the absence of a political will and politically acceptable means to contain them. As a consequence, I assume that the structural changes will become ever more pronounced. They will almost inevitably lead to two-tier systems in most fields, from income maintenance to health and education. Some of these features are already emerging.

In this region, formal similarities with Bismarckian insurance and Swedish public financing still remain. However, the essence of the 'European model' – an attempt to control inequalities, to pay increasing attention to ethnic and gender issues, to strengthen social rights so as to assure the emancipatory potential of the welfare system, to underpin social rights by labour rights, to put social integration on the agenda – is almost totally absent. Compounding this trend is the fact that the European Union does not seem particularly keen on enforcing the 'European model'.

It is clear that the interests behind the neo-liberal agenda, inasmuch as it was implemented, are manifold. The new propertied strata, the managers in the private sector and foreign capital, have relatively high stakes in its success. The interests of international capital should not be forgotten, especially if the links with the process of (economic) globalization are to be highlighted, even though these interests seldom become visible. It is, therefore, interesting to note instances when they are. For instance, it was considered a major achievement by the World Bank that the deadlock that prevented the privatization of large public utilities in Hungary for a long time, was overcome with the help and advice of the World Bank.

If we now return to the four trends in the welfare politics of the region suggested above, we may argue that the dominant one in the CEE countries is residualization, though it has not yet fully unfolded. However, one may paraphrase Esping-Andersen, who concluded in 1996 after a similar review of existing trends that in Western Europe 'the cards are very much stacked in favour of the welfare state status quo' (Esping-Andersen, 1996a, p. 267). I would venture to suggest that in the east of Europe, the cards are, rather, very much stacked in favour of a neo-liberal, residualist welfare strategy.

The Reception of 'Globalizing' Forces in the East and the West of Europe

There seems to be a significantly higher degree of compliance with the new ideology of globalization in the transition countries than in most developed democracies of Western Europe. This more assertive neo-liberal ideological style, as well as weaker local resistance, may have many causes. Some of these are as follows.

Firstly, most of the transition countries are poor. These countries all belonged to the world's middle-income countries with an average per capita GDP of around 4,000 US dollars (USD) in the mid-1990s (as against USD 23,000 in the high-income countries). Their economic situation deteriorated with the transformation crisis. Of the transition countries only the CEE countries are recovering from this crisis after a decade, but they are still among the middle-income countries due to the fact that state revenues have dwindled more rapidly than expenditure (see Table 7.2). Because the relationship between the government and individual citizens is not based on mutual trust, and because services have deteriorated, citizens are less willing to pay taxes and insurance contributions.

Secondly, in the short term, cutbacks in state spending are an economic necessity. This does not fully explain, however, why the welfare system had become the main target of cutbacks, and why the cuts are implemented in a way that affects the long-term commitment in all areas of public well-being. One tentative explanation is that the governments of this region are yielding more easily than elsewhere to the globalizing pressures because they desperately need the 'goodwill' of foreign capital and supranational agencies. The countries that are most heavily in debt are particularly vulnerable because of this 'need'. Political leaders, especially those who have a 'socialist' past, have also a strong political will to prove that they have made a clean break with the 'tainted' political past of the country. In short, there are political and ideological reasons for the cutbacks, over and above the economic reasons that have been emphasized.

Thirdly, there may also be structural reasons for the shift to neo-liberalism and weak local resistance to exogenous pressures. Totalitarian systems (even in their later, less dictatorial period) had a stifled social structure.

The ideological and political system prevented the realization of capitalist developments (competitiveness, search for ownership and for profit-making activities). These tendencies existed, though, and are now emerging in an amazingly uninhibited way. Increasing wealth and income inequalities are seen not only as 'natural' in a capitalist economy or beneficial for incentive purposes, but also as a justified 'correction' of former politically enforced 'egalitarianism', or rather, of the ban on private ownership. The new 'upper class' shares the interests and ideologies that are currently undermining public responsibility for social welfare.

Fourthly, one of the fundamental reasons for the current situation might be that the practices of socialist dictatorships delegitimated or corrupted the values underpinning social policy more so than in the Western liberal democracies. In most former 'socialist' countries it is almost impossible to support traditional social democratic ideals – one is immediately suspected of nostalgia for a statist, communist or paternalistic past. Responsible (even socialist) politicians argue against the bogus enforced solidarity embodied, for instance, in large-scale pension and health systems. Others simply redefine the old terms to fit their purpose if they realize that citizens still value them. Thus the economist János Kornai defined two 'ethical principles' governing his social reform recommendations. One of them is autonomy interpreted as freedom of choice. The other one is solidarity interpreted only as charity.

The function of this new discourse is to present the neo-liberal agenda as belonging to the European tradition and, by so doing, to assure public acceptance for it. A series of public opinion surveys showed that the majority of CEE citizens are indeed very much in favour of the fully-fledged 'European model' and would like to see not only a regulatory and disciplinary, but also a citizen-friendly, public-good minded state (Svallfors and Taylor-Gooby, 1999).

A fifth reason for the trends is that civil society as a political force is still weak. One of the most important and most positive results of the change in the system is the advent of political democracy, and the (re-) emergence of civil society. However, the servicing function of the 'third sector' is more prevalent than its political or 'voice' function. It will take some time before civil society becomes strong enough to be able to defend itself and the rights, social rights included, which it considers essential. Also, most new democracies are still 'illiberal democracies' (Zakaria, 1997). To counter these trends, civil society will need to bring pressure on government to let it freely develop its 'voice potential', and then press for better social policy. It is not up to this dual task yet.

The enlargement of the European Union may awaken some hope for the improvement of the social policy of the CEE countries. The conditions of access relating to public or state responsibility for public well-being are, however, not very stringent. At present, the Union requires, as membership conditions, legal dispositions in the labour and social field concerning the equal treatment of men and women and the endorsement of certain health and safety standards. The various programmes of the EU, e.g. PHARE, were never successfully used to promote the European social model. The lack of concern shown by the EU, and the absence of public discourse relating to European integration in CEE, contribute to the relegation of social policy issues to the background. The consequence may be that the countries that would like to join the EU may destroy institutions that can ultimately become conditions of admittance. I do not know of any instance in which this dilemma has been pointed out by responsible agents of the Union to those seeking admittance.

In summary, the balance sheet of the transition, at present, reflects only an interim situation: the story is still unfolding. After ten years, it seems that in the CEE countries with relative stability the political gains serve almost everybody, whilst the economic gains favour a minority. The negative aspects include the fragmentation of the integrative institutions; weak concern with welfare rights; the demolition of collective structures of 'social property' (Castel, 1995) that could counterbalance the weak position of the groups that have been left out of the privatization drive; the massive increase in poverty, insecurity and inequality; and the withdrawal of the state from its civilizing and welfare functions.

The region is seen by many as a laboratory for experiments in 'the individualizing of the social'. The adjustments or alterations already implemented prove the feasibility of this project without major upheavals in the majority of the countries. Yet quiescence does not necessarily mean acceptance: resignation may be a more appropriate term. A shared feeling of powerlessness is prevalent everywhere.

8

Globalization and the Nordic Welfare States

PEKKA KOSONEN

Introduction

In comparative welfare state research, the Nordic countries have often been treated as a distinctive group. During the golden age of capitalism and into the 1980s, they were counted among the most developed and successful welfare states. However, in the 1990s these countries, and in particular Finland and Sweden, faced severe economic and social problems, and welfare arrangements were claimed to be a part of these problems. In this chapter, these developments are related to the new stage of globalization as well as to internal changes in these countries.

Four Nordic countries are studied.[1] These are Denmark, Finland, Norway and Sweden. Esping-Andersen (1990, 1999) sees them as representatives of the social democratic welfare regime. This regime is characterized by the principles of universalism and de-commodification of social rights that are extended to all social groups. Also, it promotes an equality of the highest standards, and not only an equality of minimal needs. Esping-Andersen's typology, and his description of the Nordic welfare states, is essentially adopted in the chapter. However, since the role of social democracy has been more limited in Denmark and Finland than in Norway and Sweden in the post-war era, a more neutral notion of the *Nordic* welfare model is used. Furthermore, although the Nordic welfare states are based on common principles, in practice they have many dissimilarities that must also be outlined. It can be argued that differences increased rather than diminished during the 1990s.

There is a general agreement that in the post-war period there was a positive correlation between the openness of a country's economy and welfare statism (e.g. Cameron, 1978; Huber, Ragin and Stephens, 1993). However, these overall comparisons, based mainly on levels of welfare expenditure, are not without problems. First, the best indicators of changes in welfare policies are not necessarily welfare expenditure, since total expenses may increase even if cuts and alterations are made in benefits. Second, research from the 1970s and 1980s does not necessarily show whether new forms of internationalization changed the picture more radically in the 1990s. In what follows, the notion of a Nordic normative legacy is first introduced, and the development of the Danish, Finnish, Norwegian and Swedish welfare states is briefly outlined. Secondly, changes in economic and social policies are examined from the viewpoint of external changes such as participation in European integration and liberalization of international capital movements. Finally, the question of the Nordic model in a globalized world is discussed.

Nordic Welfare States: Main Ideas and Arrangements

(a) The Nordic Normative Legacy

In analysing the Nordic economic and social policies, country-specific models are used in order to understand in what way economic and social tensions and transformations been controlled in each country. These economic-political models are an effort to outline the complex interplay between economic structure, economic and social policies, and a political-institutional framework (dependent on class structure and political mobilization). From this point of departure, the distinctive features of four Nordic models can be underlined (see Kosonen, 1991).

The post-war *Swedish* model can be characterized by full employment, active labour market policy, solidaristic wage policy, redistribution of incomes, and social democratic hegemony. The specific feature in the *Norwegian* model is that the state has directly regulated incomes and investments. The twin goals of structural change and the maintenance of an institutional welfare state were underpinned by a system of fiscal and monetary policies that has been termed 'fiscal socialism' (Fagerberg, Cappelen and Mjøset, 1992). In *Denmark*, there have been few elements of economic management by the state, and the liberalist tradition has been stronger than in other Nordic countries. On the other hand, the public

expenditure share of GDP rose very rapidly in Denmark from the mid-
1960s. Finally, in a Nordic comparison the distinctiveness of the *Fin*
model can be seen in the central status of competitiveness and inte
mediation. This means that social expenditure is allowed to incre
within the limits of economic growth, as long as this increase does
endanger the main political target – the competitiveness of the exp
sector (Andersson, Kosonen and Vartiainen, 1993).

The international shocks of the 1970s and early 1980s put a great strain
on the social security and employment systems in many countries, but
these Nordic models survived with some modifications. It seems that the
Nordic models incorporated national modes of development which could
also work during periods of uncertainty. This might partly be explained by
strong, nationally controlled export sectors, but also by the national coordination of incomes and public expenditure between all interest groups.

Although differences between the four countries are emphasized here,
they have many common features. In the present context, I try to distin-
guish typical Nordic features by the notion '*Nordic normative legacy*'. It
refers to a set of important objectives, especially an egalitarian distribution
of income, the provision of welfare state services as rights possessed by all
citizens, and full employment. The argument is that these goals were institutionalized in the Nordic countries during the post-war decades, but they
were not necessarily realized. Rather, they act as legitimation pressures, as
a constraint on political action. The 'Nordic normative legacy' can be
defined as certain goals that exist or, at least, have existed as legitimating
requirements in economic and social policies. These are:

- universal social rights
- responsibility of public (governmental) power
- equality (both income and gender equality)
- full employment target

Universalism in welfare policy suggests that services and social transfers cover all citizens living in the country. In the Nordic countries, the
goal has usually been to include both a basic amount and an income-
related component in social entitlements. In addition, the responsibility of
government is reflected in the fact that the role of the public sector is fundamental both in social insurance and service production and other sectors
play a minor role. For this reason, universalism and 'statism' have often
been named as typical features of Nordic welfare states (e.g. Alestalo and
Flora, 1994).

The third goal, equality, is, of course, a multidimensional and complicated concept. However, in order to analyse the normative legacy, we need to discuss the different terms used in public discourse. According to Therborn (1995, pp. 150–1), there is a British or Anglo-Saxon focus on poverty, on the exclusion of a part of population from the normal standard of living. In many countries of continental Europe, in contrast, the main focus of distributive discourse has centred on justice, or income maintenance. Distinct from both of these, Nordic discourse, since the late 1960s, has centred on equality, meaning both income distribution and gender equality.

It is debatable whether or not the fourth target, full employment, was institutionalized in the whole Nordic area. In Therborn's (1986) classification, 'full employment commitment' has been strong in Norway and Sweden, but weaker in Denmark and Finland. However, some sort of full-employment target can be seen in all four countries. At least as important is high labour force participation (by both men and women), and high employment rates have been regarded as essential, not only as a goal in itself but also to guarantee the financing of welfare policies.

These common traits are based not only on common ideas, but also on similarities in economic and political structures, which are important in explaining similarities as well as differences in Nordic welfare policies (see Salminen, 1993). For instance, all Nordic countries are small open economies, and have developed national productive systems that are export-oriented and based on a high level of national knowledge. Politics have been characterized by strong social democratic and agrarian (centre) parties, which reflect the share of workers and farmers in the class structures. In addition, female labour force participation has been high.

(b) Welfare Arrangements: Similarities and Differences

First, some Nordic labour market characteristics should be mentioned. One distinctive feature has been the high participation rates of women in paid employment. Female participation rates varied between 55 and 60 per cent in the late 1960s, and increased to more than 75 per cent during the 1980s. The only exception was Norway, where female participation rates remained below 50 per cent until the mid-1970s, but since then have increased rapidly (OECD, 1997b). Secondly, low levels of unemployment have lasted for several decades, right through to the late 1980s. Thus, the target of full employment remained viable. The third element is the extent

of unionization and corporatism. Union density has been pe
in Sweden and Finland (more than 80 per cent), and corporatism a.
tralized collective bargaining systems can be seen as a part of economic
and social policies in all Nordic countries.

Since the notions of universalism, equality and responsibility of government have dominated Nordic welfare policies, it is interesting to evaluate
some basic welfare schemes from this perspective: these include pension
schemes and public welfare services, as well as income equality. Public or
state pension schemes are extensive in all Nordic countries. In old-age
pensions, two main systems can be distinguished. Basic pensions, called
people's pensions, follow the citizenship principle, while the basis of
occupational pensions is the work performance model (Palme, 1990). In
addition to the public pension systems, private and collective arrangements exist, but their role is small compared with many other European
countries. The structure of basic pension schemes is quite similar in all
four countries. These minimum, flat-rate pensions can be seen as a part of
universal welfare policies. On the other hand, there are clear-cut differences in the making and structure of occupational, supplementary public
pensions between the countries (Salminen, 1993). A work-related and an
earnings-related state pension scheme exist in Finland, Norway and
Sweden, although the systems have different characteristics. Denmark,
however, has a flat-rate supplementary pension scheme. The relative level
of minimum pensions has been high in Denmark, while average levels of
all public pensions have been highest in Norway and Sweden.[2]

The distinctiveness of Nordic welfare policies is reflected also in the
supply of public services. The state has a responsibility to finance and
often also to provide (via local bodies, municipalities) services in education, health care and social care. Correspondingly, the role of private organizations has remained small. This has been justified by the idea that
universalism and equality, both regionally and between various social
groups, require public responsibility. In particular, Denmark and Sweden
have developed a very extensive public service network, which provides
services to all citizens. As the public sector employs women in the main,
this contributes to high female employment rates.

So, have the Nordic welfare states succeeded in maintaining or increasing income equality? At least in an international comparison, this seems to
be the case. The distribution of household disposable income can be measured by the Gini coefficient (Table 8.1). In the mid-1980s, these four
countries – together with the Netherlands – proved to have the most equal
income distribution, and in the mid-1990s the very same countries contin-

TABLE 8.1   *Income inequality in 13 OECD countries in the mid-1980s and mid-1990s, indicated by the Gini coefficient*

	Mid-1980s	Mid-1990s
Italy	30.6	34.5
United States	34.0	34.4
Australia	31.2	30.6
France	29.6	29.1
Canada	28.9	28.4
Germany	26.5	28.2
Belgium	25.9	27.2
Japan	25.2	26.5
Norway	23.4	25.6
Netherlands	23.4	25.3
Finland	21.2	23.1
Sweden	21.6	23.0
Denmark	22.9	21.7

Source: Burniaux *et al.* (1998, p. 35).

ued to be in the lead. This is in contrast to many other European countries, which can also have huge income differentials (e.g. Italy and the UK). This outcome can be explained simply by the different models of redistribution. Progressive income taxation and, especially, income transfers have a redistributive influence (Gustafsson and Uusitalo, 1990).

It is evident that these kinds of welfare state require a high level of social expenditure and high taxation. Indeed, with taxes calculated as percentage of GDP and of income taxes on earnings, the Nordic countries keep their positions as the countries of highest taxation. But of course, high taxation is not an end in itself; taxes are used for redistribution by means of income transfers and providing a wide scope of public services. However there is also some variation between these four countries in this respect (see Table 8.2). In the financing of social security, Denmark has relied mainly on general tax receipts. General taxation is important in the other three countries too, but Finland and Sweden, in particular, have financed social security (e.g. earnings-related occupational pensions) by employers' social security contributions as well. In Norway, both employers and the insured have participated in the financing (Norway is closer to continental European countries here). Therefore, there is no clear-cut 'Nordic financing model'.

TABLE 8.2   *The distribution of the financing of social expenses (%), Nordic countries, 1975–95*

	Public authorities			Employers			The insured		
	1975	1984	1995	1975	1984	1995	1975	1984	1995
Denmark	88	85	70	10	11	11	2	4	19
Finland	38	47	48	51	45	37	11	9	14
Norway	30	46	62	47	35	22	23	19	15
Sweden	65	51	54	24	48	43	11	1	3

Source: *Social Security in the Nordic Countries*, various years.

Nordic Welfare Debates in the 1990s

As long as economic growth continued, unemployment rates remained low, social entitlements were increased rather than reduced, and some kind of political stability characterized the Nordic countries. In Denmark, stability was threatened in the mid-1970s due to high taxation and increasing unemployment. In the other three countries, economic downturn, unemployment problems and public indebtedness appeared only in the late 1980s and the early 1990s. Not surprisingly, the weaknesses of a large welfare state and regulated labour markets were seen as the main causes of these problems. In Denmark and Norway, anti-tax protest parties, known as 'progress parties', were established in the 1970s. The Danish party claimed a staggering 16 per cent of the vote in the 1973 election, but it lost most of its support relatively soon after. In Norway, the 'progress party' has survived for a longer period, and it obtained some 15 per cent of the vote in 1997. In the other two Nordic countries, similar anti-tax parties have been weaker: one example was the 'New Democracy' party in Sweden in the 1990s. (Arter, 1999, pp. 103–7).

Despite these changes, the social democratic parties have not surrendered their dominance. However, in the 1990s they adopted more market-oriented views, and the general political atmosphere has changed. At the same time, conservative and liberal parties have strengthened their criticism of taxation and welfare statism, although strong neo-liberalism has not become a dominant doctrine. In each Nordic country, bourgeois parties formed governments in coalition with other parties in the 1980s and 1990s (including a left-wing party in Finland). However, due to internal divisions within the bourgeois bloc (conservative, liberal and centre parties), these coalitions have usually been unstable. In the welfare debate, the issues have been similar to those discussed in other capitalist countries, often showing the influence of international neo-liberal discourse. These include questions on the relationship between welfare statism, competitiveness and effectiveness, arguments about inflexibility and disincentives in the labour market, and criticism of welfare bureaucracies and misuse of benefits. This is not to dismiss the many defenders of the Nordic normative legacy described above. A central topic in the discussion has been the relationship between welfare statism and competitiveness. It has been argued that the welfare state, from an economic point of view, is a costly luxury that the Nordic countries could afford so long as they were not too involved in economic competition with countries which did not have this 'luxury' or which had quite low social costs. Today, global competition is more open, and social costs are seen as an obstacle in this competitive environment. In particular, many economists and representatives of employers have named high taxation, equality and regulation as obstacles to economic growth and efficiency in the Nordic countries. In Sweden, where economic growth remained low, this issue was debated during the 1980s. When Finnish and Swedish economic growth stopped in the early 1990s, the criticisms of welfare spending intensified.

The Nordic welfare systems have also been criticized for the 'inflexibilities' that create disincentives to work and entrepreneurship. These disincentives are deemed to come from high income taxation and generous social entitlements. Some politicians and academics argue that these 'inflexibilities' have produced increasing levels of unemployment, while others suggest that they prevent the reduction of unemployment rates once these have increased. Disincentives to work have been explained partly in terms of high marginal taxes, since these have been particularly high in the Nordic countries. According to an OECD comparison (1995b) the marginal tax rates at average income in the mid-1980s were highest in Denmark and Sweden. After the tax reforms of the late 1980s, however, marginal tax rates decreased substantially in Norway and Sweden. Immediately after these reductions, unemployment rates began to increase in Sweden, and it was acknowledged that macroeconomic development was more important than the structure of taxation. In any case, taxation has been a permanent political issue in all four countries since the late 1980s. Also, high levels of unemployment are seen to be associated with generous unemployment benefits and other social entitlements. All in all, the change in welfare debates reflects both the new and more difficult economic environment for the Nordic countries, and also often comes from outside sources.

The Nordic Countries, Globalization and Europeanization

We now ask the questions : how have the four Nordic countries participated in the international division of labour in the 1980s and 1990s, and how has this particular process of globalization affected the basis of welfare policies in these countries? The following analysis uses comparable statistical data on small OECD countries as well as data from Nordic studies such as the Finnish research project 'Globalization, Welfare, and Employment', summarized by Väyrynen (1999). The two main issues to be discussed are: (i) the internationalization of enterprises, and (ii) deregulation of capital markets and EMU requirements.

Internationalization of Enterprises: Foreign Direct Investments

International capital mobility has clearly increased during the last two decades. This has been a global process, and the Nordic countries have participated in the process since the mid-1980s in particular. In this section, foreign direct investments (FDI) are examined.

In Figure 8.1, Nordic FDI is compared with that of other small OECD countries: Austria, Belgium, New Zealand, the Netherlands, Portugal and Switzerland.[3] Since the 1960s, the Netherlands and Switzerland have invested largely abroad, whereas Ireland has been the object of inward investments. In the 1980s, Sweden became a big investor in relative terms, and FDI from Finland and Norway also increased.[4] The Finnish and Swedish FDI diminished due to the recession in the early 1990s, but a new wave of enterprise internationalization has occurred since the mid-1990s.

As a result of this kind of internationalization, the importance of purely national enterprises has diminished, and that of multinationals has increased in the Nordic countries, especially in Sweden. Of the 30 largest industrial firms (ranked by employment) from the four Nordic countries, the major part of their personnel works abroad, so that in Denmark, Finland and Norway, in the mid-1990s, they had some 40 per cent of their employment abroad, and in Sweden it was over 60 per cent (Braunerhjelm, Heum and Ylä-Anttila, 1996).

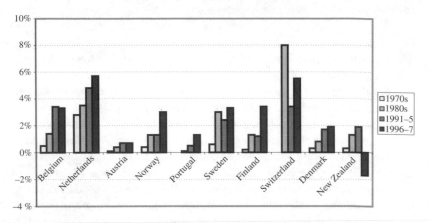

FIGURE 8.1   *Foreign direct investments: outflows, as % of GDP in 10 OECD countries, 1970–97*

The Nordic countries have also received investments from abroad, although capital import has remained smaller than capital export. However, foreign investors nowadays buy shares in Nordic enterprises. This has aroused anxiety, especially in Finland.[5] The internationalization of firms has essentially changed the character of 'national economies' as decision-makers tend to take account of the reactions of potential investors in reaching their solutions (Pajarinen *et al.*, 1998). On the one hand, they try to keep domestic enterprises at home in order to guarantee tax receipts and work places. On the other, they attract foreign enterprises to locate into their country by beneficial tax treatment and extensive infrastructure. In this global competition, the Nordic public sectors have increased their stakes in (technological) research and development and education, while other parts of the public sector (such as social security) seem to have diminished in importance.

This kind of internationalization is also likely to weaken corporatist structures, at least in the long run, by creating diversity of interest both on the employers' side and on the workers' side, thereby increasing the difficulty of maintaining compromises over labour market policies and welfare policies. This would be a significant change, especially in the Nordic countries, where labour market and welfare policies have been built on the basis of 'social corporatism' in the post-war period.

Deregulation of Financial Markets and EMU Rules

The other – and, from a Nordic perspective, the more important – aspect of capital market liberalization, has been deregulation of financial markets. Previously, the traditional view was that the central bank should maintain low and stable interest rates and fixed exchange rates. Credit rationing was widespread and monetary policy was predominantly passive. During the 1980s, rationing and regulation were replaced by flexible interest rates and central bank operations in open markets, and the size and interest sensitivity of capital flows increased. Denmark was in the lead in the deregulation process: in 1982–3 it embarked on a hard currency option, and deregulation was completed in 1987. Norway followed in 1984 with the lifting of direct regulations on banks and insurance company lending. In Norway, and in Finland and Sweden, deregulation was practically completed in 1990–1, when all restrictions on international capital movements had been lifted.

In Figure 8.2, the reduction of restrictions on capital movements has been compared amongst small countries. Measured by the IMF criteria

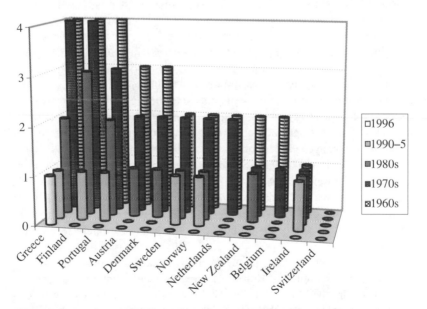

FIGURE 8.2   *Restrictions on international capital movements in 12 OECD countries, 1960–96*

(maximum 4 restrictions), there were 2 or 3 restrictions on average in the 1960s.[6] Regulation was strict in the Nordic countries. In some countries, liberalization happened in the 1970s, but in the Nordic countries some-what later, in the 1980s and early 1990s, when the reversal of previous practices was quite sudden.

What is important in this context is the impact that the deregulation process had on economic expansion and recession in Norway, Sweden and Finland. During the latter part of 1980s, free capital movement led to an overheating of the financial sector and to a heavy competition between the banks. A consumption and investment boom followed, consumer borrow-ing increased, and household savings ratios fell dramatically. As there were generous rules for tax-deductions, housing investments expanded, as did house prices. When the recession began in 1989–90 with export prob-lems, interest rates went up and foreign debt expanded. The policy of fixed exchange rates and hard currency failed in Finland and Sweden. Due to high interest rates, budget deficits and growing foreign debts, these coun-tries had great difficulties in balancing their economies.

First in Norway in the late 1980s, and then in Sweden and Finland in the early 1990s, a severe banking crisis occurred. Due to credit losses and a liquidity crisis, many banks needed state support. It was feared that the whole financial system would face chaos if the state did not intervene in the process. In Norway, the banks undergoing the most serious crises were 'socialized' (but then again privatized), whereas in Finland and Sweden banks received generous monetary support from government. The public support to the banks was most important in Finland. This support policy quickened cuts in other items of state expenditure, including welfare expenses. The banking crisis as such was a relatively temporary phenome-non. However, this episode had a more constant real effect in the Nordic economies. Changes in economic structures and institutions took place, and (especially in Finland and Sweden) a new kind of structural long-term unemployment emerged. Also, the level of public debt increased, and this has been used to justify many changes and cuts in social entitlements. It seems that financial liberalization and the way it was implemented, changed some of the basic premises of the Nordic models in an irre-versible way.

In the 1990s, the Nordic EU members, Denmark, Finland and Sweden, also faced the challenge of European economic and monetary integration, especially after the Maastricht Treaty. Economic and Monetary Union can be seen as a response to the globalization of financial markets, but EMU membership also creates new pressures on public policy. This impact has been most pronounced in Finland which struggled to fulfil the convergence criteria to enter the third stage of EMU. The other three countries may or may not join EMU (Denmark is allowed to stay outside, Sweden has decided to wait and see, and Norway is not a European Union member-state), but they too are affected by economic and monetary harmonization. In practice, the Nordic countries have tried to follow EMU criteria from as early as the early 1990s. This was reflected in tight fiscal policies and cuts in public expenditure as Danish, Finnish and Swedish governments attempted to reduce the high levels of public debt to fulfil EMU criteria. Therefore, the target of full employment became weaker than the targets of price stability and a balanced budget, and meeting these contributed to rising unemployment rates.

Moreover, the tight criteria set for the conduct of fiscal policy in EMU imply that countries with high public spending will be obliged to continue cuts in their public expenditure in order to reduce their indebtedness. In particular, the EU's *Stability and Growth Pact* is designed to secure fiscal prudence in the Euro-zone by levying penalties on EMU members running excessive deficits. Fears have been expressed that this will result in the operation of pro-cyclical fiscal policy: countries experiencing a recession could find themselves in the position of having to raise taxes and cut public expenditure either to avoid breaking the fiscal rules of EMU or to pay the fines imposed upon it by EU authorities (Teague, 1998).

In the Euro-zone, efforts to harmonize taxation are likely to be intensified. Since Finland, as well as Denmark and Sweden, have high value-added taxes and excise duties, even partial harmonization implies a reduction in their tax rates. This, in turn, means additional pressures to cut welfare expenditure.

Labour Market and Welfare Policies: Facing the Challenges of Globalization

Policy Changes in the Four Countries

In the late 1980s and in the 1990s, the Nordic countries faced new kinds of problems, due to both internal and external pressures. Economic recession hit Norway in the late 1980s, but more serious crises were felt in Finland and Sweden in the early 1990s. In Denmark the development has been more stable, although unemployment rates remained high until the late 1990s. In all four countries, the use of labour market and welfare policies has alternated. Replacement rates have been cut, waiting days introduced, qualifying conditions tightened and public services reduced (see Kosonen, 1998). In addition, activation strategies and the focus on work-centred welfare policies (the 'work approach') are emphasized.

Certain forms of globalization and Europeanization have directly or indirectly affected policy changes. In Finland and Sweden, the way in which capital market deregulation was implemented since the mid-1980s, and problems of indebtedness and unemployment that followed, can be seen as a background for tight economic and social policies. This effect is strengthened by the fulfilment of EMU criteria. The direct influences of internationalization of enterprises are more difficult to assess, but in the reorientation of tax policies, for instance, this influence can be seen. However, it is clear that explanations must also be sought in domestic institutions and political shifts.

Reorientation occurred first in Denmark, during the early 1980s (see Plovsing, 1994). Denmark had Conservative-led governments during 1982 to 1992, and combating inflation and reducing interest rates and the deficit on public budgets had high priority. This involved a programme targeted at public sector efficiency. In the 1990s, Denmark diverged from other Nordic developments in that the Social Democratic-led government decided on a number of social reforms. These include labour market reform and initiatives to promote employment. The main elements of the labour market reform, initiated in 1994, are active labour market policy, leave entitlements, changes in employment benefit rules, and renewal of labour market training. This activation orientation implies that the public sector is responsible for giving the unemployed more opportunities for work and training, and that the unemployed are obliged to accept these offers.

The goal of the Finnish Centre-Conservative government in the early 1990s was an equal spread of cuts entailing a variety of minor adjustments and cuts in various welfare schemes and services. According to the Finnish economic-political model, 'economic imperatives' were sufficiently serious to justify cuts and alterations in social benefits and services. Under the Social Democratic-led 'rainbow coalition', policies of cuts and reductions have continued since spring 1995, and because unemployment has remained at a very high level, further cuts have been proposed. In particular, the need for structural changes in the labour market has been emphasized. Unemployment insurance has been reviewed by tightening the entitlement rules for unemployment benefits, and the support paid to young people (under 25) has been reduced if they are not enrolled in training or educational programmes.

The shift in welfare policies has also been drastic in Sweden. No single welfare programme appears to be left out of the reforms; reductions in replacement rates are planned or already accepted for almost all social insurance benefits. Under the four-party bourgeois government 1991–4, many expert groups were created to assess unemployment benefits, pensions, sickness benefits and social assistance. Sickness benefits were the main target for cutbacks, and many alterations were decided. From 1994, the Social Democratic government by and large continued these policies, although in a more pragmatic way than was the case with the previous cabinet led by Bildt.

The 'work approach', instead of passive support (*trygdelinje*) is emphasized also in Norway (Lødemel, 1994). Reforms leading to greater selectivity and increased emphasis on incentives have been proposed, with the aim of achieving the ideals of the employment-orientated welfare state. The change of approach is evident in reforms in the areas of benefits for sickness, disability, old age, single parenthood, unemployment and social assistance. Despite expanding economic resources, the Social Democratic government stressed savings in welfare policies. Paradoxically, the bourgeois parties criticized Social Democrats in the 1997 election for inadequate welfare arrangements, and the result was a change of government.

What Has Happened to the Nordic Normative Legacy?

It is interesting to note that the main lines of economic and welfare policy are not affected significantly by changes in national governments in the Nordic countries. This indicates that there are common pressures and ideas behind the new policies. The question is, to what extent have the Nordic welfare states preserved their specific characteristics? To answer this, we must look at changes in the Nordic normative legacy. It is clear that new tendencies in welfare policies cannot simply be attributed to economic necessities or 'globalization'. Rather, they depend to a large extent on the normative and political basis of welfare states. The question, then, is whether previous goals continue to exist as legitimation requirements and as constraints on political action, or whether they are reducing in importance.

The full-employment target clearly has lost its primacy in favour of goals such as price stability and a balanced budget, even though all governments formally have the reduction of unemployment as one of their targets. Full employment, however defined, is still important in economic and political rhetoric, but in reality the target is not defended as convincingly as in the past. In Nordic employment policies, a tendency towards activation policies and a new 'work approach' can be seen. Both in labour market policies and social policies, the so-called 'work line' has been underlined, and the young unemployed are obliged to accept education or work offers instead of passive support, i.e. benefits. It must be noted, however, that in Sweden in particular, though partially adopted in other Nordic countries too, active labour market policy has encouraged the unemployed to participate in training and employment schemes since the 1960s.

These labour market changes are associated with the second issue referred to at the beginning of this chapter, the position of equality among societal goals. In every Nordic country one can find an increasing acceptance of wider income differentials and low-paid jobs for young jobseekers (but not necessarily for other employees). There is also a willingness to reduce marginal taxes especially at higher income levels, and concrete decisions to do this have already been made in Norway and Sweden. These measures and plans are advanced in order to create incentives to work and entrepreneurship, which reflects the fact that there is a widespread acceptance of a correlation between incentives and levels of incomes and taxation. At the same time, equality is cherished as a basic value in Nordic societies. Thus one can still claim that equality exists as a legitimation requirement in political programmes. This is confirmed by international comparisons that show that income inequality has remained at a relatively low level (Table 8.1) in Nordic countries. The reason why these countries could maintain a relatively equal income distribution, despite rapidly increasing unemployment, can be found in large, universal income transfers (Gustafsson *et al.*, 1999).

Views on the responsibility of the public sector have varied but not changed completely. Private or collective (labour market based) solutions have become stronger, especially in social insurance. There is also a tendency towards insurance contributions instead of tax financing, at least in Denmark and Finland (Table 8.2). In public services, user charges have been introduced, and, what is more decisive, the workforce in public services has been reduced everywhere in the name of efficiency and, in Finland and Sweden, as a part of savings measures. But even if this strengthens the other components in the 'welfare-mix', there is still a rather firm belief in the responsibility of the public sector for service provision and in basic social security. Thus, universal social rights are still supported by almost all social groups and political forces. In normative and ideological contexts the principle of universalism is often referred to as one of the Nordic achievements. In practice, however, one can detect a shift of emphasis from basic security to income-related insurance. The problem is that for the first time, the long-term unemployed tend to be excluded from these benefits and new divisions are created in society.

Global Pressures: Vulnerability versus Sustainability of the Nordic Models

In the past, it was thought that large-scale welfare arrangements could be combined successfully with good economic performance. Today, it is increasingly argued that these two contradict each other, and that economic recessions and low economic growth can be explained by this contradiction. Since the levels of social expenditure and taxation are high in the Nordic countries, they are supposed to be particularly vulnerable in the global marketplace. This conclusion is too simplistic. There are good reasons to argue that economic slowdown in Finland and Sweden in the early 1990s was not caused solely by the size of the welfare state (in fact, before the recession welfare expenses were on an average at Western European levels in Finland), but by the failure of deregulation and macroeconomic policies. Second, developments in Danish employment levels and in the economy generally were quite satisfactory during the 1990s, even though very high levels of social expenditure and taxation were maintained. In the Norwegian case, oil production had played a crucial role. These comparisons seem to imply that the content of welfare policy, and its connection to labour markets and overall economic policy, are more important than the size of welfare expenditure. This is especially true if the country is experiencing the process of globalization. In this sense, the Danish experience is especially worth studying.

How vulnerable are the Nordic type of welfare states to global pressures? The answers, I suggest, may be found in a discussion of labour market changes, the financing of social expenditure and political support. In the Nordic labour markets, Europeanization and globalization are likely to create more uncertainty and to strengthen demands for flexibilization. Under global conditions, governments have fewer instruments for the maintenance of high employment than earlier. Also, global competition is expected to favour highly skilled employees, while less-educated job-seekers meet increasing difficulties in getting jobs. It has been argued that more low-wage jobs are needed to employ less-skilled workers, whereas highly educated experts should be rewarded. If this thinking is accepted, the Nordic policy of equality will be under threat.

A vital problem raised in the globalization debate deals with funding structures, that is, the way in which welfare policies are financed. The Nordic welfare systems rely heavily on general taxation, although more so in Denmark than in the other three countries. It has been argued that these kinds of system are less vulnerable than systems based on social insurance contributions, because contributions and indirect labour costs are seen as harmful to international competitiveness. While this is true, globalization is also said to require reductions in direct income taxes, reductions that would lead to a decrease in revenues from general taxation. It is not in fact 'globalization' but rather, of course, politicians and economists who formulate these requirements in relation to taxation. It must also be remembered, however, that Denmark, Finland and Sweden have increasingly financed social security from social contributions. When the employers' share decreased (and this has been done in the name of international competitiveness), the share borne by employees and other insured persons increased correspondingly in the 1990s. In all of these countries, large pension funds exist.[7] However, it is doubtful whether these funds are large enough to meet future demands because the number of pensioners is set to increase rapidly in the coming decades. The global issue here is, how can public funds be invested profitably in international bond markets without making pension funds more vulnerable to global fluctuations?

One of the strengths of the Nordic welfare states is the popular support they enjoy (Goul Andersen *et al.*, 1999). In Sweden, there is broad support for most aspects of welfare policies, although some criticism of bureaucracy and suspicions of abuse can be found. In Denmark, the decline of welfare state support in the 1970s was only temporary, and today one can find a relatively positive attitude towards welfare arrangements (combined with a criticism of social abuse of welfare entitlements). This pattern of Nordic opinion is reflected in government policies: all major parties want to maintain the basic pillars of the welfare state, and savings are made mainly because they are argued to be necessary in terms of fiscal policy. However, the process of globalization may affect these attitudes too. There is a potential threat of a clash between the globally-minded and market-oriented elites and voters, who continue to value high employment and generous welfare arrangements.

Conclusion

The Nordic welfare states have undergone a substantial reorientation since the late 1980s. Unemployment rates have increased, welfare benefits have been cut, and a tendency towards a 'work approach' can be observed. In this chapter, these changes have been related to the ongoing globalization process, in particular to internationalization of enterprises, to liberalization of capital markets and to EMU. The chapter has argued that the background to the Nordic economic and unemployment problems in the first half of the 1990s is to be found in the sudden deregulation of financial markets. This led to the overheating of the economy, indebtedness, a banking crisis, and a recession in Norway, Sweden and Finland. In addition, the attempt to fulfil the EMU convergence criteria led to tighter fiscal policies and cuts in public expenditure in Denmark, Finland and Sweden. Thus, deregulation decisions and macroeconomic policies, rather than foreign investments or globalization *per se*, may be regarded as the main reasons for changes in labour market and welfare policies.

It is not clear if the events of the 1990s reflect permanent shifts in the Nordic type of welfare state. It is possible that these were problems of transition, which may not continue in the same way in the future. In the second half of the 1990s, economic development was favourable in all four countries, unemployment rates reduced, and even some benefit improvements were made. The scene has changed, undoubtedly, but most of the characteristics of the Nordic welfare states have been maintained. Yet, deregulated capital markets, internationalization of enterprises and Europeanization set tighter limitations upon economic and social policies, so that the pressures of globalization are likely to push the Nordic countries to re-evaluate their welfare policies. The internationalization of enterprises has an impact especially on the social and political basis of the Nordic models, since it is likely to increase the difficulty of maintaining compromises over labour market policies and welfare policies. Corporatist negotiations continued in particular in Finland and Norway during the 1990s. However, national pay agreements have been designed to constrain wage rises, both in nominal and real terms in these countries. This reflects a shift from 'social corporatism' to what has been termed 'competitive corporatism' (Rhodes, 1998; Teague, 1998).

The Nordic welfare states also have some specific strengths in terms of global competition. These include societal consensus, high levels of social inclusion, as well as relatively high levels of education and technology. If these are maintained and developed further, these small countries can combine large-scale welfare arrangements and as well as economic performance in the globalizing world economy.

Notes

1. The notion of Scandinavia can also be used. In this chapter the term 'Nordic' is preferred so as to include Finland, which in a geographical sense is not part of Scandinavia.
2. Replacement rates are published annually in *Social Security in the Nordic Countries*.
3. FDI outflows are not reported from Greece and Ireland.
4. In the Finnish case, foreign direct investments remained at a relatively low level until the mid-1980s (which is reflected in the average for the decade), but in the last years of the 1980s all big enterprises started to invest abroad on a large scale.
5. In many big Finnish enterprises, already more than half of the shares (and in Nokia more than three-quarters) are owned by foreign investors. Foreign investors are usually institutional investors, such as mutual and pension funds. Also, important mergers between Finnish and Swedish banks and industrial firms have been made. These arrangements have been widely debated in Finland, also in the parliament, especially the merger of Enso (formerly a state-owned company) and Swedish Stora (both firms are from the paper industry).
6. In the case of Switzerland, information is missing from the 1960s and 1970s.
7. The funds are organized in rather different ways (Salminen, 1993). In Norway and Sweden, funds are handled by a centralized state organization. Labour market organizations have a strong grip on the independent and centralized pension fund that handles Danish supplementary pensions. In Finland, these pensions are decentralized to separate sectoral schemes, which are handled by private insurance companies and pension funds.

9

Globalization and the Liberal Welfare States

NORMAN GINSBURG

This chapter discusses the role of globalization in social policy developments in Britain and Ireland over the past two decades. In both countries, governments in the 1980s pursued macroeconomic and industrial policies explicitly designed to expose their economies to the forces of global economic competition. In so doing, however, they adopted contrasting approaches to social policy. In Britain the dominant neo-liberal discourse led to a restrictive restructuring of the welfare state, based on the view that social expenditure undermines the competitiveness of both the individual and the firm. In Ireland some neo-corporatist agreements and policies, embracing the European social model, were developed to compensate to some extent for the increasing social risks associated with global competitiveness. This illustrates very clearly how national social policy responses to economic globalization can vary enormously even within one regime type.

'Economic globalization' is used here to describe the increasing extent and speed of global flows of money, goods, technology and services, which both governments have sought to facilitate in the drive for economic growth. The economic globalization thesis suggests that this is a permanent, possibly irreversible process, which is undermining both the extent of and the distinctiveness of national welfare systems. As many commentators have pointed out, including Clarke and Hay in this volume, this thesis underestimates the continued diversity of national and subnational welfare systems as well as undervaluing more positive effects of globalization, especially when conceived less narrowly and economistically. Here the discussion is confined to examining significant changes in social policy outcomes in Britain and Ireland that are commonly attributed to the forces of globalization.

The chapter opens with a review of what is meant by the term 'liberal welfare states' followed by an examination of the extent to which the welfare state in Britain and Ireland has conformed to the abstract model, suggesting a rather awkward fit in both cases. The chapter then goes on to outline the contrasting directions taken by social policy in the 1980s and 1990s in the two countries, showing that government enthusiasm for economic globalization can lead in somewhat different social policy directions. This is followed by a detailed consideration of some critical effects of policy in the case of Britain, effects that are often attributed to economic globalization. It is suggested that while there has been a distinct shift towards a more purely 'liberal' model in Britain, this has come about as a result of the explicit neo-liberal influence in politics rather than exogenous globalization forces, though this distinction often becomes blurred in practice.

The Liberal Welfare States

Before considering Britain and Ireland as examples of liberal welfare states, it is essential to consider what are the key elements of the liberal model of the welfare state, drawing on but expanding on the Esping-Andersen (1990) approach. Key parameters of the liberal regime in comparison with the other regimes examined in this book seem to be:

- a low level of social expenditure as a proportion of GDP
- low social protection from the risks and needs arising from unemployment, sickness, old age, pregnancy/maternity, lone parenthood
- high exposure of households with below-average incomes to the full market costs of housing, health care, care of dependants, lone parenthood
- low replacement levels of income by state benefits and pensions
- exclusionary, restrictive and deterrent qualification for social insurance
- high levels of income inequality and relative poverty
- a central role for means-tested benefits
- stigmatized, underfinanced and low-quality public social services
- loose regulation of and low or no subsidy for private welfare provisions
- a culture of reliance on self-financed, family support and care, supplemented by charity and occupational provision

In the wake of feminist analysis initiated by Lewis (1992) this list can be supplemented by liberal regimes' predominant 'male breadwinner' policy discourse which continues to shape policy towards pre-school child care, support for lone mothers, women's independent rights to benefits, institutionalized gender discrimination in provision of benefits and services and many other aspects of policy.

Britain as a Liberal Welfare State

The so-called 'classic' British welfare state of the 1940s to 1970s conformed only very partially to the liberal model as sketched above. In particular, the mass provision of low rent social housing, the national health service (NHS) and publicly organized personal social services provided very considerable protection from the market costs of decent housing, health and social care. The protection and replacement of income offered by the British social insurance system certainly lagged significantly behind both the Nordic social democratic and the Bismarckian systems. However, this was accompanied by the development of a safety-net role for means-tested benefits. This offered a nationally uniform, comparatively unstigmatized right to subsistence income for almost everyone, including single people and the long-term unemployed. In terms of the decommodification effects of social insurance benefits, the UK in 1980 just fell within the liberal grouping, according to Esping-Andersen. However, in terms of his 'clustering of political welfare regimes', the UK displayed a 'degree of liberalism' which was only about average among OECD states, below that of Denmark and of all the Bismarckian states except Austria (Esping-Andersen, 1990, table 3.3). British social expenditure as a percentage of GDP was a little above the OECD average in 1960 and a little below it more recently. In 1990, amongst twenty OECD states, social expenditure in the UK ranked twelfth, just behind Germany and some way above the other Anglo-Saxon, liberal regimes (Hill, 1996, table 3.1). The UK also had a middle-ranking position in terms of household income inequality up to the 1980s. In the early 1970s, the UK had the second lowest poverty level among the twelve EC states. Comparative analysis of 'child benefit packages' in the early 1980s put the UK in a 'middling' group of states, neither particularly generous nor parsimonious alongside Denmark, Germany, Australia and the Netherlands (Bradshaw *et al.*, 1993). By the 1970s a welfare culture was in place in which social rights to a basic, universal level of welfare provision and protection within a male breadwinner discourse had been clearly established in the popular imagination, though by no means perfectly realized in practice. Elsewhere, I have described this peculiar mixture of social democratic, conservative and liberal policy as Liberal Collectivism (Ginsburg, 1992).

Ireland as a Liberal Welfare State

The Irish welfare state is even more difficult to pigeonhole in the liberal camp. Esping-Andersen's decommodification index places Ireland among the liberal Anglo-Saxon regimes, but his analysis of its welfare politics puts it closest to the conservative, Bismarckian camp. McLaughlin (1993) describes the Irish regime as Catholic Corporatist, tracing its origins to the creation of the 'integral Catholic nation-state' before the Second World War and, more recently, to the development of tripartite corporatist structures since the early 1960s embracing national pay agreements and 'National Understandings for Economic and Social Development' (McLaughlin, 1993, p. 214). These neo-corporatist developments were an essential part of the deliberate policy shift opening up Ireland to the global economy in the 1960s, with fiscal and development measures designed to attract transnational corporate investment. In many respects, this was an early example of a state-orchestrated opening of the economy to the forces of globalization. In the wake of the new corporatism, the 1970s saw the introduction of more comprehensive social insurance and social assistance schemes. During the 1970s and 1980s, considerably increased public investment was made in health care, education and social care services. However, a substantial proportion of these services continue to be provided by private and voluntary organizations, predominantly those of the Catholic Church. Hence, by the 1980s, the Irish welfare state had been modernized and had acquired some traits of the mainland European social model. The Irish welfare state also has some traits of the Southern European model, such as its historical level of economic development, the influence of Catholicism, and the role of third sector organizations in service provision. In other respects, such as national policy uniformity and the absence of political clientelism, it is quite different from southern Europe (see Ferrera, 1996; Guillén and Álvarez in this volume). Irish social policy also shares some features with the British variant of the liberal model, such as comparatively low coverage of social insurance, comparatively strong emphasis on means-tested benefits, and comparatively high levels of relative poverty.

Having discussed the applicability of the 'Liberal' regime type to the British and Irish welfare systems, it is now time to consider recent changes in social policy in both countries and the role of globalization.

The New Politics of Social Policy in Britain

The Conservative government led by Margaret Thatcher came to power in May 1979. In retrospect this constituted a great watershed in British politics with a significant effect upon social policy. Initially, however, the Conservative government was rather cautious in its approach to social policy. It concentrated more on the development of monetarist economic policy and the undermining of the power of the labour movement. While some neo-liberal advisers such as Hayek advocated a clean break with the welfare state Chile-style, the government remained pragmatic, knowing that the welfare state provided an essential cushion against the shocks of rapidly rising unemployment, social inequality and household insecurity.

The government's pragmatism was allied to what was described by Hall (1988) as an 'authoritarian populism' around issues such as tackling inflation, trade union power, law and order, inefficiency and bureaucracy in the public sector, empowerment and choice for consumers of public services, cuts in direct taxation, expanding home ownership and developing popular share ownership through privatizations. Behind its pragmatic and populist approach, however, the government was increasingly driven by neo-liberal thinking. Four elements, at least, of this neo-liberalism bore down heavily on the welfare state:

- *Monetarism* Elements of monetarism had already entered into economic policy under the Labour government during the 1970s. However, this was greatly extended in the 1980s: the control of inflation replaced 'full employment' as the principal goal of economic policy. This was to be achieved by tight control of the money supply, using interest rate rises and severe restraint of public expenditure.
- *Supply-side policies* These were particularly inspired by Reaganomics in the USA and included: freeing-up the supply of capital and labour by deregulation; abandoning foreign exchange controls; tax cuts particularly for business; anti labour union measures; utility privatisation; cuts in eligibility for and levels of social security benefits; and the removal of minimum wage legislation.

- *Anti-public provider/pro-consumer discourse*   This discourse attacks the legitimacy of direct provision of services by public bodies, particularly local government, undermining the pay and status of public sector professionals, e.g. school teachers, nurses, university teachers and social workers. It also involves some efforts to empower parents, social services clients, and patients.

- *Restructuring*   This includes efforts to move from direct public provision of benefits and services towards the 'contract culture' of provision by 'independent' agencies and providers (profit and non-profit); dispersal of welfare administration under the (more or less) regulatory state; 'new managerialism' in the public and third sectors. These changes are more cost-driven, performance sensitive, commercially minded and union hostile.

The Thatcherite government was remarkably unconcerned about the effects of its policies in generating greater social inequalities. The notion of 'trickle down' was widely invoked during this period to legitimate the visible and rapid increase in social inequalities. Governments since 1979 explicitly presented mass unemployment as a necessary evil in an economic policy framework with anti-inflation strategy at its heart. This strategy was allegedly the key to making the British economy globally competitive. Thus, a barely disguised strategy of mass unemployment underpinned macro-economic policy. However, this argument merely explains the lack of urgency amongst policy makers in tackling unemployment. The high levels of UK unemployment are, of course, the result of the brutal shake-outs of British industry in the pursuit of global competitiveness. Much of this restructuring has been directly organised and overseen by governments in basic industries such as steel, coal, railways, telecoms and energy. Public expenditure restraint has meant that, even if it were that simple, unemployment could not be soaked up in public service employment. The growth of private sector services and self-employment has generated new jobs, but many are part-time, casualized and insecure (see below). These processes are also apparent in all European states, but they have been particularly strong in the UK, nourished by neo-liberal thinking. While mass unemployment appears to be a universal experience in most of the western world, the neo-liberal government in Britain exacerbated the problem.

Some of the most important Thatcherite reforms were:

- In 1980 social assistance and the basic state pension became indexed to retail prices only, not to wages. These benefits are the bedrock of the welfare state, providing the only source of income to millions of households. As a result, their relative standard of living fell dramatically over the whole period.

- In 1986 contributions to and benefits from the State Earnings Related Pension were halved, as the government tried to encourage workers into private personal and occupational pension schemes.
- From 1980 onwards, eligibility for and benefits from the national unemployment insurance scheme were gradually reduced, culminating in its abolition in 1996, when it was replaced by a more restrictive Jobseekers' Allowance.
- In the early 1990s, internal or quasi markets for the provision of health care and social care were introduced, involving the separation of purchasing agencies from providing contractors, with managed competition amongst providers.
- From 1980 onwards, the sale of 1.7 million local authority rented homes to their occupants, and the transfer of another 300,000 to the third sector ended the role of local authorities as direct developers and managers of new rented housing.
- In 1989 a national, ethnocentric curriculum for schools was introduced, with tougher regulation of school performance, publication of school performance league tables, and some dispersal of power from local councils to individual schools.

Despite Mrs Thatcher's neo-liberal instincts, the Conservative government never went as far as overtly advocating private health insurance, private schooling, university tuition fees, market rents for housing unprotected by housing allowances, or the phasing out of means-tested assistance. The greatest irony is that the Conservative governments' monetary and supply-side policies deepened the recessions of the early 1980s and early 1990s, and it was the latter which led to their downfall. Their policies increased welfare needs, demands and risks and at the same time attempted to withdraw the very benefits and services designed to meet them.

Interpretations of the Changes

In the social policy field there are two possible interpretations of the changes initiated by the Thatcher governments and carried forward by subsequent governments, including New Labour. A *resilient modernization* view, as implied, for example, by Glennerster (1992) and Pierson (1994), suggests that the classic welfare state has robustly survived, in some ways battered and in other ways modernised. According to this view, policy change has developed pragmatically, achieving an adaptation to wider circumstances, not least of which are more competitive global economic conditions. From this perspective, the managerialist restructuring of the welfare state has achieved gains in efficiency and effectiveness, while providing vital basic protection to people directly affected by economic restructuring, thus preventing social upheaval. A *residualization* view, as in George and Miller (1994), suggests that a deeper transformation has taken place towards a cut-down, 'affordable' welfare state, which has opened the way for a further transformation to a more 'residual' social policy, much closer to the liberal regime type. From this perspective, policy change has been driven explicitly by neo-liberal discourse, legitimated by arguments about the inevitability of and economic advantage derived from economic globalization. Perhaps both residualization and modernization processes were at work. Certainly Thatcherism itself was driven by a residualisation strategy, but in its pragmatism and its recognition of popular support for the classic welfare state, the Conservative government was driven towards modernization. Hence, the British welfare system has perhaps shifted towards a post-classical welfare state that awkwardly combines residualisation and modernisation.

The advent of the New Labour government in 1997 has increased emphasis on the modernization elements and reduced the emphasis on residualisation without decisively abandoning the latter. Post-classical social policy under New Labour incorporates the following elements:

- economic competitiveness: a continuation of monetarist and supply-side policies
- workfare/labour market policies, with the strongest emphasis on raising the incomes of people in low paid employment through the minimum wage, working families tax credit, child care tax credit, wage subsidies
- interventionist, regulatory governance embracing, rather ambivalently, both public service and private finance and contracting for welfare provision
- modest measures to bolster social cohesion and diminish social exclusion

The first three of these elements were also essential to the Thatcherite strategy in practice, but New Labour is considerably more interventionist in terms of workfare and the regulated mixed economy of welfare. It is still too early to assess what impact New Labour's measures will have on social justice and social inequalities.

The New Politics of Social Policy in Ireland

The contemporary scene in Ireland is perhaps dominated by particularly rapid and dramatic socio-economic changes since the late 1980s. These have led to Ireland being dubbed the *Celtic Tiger*. GDP growth averaged 9 per cent a year between 1994 and 1998, a growth in national income of over 50 per cent over the period (Atkinson, 1999, p. 29). Ireland is no longer a relatively poor country within the EU. In 1980 income per capita was 60 per cent of the EC average, but by 1996 it was 94 per cent of the EU average and rising rapidly (Sweeney, 1998, p. 52). The Irish economy now has a very high level of dependence on trans-national corporate investment, encouraged by government policies such as tax-free industrial zones, duty-free shopping and zero tax on export profits. The recent period of growth began in the late 1980s, as the Irish government keenly embraced the European model of the social market economy in the run up to the single market and the Maastricht treaty. A package of measures was adopted, including major investment in infrastructure through the EU structural funds, tax cuts and public spending restraint, legitimated by a strengthening of the neo-corporatist structures. Since 1987 a series of three year agreements between the social partners has 'brought Ireland to more than a decade of negotiated economic and social governance' (O'Donnell and Thomas, 1998, p. 118). The agreements have given the trade unions 'a say on take-home pay – that is on the level of income tax [which] ... ensured that take home pay of workers increased in real terms' (Sweeney, 1998, p. 90).

Despite the tax cuts and social expenditure restraint, social spending has increased in line with the economic growth, more so in areas such as health care, education and active labour market measures. In 1990 Ireland ranked thirteenth out of twenty OECD states in terms of social expenditure as a percentage of GDP, above all the other Anglo-Saxon states except the UK and above all the southern European states except Italy (Hill, 1997, table 3.1). Cousins (1994, p. 24) describes the period between 1980 and 1994 as being one of 'crisis and consolidation' for the Irish welfare system in the vice-like grip of tight expenditure restraint and very high levels of unemployment. In contrast to Britain, the 'crisis' was seen as exogenous to the welfare state, so that the growth of social expenditure was perceived not as a major causative factor in the economic crisis but more as a means of weathering it. The consolidation of the benefits system in response to the explosion of unemployment did not involve a 'large-scale assault' (Cousins, 1994, p. 24) but it brought about a significant shift towards assistance benefits and away from social insurance. This was accompanied by the abolition of earnings-related benefits in 1994 and the taxation of benefits since 1993.

One of the most prominent features of the recent period in Ireland has been the enormous growth of unemployment in the 1980s, followed by an almost corresponding fall in the 1990s. In 1973, 5.7 per cent of the labour force was unemployed on the ILO definition. This rose to a peak of 17.5 per cent in 1987, and fell back to under 7 per cent in 1998 (Collins and Kavanagh, 1998, table 9A.3; Murray Brown and Chote, 1999, p. 21). As Sweeney (1998, p. 169) points out, the ILO definition does not include discouraged workers, the comparatively large numbers on employment schemes and the 49 per cent of married women who were not in the labour force in 1996. Nevertheless, it is clear that the current economic boom, facilitated by the state's neo-corporatist strategy, has succeeded in reducing both unemployment and inflation to levels not seen since the early 1970s. Whether these achievements can be sustained is an issue for debate (Atkinson, 1999; Murray Brown and Chote, 1999).

Data on poverty, measured as the proportion of individuals in households with incomes of less than half the average, suggest much higher levels of poverty in Ireland over the past 25 years when compared with Germany, Sweden and the UK. In 1994, the proportion was 22 per cent compared with 15 per cent in 1973 (Callan and Nolan, 1998, p. 149). This represents a slowly rising trend in the 1980s, similar to that in Germany and Sweden, but in sharp contrast to the marked rise in the UK in the 1980s (Atkinson, 1998, fig. 1.14). Collins and Kavanagh (1998) suggest that there has been a significant increase in the inequality in market incomes in the 1980s (though not as great as that in the UK), but that inequalities in disposable income increased only very modestly. In a comparative analysis of old-age pensions, Korpi (1992) demonstrates that the income replacement rate in both the UK and Ireland in 1985 put them into a middle category of OECD states. However, while state pensions coverage was nearly universal in the UK, coverage was only around 50 per cent in Ireland, one of the lowest levels amongst the OECD states. Comparative analysis of 'child benefit packages' in the early 1980s put Ireland in the 'least generous' group of states, alongside Portugal, Spain and Greece (Bradshaw *et al.*, 1993). As Lewis (1992) suggests, Ireland has had a strong 'male breadwinner' policy discourse and practice, particularly in its social security system, and as Cousins (1994) demonstrates, it has been modified just enough to conform with the EU 'equal treatment' directives. Barry (1998, p. 368) concludes, from a review of the impact of recent policy on Irish women, that 'equality issues are still not being centrally addressed in critical areas of public policy' such as the provision of care services, support for carers, parental leave, pre-school child care, and reproductive choice.

Cousins (1997, p. 232) concludes that Ireland is neither exceptional nor an example of another distinct regime, but that 'there are more worlds [of welfare capitalism] than we have dreamt of'. State-managed high exposure to economic globalization appears to have paid great dividends for the Irish economy, since it has sustained social expenditure alongside comparatively high levels of poverty and income inequality, an extreme unemployment cycle, a predominantly male breadwinner approach to family policies and a UK-style deregulated labour market. While neither the British nor the Irish welfare regimes are anything like clear examples of the liberal model, they certainly have many liberal features that have been enhanced by their state-sponsored exposure to economic globalization in the 1980s. The style and substance of that state sponsorship has, in many respects, differed substantially, with the Irish government adopting a neo-corporatist managerialist approach and the British government taking a more hard-nosed anti-corporatist, neo-liberal approach.

We now turn to examining the British social policy of the past twenty years, where there has been a much more distinct shift towards the liberal model than in Ireland.

Effects of Policy Changes and Economic Globalization in Britain

If globalization is predominantly associated with the neo-liberal project, then its impact on British social policy has been enormous. If globalization lies behind the 'cuts' in social spending, the rise in unemployment, increasing income inequality, the growth of the flexible labour market and welfare privatization, then it is unquestionably true that these effects have been felt particularly strongly in the UK. These are phenomena common to all western industrial states, but they appear to have taken a particularly emphatic direction in the UK. Here the UK is taken as a case example of the possible effects of globalization, and the following parameters are examined briefly: social expenditure and taxation restraint; increasing inequality; increasing labour market flexibility and deregulation; privatization of welfare consumption and services.

Social Expenditure and Taxation

Social expenditure as a proportion of UK GDP rose steadily from around 10 per cent after 1945 to around 25 per cent in the mid-1970s. Since that time it has remained around this level, fluctuating between a peak of 26.6 per cent in 1993/4 and a low of 21.6 per cent in 1989/90, the fluctuations reflecting the economic cycle (Glennerster, 1998a, table 2.1; Glennerster, 1998b, table 8.1). UK social spending has always been below the OECD average, but the disparity has increased over recent times. Hence in the period 1981–93, average social spending as a share of GDP for 19 OECD countries increased from 25 to nearly 30 per cent (Hills, 1997b, Fig. 4). Not surprisingly, social spending grew most in the 'social democratic' states and least in the 'liberal' states, with the 'conservative' states in the middle-range. Hence, in terms of the modesty and stability of social expenditure between 1981 and 1993 (Hills, 1997b, fig. 8), the UK ranks alongside Japan, Ireland and the US.

Significant changes have taken place in the deployment of social expenditure since the mid-1970s in the UK. There has been a marked increase in the proportion of spending devoted to transfers (i.e. pension and benefits) and a marked decline in the proportion devoted to capital expenditure (i.e. buildings and major plant). Public expenditure on housing and, to a lesser extent, on education has fallen, while expenditure on transfers and, to a lesser extent, on health and social care has risen. Much of the growth in benefits spending resulted from the great rise in unemployment, including the costs of greatly increased numbers claiming early and sickness retirement benefits.

Ever since the mid-1970s, the restraint of social expenditure has been legitimated in considerable measure by globalization arguments. Lower levels of personal taxation are allegedly required both to prevent workers from being priced out of jobs and to preserve incentives for top earners in globally competitive labour markets. Britain's particular dependence on overseas trade allegedly necessitates lower levels of corporate taxation to keep exports competitive. Gray (1997, p. 6), amongst others, links these arguments to fundamental implications of globalization for economic policy beyond the abandonment of Keynesianism, arguing that 'the growing global mobility of production of both businesses and people, is enforcing a downward harmonisation of levels of personal and corporate taxation throughout the world'. It is certainly true that personal and corporate taxation have been significantly reduced in the UK, but indirect taxation has substantially increased since the 1970s, as is also true of the

US (Krugman, 1994, pp. 155–6). In the UK the tax ratio, that is the ratio of total taxation to GDP, has 'varied little over time, while the ratios in other high tax and low tax countries have risen steadily' (Hills, 1997a, p. 240). The UK has therefore moved from having a tax ratio around the average for western states in the 1970s to having one significantly below the average in the 1990s.

The New Labour government has embraced a key element of the Conservative orthodoxy by emphatically ruling out 'tax and spend' policies, with constant reminders of the virtue of 'prudence' in public finance. The government's plans to cut the biggest spending programme (pensions and welfare benefits), have been quite effectively challenged by pressures from and on behalf of lone parents, disabled people and pensioners. Increased spending on welfare-to-work, the health service and education is being financed by indirect taxation increases on vehicle fuel, tobacco, occupational pension funds and the privatized utilities, and by reallocation of some defence spending. Hills (1998b, p. 25) estimates that the cost of the new measures is equivalent to a rise in standard income tax of two pence in the pound.

The extent to which globalization can be said to have contributed to the restraint of social expenditure and taxation in Britain is almost impossible to measure. The political elite's belief has been that to be globally competitive, the British economy requires stable if not falling social expenditure and direct taxation. This has been achieved.

Increasing Inequality

In the post-war period, incomes in the UK started becoming more unequal in the mid-1970s, with a particularly rapid rise in the late 1980s, followed by a modest fall in the 1990s (Hills, 1998a, p. 16). Here the UK stands out from other countries, including the USA. This trend may possibly undermine the crude globalization thesis. According to Atkinson (1996, p. 11), the UK 'stands out for the sharpness of the rise in recorded income inequality in the 1980s' when compared with Sweden, Germany, Italy, France and the USA. Hills (1998, p. 17) demonstrates that from the mid-1980s to the early 1990s rising inequality was by no means a universal trend. It actually fell in Belgium, Norway, Holland, Italy and Canada. Data on relative poverty also show a dramatic increase in the UK compared with other EU states. The proportion of the UK population living on incomes of less than half the average almost tripled under the Thatcher governments, increasing from 9 per cent in 1979 to 25 per cent in 1990, and remaining at a little below that level ever since (Brindle, 1998, p. 7). However, recent New Labour policies will certainly achieve a positive redistributive effect, particularly in favour of low-income households with children. These measures include a Working Families Tax Credit, a new Child Care Tax Allowance, increases in Income Support for families and a 20 per cent increase in Child Benefit for the first child.

Reviewing explanations for the rising earnings dispersion in the UK, Hills and Atkinson cite a number of factors: the absence of a minimum wage, the decline of trade union membership, falling benefit levels, and rising unemployment. With the possible exception of the latter, all these factors were either specific to or particularly strong in the UK in the period since the mid-1970s. Additionally, most were either linked to government policies or directly caused by them. There is a global phenomenon of rising earnings dispersion linked to the decline of unskilled employment, technological change and the rise of credentialized, high-wage white-collar employment. Reich (1992) links this to globalization, suggesting that in the increasingly globalized labour market, there is an oversupply of unskilled labour and a scarcity of highly educated labour. Vandenbroucke (1998, p. 24), however, cites American evidence showing that international 'trade and immigration only accounted for about one tenth of the gross unequalising pressures over the past two decades'. Globalization sceptics such as Krugman (1994, p. 148) also point out that 'workers in the "typical" US trading partner are paid almost 90 per cent of the US wage rate' and that much of the growth in inequality is 'fractal', that is, within distinct occupations. Similarly, Atkinson (1996, p. 13) suggests that in the UK and the US in the 1980s 'however narrowly one defines [occupational groups] one still finds an increase in dispersion', amongst school teachers or police officers, for example. It may therefore 'have become socially acceptable to have larger differentials within the workplace ... [or] as more people are remunerated outside the conventional norms, so adherence to these norms becomes weaker' (Atkinson, 1996, p. 15). Maybe this is part of the culture of globalization, a growing culture of greed in which top managers and professionals have created a 'market' where exorbitant salaries are the global norm.

As Vandenbroucke (1998, p. 49) suggests, if economic globalization was a major factor in explaining the growth of inequality in the US and UK, we would expect to see such a phenomenon in economies even more exposed to global economic forces, such as the Netherlands and Switzerland, but this is not the case because they have retained their 'distributive social institutions'. Certainly globalization can be detected in the dispersal of market incomes, but governments can mitigate such effects substantially, if they choose to do so, without damaging competitiveness.

Labour Market Flexibility and Deregulation

Governments since 1979, including New Labour, have enthusiastically embraced the notion of the flexible labour market as essential to Britain's global economic competitiveness. For the Conservative government, flexibility was more or less synonymous with deregulation, the strategy of 'freeing' the labour market by encouraging non-standard conditions of employment such as part-time, casualized, temporary, freelance and fixed-term contracts. A range of explicit policies were implemented under the Conservatives to further this strategy. These included measures to reduce union power, to increase work incentive pressures on benefit claimants, to abolish minimum wages regulations in low-pay industries, to contract out public services and the decision not to sign up to the EU Social Charter. However, if labour market regulation is interpreted more narrowly as the employment rights of standard workers, then it can be argued that 'there has been no overall shift to greater deregulation in the UK since 1979' (Robinson, 1999, p. 98). This is because European legislation has enhanced some workers' rights, while national legislation has diminished others. At least three cross-national studies cited by Dex and McCulloch (1995, p. 3) suggest that the British labour market is one of the least regulated amongst the OECD states, alongside the USA.

There is little doubt that the weakening of the broader institutions of labour organization and workplace power has in itself 'deregulated' the labour market (Cousins, 1999, pp. 62–3). The decline in trade union membership and influence in Britain is justifiably cited as a major factor in explaining both growing income dispersion and labour market deregulation, but it is notable that unions still represent around one-third of the labour force, a higher proportion than in Germany, Holland, Spain and, above all, in France where union density is less than 10 per cent.

Flexibility is, of course, a much broader concept than deregulation. It may include general labour mobility, functional flexibility (multi-tasking) and place of work flexibility. Available data and research focuses on 'numerical flexibility' which is 'the ability of firms to adjust the number of workers they wish to pay' according to demand (Dex and McCulloch, 1995, p. 6). Dex and McCulloch (1995, p. 132) also found that 'at least one quarter of men and one half of women of working age held non-standard jobs in 1994', a very different picture from that in the 1970s. There has been a consistent decline in the proportion of full-time, permanent employees in the British labour force for decades, but it was particularly noticeable in the recession of the early 1980s (Robinson, 1999, p. 85). Casey *et al.* (1997, pp. 148–9) found that there had been 'a substantial increase in the use of flexible working time over the last decade' but 'the extent of variation in hours within and across organisations is not great' (p. 149). So, there is strong evidence of the growth of numerical flexibility alongside the deregulation of the labour market in Britain since the 1970s, and the two must almost inevitably be connected. Casey *et al.* (1997) found flexible working-time practices more commonly in large firms than in smaller ones, indicating a possible link with globalization through the culture of transnational corporations.

When comparing the deregulated labour market regimes of the UK and US with other states, it is apparent that there is some incompatibility between flexibility and deregulation. On one index of flexibility – the incidence of temporary employment – OECD data for 1995 cited by Robinson (1999, pp. 94–5) shows that the US and the UK had significantly lower rates compared with other EU states. These included Ireland and Germany, which were around the average, and Sweden, which was well above the average. In terms of part-time employment rates, the US was around the OECD average, with the UK and Sweden well above the average, and Germany and Ireland well below. If anything this data suggests that regulation nourishes flexibilization, because the flexible worker is better protected and more willing to accept the risks of flexibility. There is therefore some evidence of a universal, long-term shift towards more flexible employment contracts across the OECD, but whether this is driven principally by economic globalization is impossible to unravel. It may also represent a cultural shift amongst employers, employees and governments towards acceptance of flexible employment patterns.

Privatization of Welfare Consumption and Provision

Changes in the level of private welfare consumption in the UK since the 1970s have not been as dramatic as might be expected. The proportion of children going to private schools has risen modestly over the past twenty years, after a long decline in previous decades. The proportion of the workforce in occupational pension schemes has remained unchanged since the 1970s. Generous fiscal concessions encouraged a boom in private personal pensions in the late 1980s, but this ended when it became clear that many people were worse off than they would have been had they stayed in an occupational scheme. Private health care insurance, mainly provided by employers and covering only certain risks, now covers 11 per cent of households, an almost threefold increase in coverage since the 1970s. Health care costs met by private insurance amount to only 3 per cent of NHS expenditure, however (Hills, 1998b, p. 9). The decline in investment in social rented housing and, more recently, in financial assistance to home owners has been the most significant shift towards privatized welfare consumption.

The provision of services and benefits within 'the welfare state' has been marketized in many different forms. These include the contracting-out to commercial organizations of particular services within central government, the NHS and local government; the publicly funded purchase of social care services from commercial and non-profit organizations; the public funding of non-profit housing associations providing social rented housing; private finance initiatives to finance capital investment in hospitals and universities; and initiatives designed to force public service bodies to raise funds by mimicking commercial behaviour. Essentially the state, including local government, is in a process of 'hollowing out' (Jessop, 1994,) or 'dispersal' (Clarke, 1996, p. 30), in which the notion of 'public service' is disappearing. Government is becoming merely the financier of privately provided services purchased by semi-autonomous agencies in quasi-markets, and the quality of these services being more or less regulated by law, or contracted out to commercial organisations. This seems to be the model of 'welfare state' towards which the UK is moving under a New Labour government as much as under its Conservative predecessors.

The outcome of all these changes is that welfare activity which is directly publicly provided fell from 52 per cent of the total spend (public and private) to 49 per cent over the period 1979–80 to 1995–6. Meanwhile welfare activity that is publicly financed and regulated, but privately provided, has risen from 6 to 9 per cent (Hills, 1998b, p. 10). If globalization is linked with the penetration of private provision (both 'for profit' and 'not for profit') into the welfare state, then the British experience is a prescient example. Long-established traditions of *pillarization* in the Netherlands and the role of quasi-public insurance funds and NGOs in Germany would suggest that the British hollowing-out presents little threat to the legitimacy of the welfare state. The frameworks of legal and administrative regulation and of public finance sustain the notion of the welfare state as much if not more than the idea of direct public provision of services. Yet the disappearance of the ethic of public service, linked to the advent of the contract culture and privatization, is widely experienced as a loss in terms of workers' wages and conditions; workers' sense of loyalty and service to a community; political accountability to consumers; and communal identity with public organizations. Residualization is not really an appropriate term to describe this process. However, the process of hollowing-out the state appears to be increasingly common and may be an aspect of globalization. Whether the welfare activity of the hollowed-out state is any more efficient and effective in meeting welfare needs is highly debatable, not least because many factors exogenous to the social welfare system have created more pressing welfare needs and wider social divisions.

Conclusion

In this chapter, globalization has been considered as a fundamental aspect of the development of the political economy of advanced capitalist societies. This involves the growing power of capital, increasingly organized on a global scale, in the form of transnational corporations, faster and bigger flows of finance capital, and global expansion of trade. This has been linked to the changes considered above, such as the declining power of labour and socialist movements, the emergence of permanent mass unemployment, and increasing inequalities and poverty. The data considered above suggest that these links are more complex and looser than is sometimes imagined. Nevertheless, there is little doubt that these forces have been experienced particularly keenly in the UK. The result has been acute pressure on the welfare state, in terms both of declining resources and of increasing demands. The most direct link to globalization has been through the political sphere, that is the use of globalization as a legitimation for governments and transnational institutions to intensify the processes in the name of competitiveness and economic efficiency gains. In Ireland, however, while the pressures of high unemployment and increasing poverty have been strong, the impact of economic globalization on social policy discourse has resulted in the expansion of social spending to improve social protection and investment in human capital within a discourse of social partnership. Hence while both governments have sponsored economic globalization, the resulting social policies have been quite different.

There is little doubt that by the mid-1990s some of the neo-liberal momentum in Britain had withered in the face of increasing popular resistance and hostility. The New Labour government, like other social democratic governments in the EU member states, is trying to maintain openness to economic globalization alongside social measures to reduce unemployment, poverty and income dispersion, while cautiously continuing with the quasi-privatization of welfare provision. In Ireland the spectacular success of the economy in recent years has further legitimated the social market corporatist system alongside the openness of the economy to globalization. While there is little belief in social partnership corporatism within New Labour, there is the possibility that, with the development of transnational social democratic governance in the EU and the political retreat of neo-liberalism, the development of a more 'socially responsible' globalization may be advanced (cf. Deacon and Daly above).

Part III

Conclusion

10

Globalization and the European Welfare States: Evaluating the Theories and Evidence

PAULINE M. PRIOR AND ROBERT SYKES

Debates about globalization are often characterized by grand, if not grandiose, claims that are rarely tested by reference to real economic, social and political developments. This is not to argue that 'globalization', in some senses at least, is not happening, but rather that if we are to have a better understanding of both *what* it is, and *how* it is implicated in current processes of change, then we need to adopt a perspective of what might be termed 'informed scepticism'. We should be sceptical of the claims made for globalization as an unavoidable force for change, creating convergence in the economies, politics and social organization of the world's nations and destroying the autonomy of national governments.

This text has attempted to investigate and discuss the evidence for such changes. Focusing on recent developments in European welfare states, it has sought (a) to describe and understand these developments, and (b) to clarify the role of globalization in bringing them about. In addition, the text has also sought to provide a critical analysis of existing perspectives on the relationship between globalization and (European) welfare states and to suggest a new approach. The following chapter attempts to synthesize the arguments and point to future trends. The discussion is organized as follows:

- *Revisiting the Perspectives*: The perspectives on the interrelationship between globalization and welfare state changes are discussed in the light of the general arguments presented in Part I, and of the country-specific evidence in Part II, with a view to coming to some conclusions as to the explanatory value of these perspectives.

- *Reviewing the Evidence*: Some of the main themes to emerge from the country-specific discussions on recent welfare state changes, and their connection or otherwise to globalizing processes, will be put forward for consideration.
- *Debates for the Future*: Many scholars are revising their models of analysis in relation to both globalization and to welfare state changes, in the light of economic and political developments, not only in Europe, but also throughout the world (for example, Esping-Anderson, 1999; Scharpf, 1999; and Streeck, 1999). In this concluding section, we will discuss some of the new ideas emerging from their work and from the material presented in this volume.

Revisiting the Perspectives

The central question raised at the beginning of this book was *How far, and in what ways, has the process of globalization been implicated in recent changes to European welfare states?* We may now suggest how each of the three perspectives might answer this question, and assess their answers against the evidence presented.

- *Perspective 1: Globalization has a significant impact on welfare states through the increasing dominance of the (market) economy.* For this view to be upheld, we would expect the direct impact of economic globalization to have led to all European countries experiencing substantial, and essentially similar, welfare state changes.
- *Perspective 2: Globalization has relatively little impact on welfare states.* In this case, we would expect globalization to have had little or no clear or direct impact on welfare state changes in individual countries. Changes that occur are likely to be slow and incremental with a high degree of continuity with the past. Furthermore, any similarities in trends in welfare state policies between countries are related to the choice of similar policy solutions by governments, rather than to the external constraints of globalization.
- *Perspective 3: Globalization has impacted on welfare systems/states, but this impact is mediated through (national) institutional structures and policy responses.* According to this view, we would expect to see

policy changes that are path-dependent, but may be quite significant. The nature of change will depend on the pre-existing national welfare ideology and the institutional framework of the welfare state in each country, but with similarities in trends within the same type of welfare state regime.

In relation to the first perspective, there is no evidence in the material presented here of a direct and essentially similar impact by globalization on European welfare states. Changes which have occurred, though they may have been indirectly related to globalization, have been mediated through national governmental policies and institutions, a process that has led to quite different outcomes.

Even in Central and Eastern European countries, where the situation seemed ripe for the neo liberal characteristics of globalization to make the strongest impact, the argument is not supported. As Ferge shows quite clearly, the policies for change came not from the unfettered forces of the global economy as these countries re-entered the capitalist fold. Rather, they came from the ideological and practical policy prescriptions of the major actors promoting the 'Washington Consensus' – international organizations, such as the World Bank, backed by the dominant world governments. Though the rhetoric of globalization was often used by national governments to legitimate the introduction of sometimes harsh social policies, their own role was crucial in terms of the interpretation of the policy changes to be made and the decision to accept the general ideological thrust of the international organizations.

There are similar problems with the second perspective, which links changes in welfare states solely to domestic factors. Whilst the significance of factors such as population ageing and the increasing cost of welfare systems should not be undervalued, it is clear that external factors, some or which were related to globalization, have, indeed, been part of the reason for changes in welfare states. Globalization is not a monolithic exogenous force that impacts directly and with equal impact on nation-states, but rather a complex set of ideological and practical processes, some of which are accepted, internalized and acted on by national governments. Within this broader view of globalization, the argument of Leibfried and Rieger (1998), that welfare state change is due more to the ideological projects of governments seeking to restructure, than to the impact of economic globalization processes, seems closer to the evidence presented here. Consider for example, the discussion on Central and Eastern European countries by Ferge, and on Nordic countries by Kosonen in relation to the impact of very different ideological stances on welfare policies.

The third perspective is broadly supported by the evidence presented in this text. Yet this perspective has flaws which limit its explanatory power. For example, according to Esping-Andersen (1996a, 1999), existing institutional arrangements and welfare commitments constrain change due to the impact of economic globalization in 'path-dependent' ways. These arrangements and commitments, and the constituencies they created, coupled with the need for governments to sustain political support, mean that welfare state responses and adaptations to globalization will be slow and piecemeal. However, this perspective does not fully account for the fact that globalization itself is experienced differently by different groups of welfare states *and* by individual nations within these groups. Welfare state changes may vary from country to country *within* similar types of welfare regime, because national governments may combine different sets of policy solutions. This can be seen, for example, in the variation within the Liberal group between the UK and Irish developments, and within the Bismarckian group between the French, German and Dutch developments.

This brings us to the fourth, or alternative, perspective proposed in Chapter 1. The central feature of this perspective is that it treats globalization not as an homogenous exogenous force impacting on nation-states and causing them to adapt their welfare states, but as a differentiated phenomenon, the character of which is constructed and interpreted differently in different types of welfare system. Furthermore, the relationship between globalization and welfare state change is conceptualized as reciprocal, not unidirectional. From this perspective we would expect the following:

1. Some significant welfare state changes associated with globalization to have occurred.
2. As globalization is not simply a homogenous external force, we should expect differentiation both in terms of responses to globalization *and* in terms of the forms that globalization may take.
3. Because national policies matter, they have a significant effect on how globalization is perceived and received.
4. Globalization should be seen not only as creating new problems for welfare states and promoting welfare state retrenchment practices, but also as providing opportunities that have sometimes been taken by certain governments to invent welfare-friendly solutions.

The evidence presented in the country-specific chapters of this text provides substantial support for this last perspective. Firstly, definitions of what constitutes globalization vary between the different families of European welfare states. The range of experience is wide. In the case of the Nordic welfare states, globalization has been constituted primarily as a process affecting the internationalization of Nordic firms within the global market and the integration of Nordic financial markets into the global system. In the Southern welfare states, globalization has primarily been about the processes of European economic and political integration, especially regarding the European Union. For the Bismarckian welfare states, globalization has been a process impacting on labour markets, affecting, in particular, the existing rigidities in occupational structures and competitiveness, but also creating problems for existing patterns of part-time and full-time employment and the gender balance in the labour force. In the Central and Eastern European welfare states, globalization has been synonomous with the process whereby the International Monetary Fund (IMF), the World Bank and other international organizations have managed to impose a completely new welfare ideology and a fundamental restructuring of welfare provision along radical neo-liberal lines. Finally, in the case of the Liberal welfare states, globalization is primarily an economic process associated with the opening of domestic economies to the full forces of the global economy in order to achieve improved economic efficiency and growth.

Secondly, it should also be recognized that for European welfare states, the role of the European Union and its various agencies in promoting different perceptions of globalization and different policy solutions has been of increasing significance in the last ten to fifteen years. This applies most importantly to the EU member states, but it also affects non-member states in Europe – such as Norway and the Central and Eastern European states. The importance of the EU as an economic and political force in the processes of globalization accounts for its increasing influence over European welfare states. Three examples may be cited as illustrations: (i) the importance of the economic criteria for membership of EU Monetary Union, (ii) the importance of meeting political criteria for membership of the EU for applicant countries, and (iii) the economic and social policy implications of EU enlargement for member-states and non-member-states alike.

Thirdly, it is clear that significant changes have, indeed, occurred in European welfare states in recent years – albeit with variation both in level and type – and that these changes are related to globalization. In some cases they could be described as retrenchment, as in the case of the Nordic, the Bismarckian and some aspects of the Southern welfare states. Though significant, they are broadly within the logic and framework of existing institutional and ideological national welfare systems, but have involved reductions in social expenditure, changes in the rules of access to benefits, and in the scope of welfare provision. In other cases, the changes are more radical and may more accurately be described as restructuring, in that they have challenged and even changed the logic on which existing welfare systems were based. Examples of this type of change occurred principally in the Central and Eastern European welfare states, but also in the United Kingdom, France, the Netherlands and, to a lesser extent, in some policy areas in the Southern welfare states. Changes have involved not only retrenchment, but also a radical altering of institutional structures *and* of the welfare ideology underpinning these structures. To suggest that either set of changes is primarily domestic in cause (Perspective 2) or relatively small and insignificant (Perspectives 2 and 3) flies in the face of the evidence.

A more detailed analysis of the similarities and differences in welfare state change across European welfare states, is presented in the next section of this chapter. This evidence supports the dialectical nature of the assumptions underlying the fourth perspective. Before proceeding to this review, it may be helpful to codify the wide range of changes described in the country-specific chapters into four broad categories. There are examples of each type of change in almost all of the welfare states discussed, although they can take different forms and occur in various combinations with the other types of change. Normally, however, one of the four types of change predominates in individual countries and in welfare family types at a given time. The four types of changes are:

- *Activation policies*: the use of supply-side measures such as education and training to improve the employability of citizens
- *Marketization*: the opening of the supply and organization of 'welfare' to market forces and privatization
- *Cost cutting*: the reduction of welfare expenditures and coverage
- *Restructuring*: a fundamental reorganization of both the ideology and the organization of welfare provision

Reviewing the Evidence

Significant Changes in Welfare States Associated with Globalization

Over the past two decades welfare systems throughout Europe have undergone significant changes, many of which have been associated with the globalization of the economy. These have ranged from changes where the link with globalization or international factors is less obvious, to radical and obvious changes. Some examples of changes less obviously linked with globalization have occurred in the welfare systems of the Nordic countries (Sweden, Norway, Finland and Denmark) and in the countries of the Bismarckian group (Germany, France, Austria, the Netherlands and Belgium). In the Nordic countries, Kosonen argues, the ideology of the welfare state remains essentially unchanged, with a continued commitment to public provision. Globalization has been synonymous with the internationalization of their financial and other markets, the deregulation of their capital markets, the attempt to meet the economic criteria for EMU membership, even for the non-EMU members, and the flexibilization of labour markets. In the Bismarckian countries, according to Daly, globalization has expressed itself primarily as an economic phenomenon concerned with increasing competitiveness between national economies. As such it has created an agenda for change for these countries, rather than directly causing adaptations or restructuring. This agenda for change, arising out of the demands for increased competition and the flexibilization of the labour force, has created 'pressure points' within the welfare systems of the countries in this group, which has sometimes precipitated change and sometimes has not done so.

In other countries, the impact of globalization on welfare state trends is more obvious – for example, in the Southern welfare states (Spain, Italy, Greece, Portugal) and in the countries of Central and Eastern Europe. In relation to the Southern countries, according to Guillén and Álvarez, the internationalization of the economies and their openness to external competition and European integration have been crucial factors in the transformation of the southern political economies in recent years. They suggest that the significance of the European Union policy of economic and monetary union cannot be underestimated, as it provides both an economic and a political rationale for the changes made to the welfare systems in these countries. The national governments made deliberate political choices to place their economies within the framework of the EMU, which involved considerable development of their welfare state programmes. The majority of political parties, employers and trade unions supported these choices.

In the Central and Eastern European welfare states, the impact of globalization though different, has also been significant. Here, Ferge argues, the 'Washington consensus', outlined by and imposed through the international agencies of the World Bank (WB) and the International Monetary Fund (IMF), has led to a total transformation of the economies, politics and welfare systems in these countries. Two aspects of this transformation are important here. The first was the promotion of neo-liberal ideology, dominated by concerns about the alleged impact of globalization. This has led to the deregulation of markets, the drive to lower direct and indirect labour costs, the privatization and marketization of former public goods and services, coupled with an attack on 'state paternalism'. Secondly, this neo-liberalism was combined with conservatism with regard to the Church, the family, and the nation. The adoption of this ideology led a radical reduction of public expenditure on the welfare state. As a result, the role of the market in welfare provision increased dramatically in housing, education and health provision, and the privatization of social insurance and most other public services has begun. The voluntary sector has undergone a rebirth in these countries as attempts are made to fill the vacuum left by the withdrawal of the state.

Globalization Takes Different Forms

It is clear from the discussion above that the experience of globalization varies widely from country to country. For the Southern welfare states, the experience is primarily one of preparing for integration into a European monetary system, while for the countries of Central and Eastern Europe it has been one of meeting the demands of international financial institutions, thus proving their commitment to economic and social development within a capitalist rather than a socialist framework of welfare services. The Nordic countries and those in the Bismarkian group, because of their stronger economic and ideological positions, have not been prone to the same level of domination from international forces. However, they too have had to take on the challenge of a changing international economic environment.

Two examples make the point clearer. For the Nordic countries, the goal of full employment has been one of the main characteristics of its 'normative legacy', along with the promise of universal social rights, the notion of the responsibility of government for welfare, and equality (both income and gender equality). As a result, these countries face the onslaught of globalization with a determination to maintain this legacy. However, Kosonen suggests that the target of full employment is increasingly losing its primacy, being replaced by an emphasis upon price stability and balancing the budget. Nordic employment policies now concentrate upon activation strategies of (re)training and education rather than job creation. Whilst there continues to be a strong belief in the role of the public sector, private and labour market based approaches in the area of social insurance are gaining ground. Charges have been introduced for some welfare services, and there are moves away from tax financing. Perhaps most significantly, there have been major cuts in public welfare service staffing. As for the principle of equality, it is now clear that increasing wage differentials and reduced tax rates have become more acceptable, though income differentials remain comparatively low due to continuing high levels of income transfer. Finally, the principle of universalism continues to be the mainstay of the politics of welfare in Nordic countries. In practice, however, this principle is being steadily eroded by moves towards income-related social insurance and the continued presence of a large core of long-term unemployed people.

In the Bismarckian group of countries, where there is also a strong commitment to a publicly funded welfare system, the demands associated with the internationalization of markets have been experienced as pressures for some change rather than for an overhaul of the system. Daly describes how in each country the nature of the existing funding and claim structures have mediated labour market policy changes, macroeconomic policy changes and social policy changes. The resulting changes vary across the Bismarckian family. In the case of the financing structure the pattern is broadly the same, with considerable change in the respective contributions of the state, labour and capital to social security revenues and programme administration across all five countries, with a general trend towards lessening employer contributions and increasing those from employees and the state. In the case of the claims structure, however, much greater variation can be found beneath the surface of apparent similarity. Daly suggest three sub-groupings: those countries seeing little or no change to their claim principles (Austria and Germany); the Netherlands which appears to have made quite significant changes to its welfare principles; and finally Belgium and France where limited changes have been seen, rather less in Belgium, rather more in France. In summary, globalization has created an agenda for change for these countries, rather than directly causing adaptations or restructuring.

National Policies Matter

The fact that national policies matter, in terms of the ways in which globalization is experienced and responded to, shows that individual states are not powerless in the face of global pressures (for an extended discussion, see Weiss, 1998). Even between countries with similar types of welfare state regime, there have been different developments in the face of these pressures. This is evident, for example, in the cases of Britain and Ireland. As Ginsburg suggests, these two nations, though not entirely similar, may be classified as having Liberal welfare states. However, their patterns of adaptation to global pressures have been quite different. Britain maintained a strong line on the need for flexibility in labour markets and restraint in social expenditure in order to enhance competitiveness (the American liberal model), while Ireland took the view that increasing social expenditure might help weather the global economic storm (the European social model). In other words, the ideological position of the individual national government determines the patterns of adaptation deemed most appropriate, and these can result in quite different models of welfare systems and employment policies.

Some nations already have a strong social ideology which they have maintained in spite of pressures from the global economy. The Nordic welfare states, according to Kosonen, may have made some changes in their welfare systems – such as the introduction of user charges in public services and the encouragement of market solutions in some areas of insurance – but politicians remain publicly committed to the ideology of social justice and equality. The characteristics of these states – social cohesion, a highly educated and technologically skilled workforce, low levels of social exclusion – are seen as contributing towards economic competitiveness. Thus, though within the Nordic group there are some real differences in adaptation to current economic pressures, not least of which are the demands imposed by the possibility of a single European monetary system, individual nations have shown their unwillingness to be passive recipients of external events, and continue to follow a well-established pattern of social protection.

Another example of the power of the individual nation to determine its own policy direction is the resistance of both Germany and Austria to changes in their external environment, described by Daly. They have reacted by adhering closely to long-standing organizational forms and principles, a characteristic, Daly argues, of the Bismarckian welfare system. This has not necessarily been either economically efficient or socially progressive for these two countries, but it has kept intact their ideological commitment to a generous system of social protection strongly linked to sustained employment.

However, this is not to say that all national policies are necessarily progressive. Welfare systems continue to reproduce the kinds of institutionalized divisions referred to by Clarke, who reminds us that even the coherent welfare state (if one exists) will produce and reproduce racialized and gendered differences. The continuation of gender inequalities in welfare systems, in spite of the major changes in the external environment, is obvious, for example in the Southern countries of Europe. As Guillén and Álvarez demonstrate, these states presuppose a strong male breadwinner/female carer model of society with the family performing a number of welfare functions not usually found in other welfare systems.

The final example of the power of the individual state in the face of the range of choices presented by developments related to globalization is Central and Eastern Europe. In a situation which Ferge describes as the 'near collapse of the state' and the growth of an 'ill-fare' rather than a welfare state, national governments have maintained a position in the face of seemingly overwhelming external pressures from international organizations such as the International Monetary Fund and the World Bank. She concedes that these countries are poor and that their governments are in a weak bargaining position (relative to the international banks and agencies) when it comes to deciding structural economic and welfare changes. However, she argues, this does not explain why their welfare system has been the main target of expenditure cuts, or why the cuts were made in a way which affects the long-term welfare of large sections of the population. A possible explanation is that these countries need the goodwill of the foreign capital and international agencies and must therefore show themselves to be completely free of links with their tainted socialist past. This, Ferge concludes, indicates that there are political and ideological reasons, over and above economic ones cited by governments, for the level and type of cost-cutting in welfare systems in these states.

Globalization May Lead to Welfare-Friendly Solutions

There is general agreement that globalization may have a negative impact on welfare systems, because of the need to reduce public expenditure to make individual countries more competitive, and of the need to make the workforce as adaptable as possible to changing market structures. However, it is clear from the evidence presented in this text that globalization can also be experienced as a catalyst for the strengthening of existing welfare provision. The best examples of this are the Southern welfare states (Spain, Italy, Greece and Portugal) and Ireland, categorized here as a Liberal welfare state.

In the Southern welfare states, Guillén and Álvarez argue that, far from being a negative pressure leading to the retrenchment of welfare provision, globalization (*qua* European integration) has actually involved positive development, a 'catching up' by these countries to a standard of welfare system already achieved in most of mainland Europe. These countries did not begin from the same level of welfare spending and institutional organization as the countries in the north of Europe, but they have seen broadly the same types of growth and development in the past three decades. What is most interesting is the fact that national governments in these countries became increasingly aware of the role of welfare systems in achieving their dual goal of European integration and of competitiveness in the world market. This led to a growing interest in a public debate on social exclusion and a move to improve social protection policies.

In Ireland, similar developments have taken place. Ginsburg shows how the development of neo-corporatist agreements and policies were used to compensate for the increasing social risks associated with global competitiveness. In contrast to the United Kingdom, Ireland increased social expenditure with the aim of strengthening the workforce. This translated as the involvement of trade unions as social partners in the setting of wages and in discussing other policies in the face of the rapid economic growth which has characterized recent years. Social expenditure has increased in line with this economic growth, especially in the areas of health care, education and active labour market measures. The Irish government's and unions' strategy seems to be based on the belief that the 'Celtic Tiger' needs a socially stable society in order to survive in the global economy.

This approach to welfare state policies reflects the ideology of those who aspire to a socially responsible globalization – an ideology discussed earlier in this text, principally by Deacon, but also by Daly and Hay. This is the notion of the welfare state as a potentially positive factor (rather than a negative one) in economic competitiveness. The central contention of those promoting socially responsible globalization is that certain firms are attracted by countries with a commitment to regulation of labour and capital and the provision of a welfare safety-net for those not in work. In this view, welfare provision and the regulation of labour can promote social cohesion that, in turn, provides a stable working population and a stable commercial environment.

Debates for the Future: Challenge and Change

This book has attempted to consider some key issues which, we argue, should underpin the analysis of the interaction between the forces of globalization and welfare states. Clarke, Hay and Deacon raised the issues as 'challenges' in the first part of this book. Yet these challenges have also been evident in the work of the contributors to the second part of the book, as they attempted to consider these theoretical and empirical issues in the light of the evidence of specific welfare state changes.

Some of the most fundamental questions were posed by John Clarke, whose critical discussion of the concepts of 'globalization', 'welfare state' and 'Europe', highlighted the complexity of the project in hand – the unravelling of the relationship between the three phenomena. For Clarke, globalization is not a single, unified causal process, but rather the effect of other national and international developments. Thus, both the experience of globalization and national responses to this experience will, indeed, differ from country to country and from regime type to regime type. Clarke's broader notion of complexity and changing nature of globalization is clearly evident in the varied experiences of globalizing forces and national responses to them across Europe – ranging from little current change in the Bismarckian countries to an overwhelming onslaught in Central and Eastern Europe.

The occurrence of different experiences and responses is confirmed not only in the work presented here but also in the recent cross-national research of Sharpf and Schmidt and their associates (see Scharpf, 1999; Scharpf and Schmidt, 2000) on adjustments of employment and social policy to economic internationalization in twelve countries (Austria, Australia, Belgium, Denmark, France, Germany, Italy, the Netherlands, New Zealand, Sweden, Switzerland and the United Kingdom). They argue that whilst in the 1970s the challenges presented by economic internationalization could be met by changes in macroeconomic management, in the 1980s and 1990s it had a more direct effect on labour markets and national welfare systems. The individual national responses were mediated through existing national structures that were extremely varied. For example, there were differences in type of welfare state, in employment structures, in public finance arrangements and in policy legacies. These features affected the degree of vulnerability to competitive pressures, and the policy options open to welfare states experiencing these pressures.

The validity of the Scharpf (1999) argument is clear when one considers the data presented in relation to a range of countries in this text. It also has some resonance with the issues raised by Colin Hay . Hay argues that existing theories of globalization have often led to false predictions as to the inevitability of retrenchment in the welfare systems of individual countries. However, it is clear that retrenchment, where it has occurred, is often not directly linked to globalizing forces, but rather to particular national economic and political choices. These choices are often ideologically-based when they involve expenditure on welfare systems. Whilst informative, we would thus take issue with Scharpf and his associates, in that they treat the link between globalization and welfare states change as an essentially one-way process, one of adaptation by national governments. Our approach stresses the political choices open to governments and other social policy actors, both in how globalization is perceived/constructed and in terms of actual policy choices and changes made.

Just as the notion of globalization is contested, so too is that of the welfare state. John Clarke argues that it would be a mistake to think of welfare states as collective actors that can 'respond' or 'adapt' to pressures such as those arising from globalization. People, rather than states, make decisions to change or introduce policies – a process that involves both political and ideological choices. He also argues that the welfare state is often mistakenly identified only with income transfer policies. Such identification leads to the exclusion of broader areas of social policy such as health, housing, education and the environment, and leads to a false analysis of developments in welfare systems.

The debate on 'what is a welfare state' may be extended to include discussion of the validity of welfare state typologies such as Esping Anderson's (1990, 1999). This model has informed many, if not most, recent studies of comparative social policy in Europe. Whilst in this text we have adapted his tripartite model and added two further groups – Central and Eastern European and Southern welfare states – his theoretical framework has provided the basis for our comparative analysis, as it has for Scharpf (1999) and others. However, the issues raised in the country-specific studies of globalization and welfare state change raise fundamental questions about the continuing utility of this model. Authors found it difficult to apply in relation to individual nations, because it either over-simplified or excluded some of the characteristics that they deemed of particular relevance to their specific welfare systems. Esping-Andersen (1999) has himself raised general questions about the nature of socio-economic change and its significance for welfare states and social policy.

One of his central arguments is that whilst the social and economic foundations of contemporary post-industrial societies are rapidly changing, their welfare systems are remaining very much as they were in the industrial past of these countries. Change is urgently needed in the welfare systems of such societies, he argues, yet various institutional and political pressures have combined to slow down such change to a snail's pace, or prevent it from occurring altogether. Esping-Andersen continues to defend the utility and applicability of his tripartite model for the study of comparative social policy, even in these circumstances of rapid social and economic change (1999, pp. 73–94). Nevertheless, he does incorporate some of the criticisms of his original work by accepting that the role of the family may be used in further differentiating welfare states. His notion of 'familialism' certainly provides a significant development to his original model. In addition, he concedes that differences in the dominant approach to the management of social risks within the labour market, the state and the family, offers an alternative way of classifying welfare states (Esping-Anderson, 1999, pp. 84–6). The question for the future is, in the light of the socio-economic changes noted by Esping-Andersen, and the sorts of welfare state changes illustrated in this text, will other models offer a more useful framework for the study of welfare state development and change?

Europe is the third and last of our contested concepts and constructs. Two of our authors, John Clarke and Bob Deacon, challenge its use as a coherent conceptual category. For example, academics often use the term 'Europe' interchangeably with the term 'European Union', seeing the latter as a central component in economic and political developments in most of the countries geographically included in Europe, regardless of their formal links with the European Union. Furthermore, a 'European social model' is taken as representing a strong commitment to a high standard of welfare provision, and the European Union itself is often regarded as presenting a strong message on the need for well-funded welfare systems. However, as Deacon points out, while international organizations such as the IMF, the World Bank and the International Labour Organization have well-articulated and highly publicized views on the role of welfare states in a globalized economy, the view from the European Union is neither coherent nor clear. Different parts of the EU – member states, Directorates, Commission, Parliament and Court – have promoted different policies, some of which have contradicted each other. Thus any discussion of Europe has to assume a changing reality. For example, in relation to the 'European social model', it is clear that systems are changing in response to economic internationalization/ globalization. Streeck

(1999) points to the differential impact of international competition on national welfare systems. In Europe, this has led to the rethinking of national patterns of social solidarity. However, this rethink has not taken place at the transnational level as, despite the existence of the EU, there is not a unified European political community. Thus, Streeck argues, how European welfare states recast their systems of social solidarity and welfare will be decided in interplay between increasingly interdependent national systems and a developing network of supranational institutions and commitments. This *new* European social model, involving both national systems and a developing system of EU social regulation, is likely to have the features of what Streeck calls 'productivist-competitive solidarity'. Individual European welfare states are not becoming part of a trans-European welfare regime, but are increasingly 'Europeanized' in the sense of being more aware of European regulatory and political context. The new system of solidarity will accommodate, rather than seek to counteract, market forces, making European social regimes more competitive and more efficient. Social cohesion will be generated not through state intervention to promote equal outcomes, but rather through attempts to foster equal opportunities in the labour market. Though framed in a somewhat different way, this notion of a shift to a more competitive and market-friendly pattern of social welfare in Europe echoes similar prognoses about the European social model made by, for example, Grahl and Teague (1997) and Rhodes (1999), and fits with the notion of a socially responsible globalization. Whether or not in the future there will indeed be a coherent economic and political Europe, dominated by an ideology of social solidarity, remains to be seen.

This work has argued that the time has come to move beyond simplistic analyses of the interaction between globalization and (European) welfare states. Globalization is both a contested notion and a contested process. Furthermore, we have argued that the relationship between the challenges presented by globalization and changes in welfare states should be seen as reciprocal rather than unidirectional. The role of different policy actors, especially national governments, is fundamental to this reciprocal process. Last but not least, we argue that when considering the relationship between globalization and welfare state change, what 'Europe' is and what it may become is of central importance.

Bibliography

Aaron, H. J. (1991) *Serious and Unstable Condition: Financing America's Health Care* (Washington: The Brookings Institute).

Alber, J. (1986) 'Germany', in Flora, P. (ed.), *Growth to Limits: The Western European Welfare States since World War II*, Vol. 2 (Berlin: de Gruyter).

Alestalo, M. and Flora, P. (1994) 'Scandinavia: welfare states in the periphery – peripheral welfare states?', in M. Alestalo, E. Allardt, R. Andrzej and W. Wesolowski (eds), *The Transformation of Europe. Social Conditions and Consequences* (Warsaw: IFiS Publishers).

Alestalo, M., Bislev, S. and Furåker, B. (1991) 'Welfare state employment in Scandinavia', in J. Eivind Kolberg (ed.), *The Welfare State as Employer* (Armonk, NY: M. E. Sharpe).

Allmendinger, J. (1989) 'Educational systems and labour market outcomes', *European Sociological Review*, vol. 5, no. 3, pp. 231–50.

Andersson, J. O., Kosonen, P. and Vartiainen, J. (1993) *The Finnish Model of Economic and Social Policy – from Emulation to Crash* (Åbo: Meddelanden från ekonomisk-statsvetenskapliga fakulteten vid Åbo Akademi Ser. A:401).

Arter, David (1999) *Scandinavian Politics Today* (Manchester: Manchester University Press).

Ashton, D. and Green, F. (1996) *Education, Training and the Global Economy* (London: Edward Elgar).

Atkinson, A. B. (1996) 'Income distribution in an international context', Annual Lecture, Centre for International Business Studies (CIBS), South Bank University, London, 9 May.

Atkinson, A. B. (1998) *Poverty in Europe* (Oxford: Blackwell).

Atkinson, M. (1999) 'The Celtic tiger burns too bright', *The Guardian*, 7 May.

Barr, N. (1998) *The Economics of the Welfare State*, 3rd edn (Oxford: Oxford University Press).

Barr, N. (1999) 'Reforming welfare states in post-communist countries', paper presented at: 'Ten Years After: Transition and Growth in Post-communist Countries', Warsaw 15–16 October 1999 (manuscript quoted with the permission of the author).

Barrada, A. (1999) *El gasto público de bienestar en España de 1964 a 1995* (Bilbao: Fundación BBV).

Barry, U. (1998) 'Women, equality and public policy', in S. Healy and B. Reynolds (eds), *Social Policy in Ireland: Principles, Practice and Problems* (Dublin: Oak Tree Press).

Baylis, J. and Smith, S. (1999) *The Globalization of World Politics: An Introduction to International Relations* (Oxford: Oxford University Press).

Bettio, F. and Villa, Paola (1998) 'A Mediterranean perspective on the breakdown between participation and fertility', *Cambridge Journal of Economics*, no. 22, pp. 137–71.

Boix, C. (1998) *Political Parties, Growth and Equality: Conservative and Social Democratic Economic Strategies in the World Economy* (Cambridge: Cambridge University Press).

Bonoli, G. and Palier, B. (1997) 'Reclaiming welfare: the politics of French social protection reform', in M. Rhodes (ed.), *Southern European Welfare States between Crisis and Reform* (London: Frank Cass).

Bonoli, G. and Palier, B. (1998) 'Changing the politics of social programmes: innovative change in British and French welfare reforms', *Journal of European Social Policy*, vol. 8, no. 4, pp. 317–30.

Bosworth, D., Dawkins, P. and Stromback, T. (1996) *The Economics of the Labour Market* (Harlow: Longman).

Bouget, D. (1998) 'The Juppé Plan and the future of the French social welfare system', *Journal of European Social Policy*, vol. 8, no. 3, pp. 155–72.

Bowles, S. and Gintis, H. (1994) 'Efficient redistribution in a globally competitive economy', paper presented to the Colloquium on Social Justice and Economic Constraints, Université Catholique de Louvain, 3 June.

Boyer, R. and Drache, D. (eds) (1996) *States Against Markets: The Limits of Globalisation* (London: Routledge).

Bradshaw, J., Ditch, J., Holmes, H. and Whiteford, P. (1993) 'A comparative study of child support in fifteen countries', *Journal of European Social Policy*, vol. 3, no. 4, pp. 255–71.

Brah, A. (1996) *Cartographies of Diaspora: Contesting Identities* (London: Routledge).

Braunerhjelm, P., Heum, P. and Ylä-Anttila, P. (1996) *Internationalization of Industrial Firms. Implications for Growth and Industrial Structure in the Nordic Countries* (Helsinki: ETLA Discussion Papers, No. 551).

Brindle, D. (1998) 'Gap between rich and poor widens again', *The Guardian*, 16 October.

Brown, G. (1999) 'Rediscovering public purpose in the global economy', *Social Development Review*, vol. 3, no. 1, pp. 3–7.

Burniaux, J-M., Dang, T-T., Fore, D., Förster, M., d'Ercole, M. M. and Oxley, H. (1998) *Income Distribution and Poverty in Selected OECD Countries* (Paris: OECD) (Economics Department Working Papers No. 189).

Callan, T. and Nolan, B. (1998) 'Poverty and policy', in S. Healy and B. Reynolds (eds), *Social Policy in Ireland: Principles, Practice and Problems* (Dublin: Oak Tree Press).

Camdessus, M. (1999) 'Looking beyond today's financial crisis: Moving forward with international financial reform', Speech to the Foreign Policy Association, 24th February 1999, New York.

Cameron, David R. (1978) 'The expansion of the public economy: a comparative analysis', *American Political Science Review*, vol. 72, no. 4.

Casey, B., Metcalf, H. and Millward, N. (1997) *Employers' Use of Flexible Labour* (London: Policy Studies Institute).

Castel, Robert (1995) *Les métamorphoses de la question sociale. Une chronique du salariat* (Paris: Fayard).

Castles, F. G. (1994) 'On religion and public policy: does Catholicism make a difference?', *European Journal of Political Research*, vol. 25, no. 1, pp. 12–40.

Castles, F. G. (1995) 'Welfare state development in southern Europe', *West European Politics*, vol. 18, no. 2, pp. 291–313.

Cella, G. P. and Treu, T. (eds) (1989) *Relazioni industriali. Manuale per l'analisi dell'eperienza italiana* (Bologna: II Mulino).

Cerny, P. G. (1990) *The Changing Architecture of Politics* (London: Sage).

Cerny, P. G. (1997) 'Paradoxes of the competition state: the dynamics of political globalisation', *Government and Opposition*, vol. 49, no. 4, pp. 595–625.

Chand, S. K. *et al.* (1990) *Aging Populations and Public Pension Schemes*, Occasional Paper No. 147 (Washington: IMF).

Clark, G. L. (1999) 'The retreat of the state and the rise of pension fund capitalism', in R. Martin (ed.), *Money and the Space Economy* (New York: Wiley).

Clarke, J. (1996) 'The problem of the state after the welfare state', in M. May, E. Brunsdon and G. Craig (eds), *Social Policy Review 8* (Canterbury: Social Policy Association).

Clarke, J. (1998) 'Thriving on chaos? Managerialism and social welfare', in J. Carter (ed.), *Post-Modernity and the Fragmentation of Welfare* (London: Routledge).

Clarke, J. (1999) 'Coming to terms with culture', in H. Dean and R. Woods (eds), *Social Policy Review 11* (Canterbury: Social Policy Association).

Clarke, J. and Cochrane, A. (1998) 'The social construction of social problems', in E. Saraga (ed.), *Embodying the Social* (London: Routledge).

Clarke, J. and Newman, J. (1997) *The Managerial State: Power, Politics and Ideology in the Remaking of Social Welfare* (London: Sage).

Clarke, J., Hughes, G., Lewis, J. and Mooney, G. (1998) 'Introduction', in G. Hughes (ed.), *Imagining Welfare Futures* (London: Routledge).

Clarke, T. and Barlow, M. (1997) *MAI: The Multilateral Agreement on Investment and the Threat to Canadian Sovereignty* (North York, Ont: Stoddart).

Clasen, J. (ed.) (1999) *Comparative Social Policy: Concepts, Theories and Methods* (Oxford: Blackwell).

Cochrane, A. (1993) 'Comparative approaches and social policy', in A. Cochrane and J. Clarke (eds), *Comparing Welfare States: Britain in International Context* (London: Sage).

Collins, M. and Kavanagh, C. (1998) 'For richer, for poorer: the changing distribution of household income in Ireland, 1973–94', in S. Healy and B. Reynolds (eds), *Social Policy in Ireland: Principles, Practice and Problems* (Dublin: Oak Tree Press).

Cousins, C. (1999) *Society, Work and Welfare in Europe* (Basingstoke: Macmillan).

Cousins, M. (1994) *The Irish Social Welfare System* (Dublin: Round Hall Press).

Cousins, M. (1997) 'Ireland's place in the worlds of welfare capitalism', *of European Social Policy*, vol. 7, no. 2, pp. 223–36.

Cremona, M. (1998) 'The European Union as an international actor: the issues of flexibility and linkage', *European Foreign Affairs Review*, vol. 3, no. 1, pp. 67–94.

Crowe, B. L. (1998) 'Some reflections on the common foreign and security policy', *European Foreign Affairs Review*, vol. 3, no. 3, pp. 319–24.

Cruz Roche, I. (1994) 'La dinámica y estructura de la universalización de las pensiones', in *V Informe sociológico sobre la situación social en España* (Madrid: Fundación FOESSA).

Daly, M. (1997) 'Welfare states under pressure: cash benefits in European welfare states over the last ten years', *Journal of European Social Policy*, vol. 7, no. 2, pp. 129–46.

De la Villa, L. E. (1985) *Los grandes pactos colectivos a partir de la transición democrática* (Madrid: Ministerio de Trabajo y Seguridad Social).

Deacon, B. (ed.) (1992) *Social Policy, Social Justice and Citizenship in Eastern Europe* (Aldershot: Avebury).

Deacon, B. (1999a) *Towards a Socially Responsible Globalization: International Actors and Discourses* (Helsinki: GASPP Occasional Paper No. 1, STAKES).

Deacon, B. (1999b) 'Social policy in a global context', in A. Hurrell and N. Woods (eds), *Inequality, Globalization and World Politics* (New York: Oxford University Press).

Deacon, B (1999c) *Socially Responsible Globalization: A Challenge for the European Union* (Helsinki: Ministry of Social Affairs and Health).

Deacon, B. (2000) *Globalization and Social Policy*, Occasional Paper No. 5, Geneva 2000 Series (Geneva: United Nations Research Institute for Social Development).

Deacon, B. with Hulse, M. and Stubbs, P. (1997) *Global Social Policy* (London: Sage).

Deakin, S. and Wilkinson, F. (1992) 'Social policy and economic efficiency: the deregulation of the labour market in the Britain', *Critical Social Policy*, no. 33, Winter 1991/92.

Deutsches Institut für Wirtschaftsforschung (1995) 'Finanzentwicklung der sozialversicherung', *DIW Wochenbericht*, vol. 62, no. 40, pp. 693–7.

Dex, S. and McCulloch, A. (1995) *Flexible Employment in Britain: A Statistical Analysis* (Manchester: Equal Opportunities Commission) (Research Discussion Series No. 15).

Durán, M. A. (1999) *El futuro del trabajo en Europa. Género y distribución del tiempo* (Luxembourg: Office for the Official Publications of the European Communities).

Ebbinghaus, B. (1998) 'European labor relations and welfare-state regimes: a comparative analysis of their "elective affinities"', paper prepared for the International Conference of Europeanists, Baltimore, February 26–March 1.

Esping-Anderson, G. (1990) *The Three Worlds of Welfare Capitalism* (Cambridge: Polity Press).

Esping-Andersen, G. (1994) 'The welfare state and the economy', in N. J. Smelser and R. Swedberg (eds), *The Handbook of Economic Sociology* (Princeton, NJ: Princeton University Press).

Esping-Andersen, G. (ed.) (1996a) *Welfare States in Transition: National Adaptations in Global Economies* (London: Sage).
Esping-Andersen, G. (1996b) 'After the golden age? Welfare state dilemmas in a global economy', in G. Esping-Andersen (ed.), *Welfare States in Transition: National Adaptations in Global Economies* (London: Sage).
Esping-Andersen, G. (1996c) 'Positive-sum solutions in a world of trade-offs?', in G. Esping-Andersen (ed.), *Welfare States in Transition: National Adaptations in Global Economies* (London: Sage).
Esping-Andersen, G. (1996d) 'Welfare states without work: the impasse of labour shedding and familialism in continental European social policy', in G. Esping-Andersen (ed.), *Welfare States in Transition: National Adaptations in Global Economies* (London: Sage).
Esping-Andersen, G. (1999) *Social Foundations of Postindustrial Economies* (London: Sage).
Europäische Union (1997) *Beschäftigung in Europa 1997* (Brussels: Europäische Union).
European Bank for Reconstruction and Development (1999) *Transition Report Update* (London: EBRD).
European Commission (1993a) *Growth, Competitiveness, Employment* (Luxembourg: Office for the Official Publications of the European Communities).
European Commission (1993b). *European Social Policy: Options for the Union*, Green Paper COM (93) 551 (Brussels: European Commission).
European Commission (1994) *European Social Policy: A Way Forward for the Union*, White Paper COM (94) 333 (Brussels, European Commission).
European Commission (1996) *European Economy*, No. 62 (Brussels: Directorate-General for Economic and Financial Affairs).
European Commission (1997a) *Employment in Europe* (Luxembourg: Office for the Official Publications of the European Communities).
European Commission (1997b). *The PHARE Programme: An Interim Evaluation* (Brussels: European Commission).
European Commission (1998a) *Social Protection in Europe 1997* (Luxembourg: Office for the Official Publications of the European Communities).
European Commission (1998b) *Social Action Programme 1998 2000* (Brussels: European Commission).
European Commission (1999) *International Rules for Investment and the WTO. Issues Paper* (Brussels: European Commission (DG1)).
Eurostat (various years) *Basic Statistics of the European Union* (Luxembourg: Office for the Official Publications of the European Communities).
Evans, P. (1997) 'The eclipse of the state? Reflections on stateness in an era of globalization', *World Politics*, 50, pp. 62–87.
Evans, R. G., Barer, M. L. and Hertzmann, C. (1991) 'The 20 year experiment: accounting for, explaining and evaluating health care cost containment in Canada and the United States', *Annual Review of Public Health*, vol. 12, pp. 481–518.

216   *Bibliography*

Fagerberg, J., Cappelen, Å. and Mjøset, L. (1992) 'Structural change and economic policy: the Norwegian model under pressure', Nordisk geografisk tidsskrift 46.

Ferge, Z. (1992) 'Social policy regimes and social structure. Hypotheses about the prospects of social policy in central-eastern Europe', in Z. Ferge and J-E Kolberg (eds), *Social Policy in a Changing Europe* (Boulder, Co.: Campus and Westview).

Ferge, Z. (1997) 'The changed welfare paradigm: the individualisation of the social', *Social Policy and Administration*, vol. 31, no. 1, pp. 20–44.

Ferguson, C. (1998) *Codes of Conduct for Business* (London: Social Development Division, DFID).

Ferguson, C. (1999) *Global Social Policy Principles: Human Rights and Social Justice* (London: Social Development Division, DFID).

Ferrera, M. (1989) 'The politics of health reform. Origins and performance of the Italian health care service in comparative perspective', in G. Freddi and J. Bjorkman (eds), *Controlling Medical Professionals* (London: Sage).

Ferrera, M. (1996) 'The "southern model" of welfare in social Europe', *Journal of European Social Policy*, vol. 6, no. 1, pp. 17–37.

Ferrera, M. (1998) 'The four "social europes": between universalism and selectivity', in M. Rhodes and Y. Mény (eds), *The Future of the European Welfare State: A New Social Contract?* (Basingstoke: Macmillan).

Ferrera, M. and Gualmini, E. (2000) 'Italy: rescue from without?', in F. Scharpf and V. Schmidt (eds), *Welfare and Work in Open Economies*, Vol. 2 (Oxford: Oxford University Press).

Fine, Ben (1998) 'The triumph of economics: or, "rationality" can be dangerous to your reasoning', in J. G. Collier and D. Miller (eds), *Virtualism: A New Political Economy* (Oxford: Berg).

Finegold, D. and Soskice, D. (1988) 'The failure of training in Britain: analysis and prescription', *Oxford Review of Economic Policy*, vol. 4, no. 3, pp. 21–53.

Finer, C. J. (1999) 'Trends and developments in welfare states', in J. Clasen (ed.), *Comparative Social Policy: Concepts, Theories and Methods* (Oxford: Blackwell).

Fisher, I. (1930) *The Theory of Interest* (Basingstoke: Macmillan).

Fisher, I. (1935) *The Clash of Progress and Security* (Basingstoke: Macmillan).

Fraser, N. (1997) *Justice Interruptus* (London: Routledge).

Fuentes, E. (1993) 'Tres decenios de economía española en perspectiva', in J. L. García (ed.), *España, economía* (Madrid: Espasa Calpe).

Fukuyama, F. (1992) *The End of History and the Last Man* (London: Hamilton).

Funk, N. and Mueller, M. (eds) (1993) *Gender Politics and Post-Communism: Reflections from Eastern Europe and the Former Soviet Union* (New York and London: Routledge).

Garrett, Geoffrey (1998) *Partisan Politics in the Global Economy* (Cambridge: Cambridge University Press).

Garrido, L. and Requena, M. (1996) *La emancipación de los jóvenes en España* (Madrid: Ministerio de Trabajo y Asuntos Sociales. Instituto de la Juventud).

George, V. and Miller, S. (eds) (1994) *Social Policy towards 2000* (London: Routledge).

Gibson-Graham, K. T. (1996) *The End of Capitalism (As We Know It)* (Oxford: Blackwell).

Giddens, T. (1994) *Beyond Left and Right* (Cambridge: Polity Press).

Gilder, G. (1981) *Welfare and Poverty* (New York: Basic Books).

Gillion, C. (1999) Speech at International Labour Organisation Transition Team seminar, Burnham Beeches, UK, January.

Gillion, C., Turner, J., Bailey, J. and Tatulippe, D. (eds) (2000) *Social Security, Pensions: Development and Reform* (Geneva: ILO).

Gilroy, P. (1993) *The Black Atlantic: Modernity and Double Consciousness* (London: Verso).

Ginsburg, N. (1992) *Divisions of Welfare* (London: Sage).

Glennerster, H. (1992) *Paying for Welfare: The 1990s* (Hemel Hempstead: Harvester Wheatsheaf).

Glennerster, H. (1998a) 'Introduction', in H. Glennerster and J. Hills (eds), *The State of Welfare* (Oxford: Oxford University Press).

Glennerster, H. (1998b) 'Welfare with the lid on', in H. Glennerster and J. Hills (eds), *The State of Welfare* (Oxford: Oxford University Press).

González, C., Merino, V. and Merino, A. V. (1985) *Análisis económico financiero del Sistema Español de la Seguridad Social, 1964–85* (Madrid: Ministerio de Trabajo).

Götting, U. (1998) *Transformation der wohlfahrtstaaten in mittel-und Osteuropa. Eine zwischebilanz* (Opladen: Leske+Budrich).

Gough, I. (1996) 'Social welfare and competitiveness', *New Political Economy*, vol. 1, no. 2, pp. 209–32.

Goul Andersen, J., Pettersen, P. A., Svallfors, S. and Uusitalo, H. (1999) 'The legitimacy of the Nordic welfare states. Trends, variations and cleavages', in M. Kautto, M. Heikkilä, B. Hvinden, S. Marklunds and N. Ploug (eds), *Nordic Social Policy. Changing Welfare States* (London: Routledge).

Grahl, J. and Teague, P. (1997) 'Is the European social model fragmenting?', *New Political Economy*, vol. 2, no. 3, pp. 405–26.

Gray, J. (1997) 'Big idea 1: Globalisation', *New Times*, 29 March.

Grossberg, L. (1999) 'Speculations and articulations on globalization', *Polygraph*, no. 11.

Guillén, A. M. (1992) 'Social policy in Spain: from dictatorship to democracy', in Z. Ferge and J. E. Kolberg (eds), *Social Policy in a Changing Europe* (Boulder, Co.: Campus/ Westview).

Guillén, A. M. (1999a) 'Improving efficiency and containing costs: health care reform in southern Europe', European University Institute: Working Papers of the European Forum, No: 99/16 (Fiesole: EUI).

Guillén, A. M. (1999b) 'Pension reform in Spain (1975–1997): the role of organized labour', European University Institute: Working Papers of the European Forum, No: 99/6 (Fiesole: EUI).

Guillén A. M. and Cabiedes, L. (1997) 'Towards a national health service in Spain: the search for equity and efficiency', *Journal of European Social Policy*, vol. 7, no. 4, pp. 319–36.

Gustafsson, B. and Uusitalo, H. (1990) 'Income distribution and redistribution during two decades: experiences from Finland and Sweden', in I. Persson (ed.), *Generating Equality in the Welfare State: the Swedish Experience* (Oslo: Norwegian University Press).

Gustafsson, B., Aaberge, R., Cappelen, A., Pedersen, P. J., Smith, N. and Uusitalo, H. (1999) 'The distribution of income in the Nordic countries. Changes and causes', in M. Kautto, M. Heikkilä, B. Hvinden, S. Marklund, and N. Ploug (eds), *Nordic Social Policy. Changing Welfare States* (London: Routledge).

Gutiérrez, R. and Guillén, A. M. (1998) 'Protecting the long-term unemployed: the impact of targeting policies in Spain', *Estudios/Working Papers*, 1998/116 (Madrid: Instituto Juan March de Estudios e Investigaciones).

Hagen, K. (1992) 'The interaction of welfare states and labour markets', in J. E. Kolberg (ed.), *The Study of Welfare State Regimes* (Armonk, NY: M. E. Sharpe).

Hall, C. (1992) *White, Male and Middle Class: Explorations in Feminism and History* (Cambridge: Polity Press).

Hall, P. A. (1993) 'Policy paradigms, social learning and the state: the case of economic-policy making in Britain', *Comparative Politics*, vol, 25, no. 2, pp. 275–96.

Hall, S. (1988) *A Hard Road to Renewal* (London: Verso).

Hall, S., Critcher, C., Jefferson, T., Clarke, J. and Roberts B. (1978) *Policing the Crisis* (Basingstoke: Macmillan).

Hantrais, L. (1999) 'Comparing family policies in Europe', in J. Clasen (ed.), *Comparative Social Policy: Concepts, Theories and Methods* (Oxford: Blackwell).

Hay, C. (1996) *Restating Social and Political Change* (Buckingham: Open University Press).

Hay, C. (1997) 'Anticipating accommodations, accommodating anticipations: the appeasement of capital in the modernisation of the British Labour Party, 1987–1992', *Politics and Society*, vol. 25, no. 2, pp. 234–56.

Hay, C. (1998) 'Globalisation, welfare retrenchment and the "logic of no alternative": why second-best won't do', *Journal of Social Policy*, vol. 27, no. 4, pp. 525–32.

Hay, C. 1999a) *Globalization, Regionalization and the Persistence of National Variation: the Contingent Convergence of Contemporary Capitalism*, ESRC One Europe or Several? Working Paper, University of Birmingham.

Hay, C. (1999b) *The Vexatious Inquisition of Taxation? Globalization and the Political Economy of Welfare Retrenchment*, ESRC One Europe or Several? Working Paper, University of Birmingham.

Held, D., Goldblatt, D., McGrew, A. and Perraton, J. (1997) 'The globalization of economic activity', *New Political Economy*, vol. 2, no. 2, pp. 257–77.

Held, D., McGrew, A., Goldblatt, D. and Perraton, J. (1999) *Global Transformations: Politics, Economics and Culture* (Cambridge: Polity Press).

Hemerijck, A., Visser, J. and Unger, B. (2000) 'Austria, Belgium and the Netherlands: renegotiating the welfare state in the face of increased international competition', in F. Scharpf and V. Schmidt (eds), *Welfare and Work in Open Economies, Vol. 2* (Oxford: Oxford University Press).

Hill, M. (1996) *Social Policy: A Comparative Analysis* (Hemel Hempstead: Prentice Hall).

Hills, J. (1997a) 'How will the scissors close? Options for UK social spending', in A. Walker and C. Walker (eds), *Britain Divided: The Growth of Social Exclusion in the 1980s and 1990s* (London: Child Poverty Action Group).

Hills, J. (1997b) *The Future of Welfare* (York: Joseph Rowntree Foundation).

Hills, J. (1998a) *Income and Wealth: The Latest Evidence* (York: Joseph Rowntree Foundation).

Hills, J. (1998b) *Thatcherism, New Labour and the Welfare State*, CASE Paper No. 13, Centre for Analysis of Social Exclusion, London School of Economics, *http://sticerd.lse.ac.uk/case.htm* © John Hills.

Hirst, P. and Thompson, G. (1996, 1999 2nd edn) *Globalisation in Question* (Cambridge: Polity Press).

Hoggett, P. (1996) 'New modes of control in the public service', *Public Administration*, 34, pp. 9–32.

Holmes, S. (1997) 'When less state means less freedom', *Transitions*, vol. 4. no. 4., pp. 66–75.

Holzmann, R. (1997) 'A World Bank perspective on pension reform', paper Prepared for the joint ILO-OECD Workshop on the Development and Refom of Pension Schemes, Paris, 15–17 December.

Holzmann, R. and Jorgensen, B. N. (1999) *Social Protection as Social Risk Management* (Washington: World Bank, Human Development Network).

Huber, E., Ragin, C. and Stephens, J. D. (1993) 'Social democracy, christian democracy, constitutional structure, and the welfare state', *American Journal of Sociology*, vol. 99, no. 3.

Hudson, R. and Williams, A. M. (eds) (1999) *Divided Europe: Society and Territory* (London: Sage).

Hughes, G. and Lewis, G. (eds) (1998) *Unsettling Welfare: The Reconstruction of Social Policy* (London: Routledge/Open University).

Hurrell, A. and Woods, N. (eds) (1999) *Inequality, Globalization and World Politics* (New York: Oxford University Press).

ILO (1997) 'The ILO, standard setting and globalization report of the Director General', International Labour Conference (85th Session), Geneva, June.

ILO (2000) 'In Focus programme on socio-economic security', *Newsletter* 2000/1, Geneva, ILO (http://www.ilo.org/ses).

IMF (1990) *Social Security Reform in Hungary*. Prepared by G. Kopits, R. Holzmann, G. Schieber and E. Sidgwick, Washington: IMF.

IMF (1998a). *Social Dimensions of the IMF's Policy Dialogue*, IMF Pamphlet No. 47, Washington: IMF.

IMF (1998b) *Issues Paper: IMF Conference on Economic Policy and Equity* (Washington: IMF Fiscal Affairs Department) June 8–9.

IMF (1998c) *International Financial Statistics*, Washington: IMF.

Jameson, F. and Miyoshi, M. (eds) (1998) *The Cultures of Globalization* (Durham, NC and London: Duke University Press).

Jessop, B. (1994a) 'The transition to post-Fordism and the Schumpetarian workfare state', in R. Burrows and B. Loader (eds), *Toward a Post-Fordist Welfare State?* (London: Routledge).

Jessop, B. (1994b) 'Changing forms and functions of the state in an era of globalisation and regionalisation', in R. Delorme and K. Dopfer (eds), *The Political Economy of Diversity: Evolutionary Perspectives on Economic Order and Disorder* (London: Edward Elgar).

Jessop, B. (1998) 'Reflections on globalization and its (il)logics', In S. Aronowitz and P. Bratsis (eds), *Rethinking the State: Miliband, Poulantzas and State Theory* (Minneapolis: University of Minneapolis Press).

Jessop, B. (2000) 'From the Keynesian welfare national state to the Schumpeterian workfare post-national regime', in G. Lewis, S. Gewirtz and J. Clarke (eds), *Rethinking Social Policy* (London: Sage/Open University).

Jordan, B. (1998) 'European social citizenship: why a new social contract (probably) will not happen', in M. Rhodes and Y. Mény (eds), *The Future of the European Welfare State: A New Social Contract?* (Basingstoke: Macmillan).

Jurado, T. and Naldini, M. (1996) 'Is the South so different? Italian and Spanish families in comparative perspective', MZES University of Mannheim Working Papers.

Kapstein, B. (1998) 'Distributive justice and international trade', paper given to the Expert Meeting on International Economic and Social Justice, Pocantico Conference Center of the Rockerfeller Brothers' Fund, 12–14 November 1998, United Nations Division for Social Policy and Development, New York.

Katrougalos, G. (1996) 'The south european welfare model: the Greek welfare state, in search of an identity', *Journal of European Social Policy*, vol. 6, no. 1, pp. 39–60.

Kaul, I., Grunberg, I. and Stern, M. (eds) (1999) *Global Public Goods* (New York: Oxford University Press).

Koivusalo, M. (1999) *The World Trade Organisation and Trade Creep in Health and Social Policies* (Helsinki: GASPP Occasional Paper No. 4, STAKES).

Korpi, W. (1992) *Welfare State Development in Europe since 1930: Ireland in a Comparative Perspective* (Dublin: Economic and Social Research Institute).

Kosonen, P. (1991) 'Flexibilization and the alternatives of the Nordic welfare states', in B. Jessop, H. Kastendiek, K. Nielsen and O. K. Pedersen (eds), *The Politics of Flexibility. Restructuring State and Industry in Britain, Germany and Scandinavia* (Aldershot: Edward Elgar).

Kosonen, P. (1998) *Pohjoismaiset mallit murroksessa* (*The tensions of the Nordic models*, in Finnish) (Tampere: Vastapaino).

Kosonen, P. (1999) 'Activation, incentives and workfare in four Nordic countries', in *Comparing Social Welfare Systems in Nordic Countries and France* (Paris: MIRE).

Krugman, P. (1994) *Peddling Prosperity* (New York: Norton).

Kurzer, P. (1993) *Business and Banking* (Ithaca, NY: Cornell University Press).

Kyloh, R. (1998) *Governance of Globalization: The ILO's Contribution* (Geneva: ACTRAV Working Paper, ILO).

Larsson, A. (1998) 'Social policy and enlargement', 14 December, 1998, speech to the Consensus Program Advisory Board, Brussels.

Lee, E. (1997) 'Globalization and labour standards : a review of issues', *International Labour Review*, vol. 136, no. 2, pp. 173–90.

Leibfried, S. (1993) 'Towards a European welfare state?', in C. Jones (ed.), *New Perspectives on the Welfare State in Europe* (London: Routledge).

Leibfried, S. and Rieger, E. (1998) 'Welfare state limits to globalization', *Politics & Society*, vol. 26, no. 4, pp. 363–90.

Lelkes, O. (1999) 'A great leap towards liberalism? The Hungarian welfare state', Manuscript quoted with the permission of the author.

Lewis, G. (1998a) 'Welfare and the social construction of "race"', in E. Saraga (ed.), *Embodying the Social* (London: Routledge).

Lewis, G. (ed.) (1998b) *Forming Nation, Framing Welfare* (London: Routledge).

Lewis, G. (2000) 'Discursive histories, multi-culturalism and the limits of social policy', in G. Lewis, S. Gewirtz and J. Clarke (eds), *Rethinking Social Policy* (London: Sage/Open University).

Lewis, G., Gewirtz, S. and Clarke, J. (eds) (2000) *Rethinking Social Policy* (London: Sage/Open University).

Lewis, J. (1992) 'Gender and the development of welfare regimes', *Journal of European Social Policy*, vol. 2, no. 3, pp. 159–73.

Lewis, J. (2000) 'Typologies of welfare regimes: the impact of gender', in G. Lewis, S. Gewirtz and J. Clarke (eds), *Rethinking Social Policy* (London: Sage/Open University).

Locke, R. and Kochan, T. (1995) 'The transformation of industrial relations? A cross-national review of the evidence', in R. Locke, T. Kochan and M. Piore (eds), *Employment Relations in a Changing World* (Cambridge, Mass.: MIT Press).

Lødemel, I. (1994) 'Recent trends in cash benefits: Norway', in N. Ploug and J. Kvist (eds), *Recent Trends in Cash Benefits in Europe* (Copenhagen: The Danish Institute of Social Research).

Lowe, L. (1996) *Immigrant Acts: On Asian American Cultural Politics* (Durham, NC: Duke University Press).

Lucas, R. E. J. (1988) 'On the mechanics of economic development', *Journal of Monetary Economics*, vol. 22, no. 1, pp. 3–42.

Mackenzie, G. A. (1990) *Pension Regimes and Savings* (IMF Occasional Papers No. 153, Washington: IMF).

Manow, P. and Seils, E. (2000) '"Adjusting badly". The German welfare state, structural change and the open economy', in F. Scharpf and V. Schmidt (eds), *From Vulnerability to Competitiveness: Welfare and Work in the Open Economy* (Oxford: Oxford University Press).

Maravall, J. M. (1995) *Los resultados de la democracia* (Madrid: Alianza).

Marquand, D. (1994) 'Reinventing federalism: Europe and the left', *New Left Review*, no. 203, pp. 17–26.

Martin, A. (1997) 'What does globalisation have to do with the erosion of welfare states? Sorting out the issues', *Arbeitspapier Nr. 1* (Bremen: Zentrum für Sozialpolitik, Universität Bremen).

Martin, C. (1997) *España en la nueva Europa* (Madrid: Alianza).

Martin, H. P. and Schumann, H. (1997) *The Global Trap: Globalization and the Assault on Democracy and Prosperity* (London: Zed Books).

Massey, D. (1999) 'Imagining globalization: power-geometries of time-space', in A. Brah, M. Hickman and M. MacanGhaill (eds), *Future Worlds: Migration, Environment and Globalization* (Basingstoke: Macmillan).

McLaughlin, E. (1993) 'Ireland: Catholic corporatism', in A. Cochrane and J. Clarke (eds), *Comparing Welfare States* (London: Sage).

Messere, K. (1997) 'OECD tax developments in the 1990s', International Bureau of Fiscal Documentation, July, pp. 298–314.

Ministerio de Trabajo (various years) *Anuario de estadIsticas laborales* (Madrid: Ministerio de Trabajo).

Mink, G. (1998) *Welfare's End* (Ithaca, NY: Cornell University Press).

Mishel, L. and Bernstein, J. (1993) *The State of Working America, 1992–93* (Armonk, NY: M. E. Sharpe).

Mishra, R. (1998) 'Beyond the nation state: social policy in an age of globalization', *Social Policy & Administration*, vol. 32, no. 5, pp. 481–500.

Mishra, R. (1999) *Globalization and the Welfare State* (Cheltenham: Edward Elgar).

Mitchell, M. and Russell, D. (1998) 'Immigration, citizenship and social exclusion in the new Europe', in R. Sykes and P. Alcock (eds), *Developments in European Social Policy: Convergence and Diversity* (Bristol: The Policy Press).

Moreiras, A. (1999) 'Hybridity and double consciousness', *Cultural Studies*, vol. 13, no. 3, pp. 373–407.

Moreno, L. and Arriba, A. (1998) 'Decentralization, mesogovernments, and the new logic of welfare provision in Spain', paper presented at the conference 'Reforming Social Assistance and Social Services: International Experiences and Perspectives', European University Institute, Florence, 11–12 December.

Morley, D. and Chen, K-H. (eds) (1996) *Stuart Hall: Critical Dialogues in Cultural Studies* (London: Routledge).

Morris, L. (1998) 'Legitimate membership of the welfare community', in M. Langan (ed.), *Welfare: Needs, Rights and Risks* (London: Routledge).

Morris, M. (1998) *Too Soon, Too Late: History in Popular Culture* (Bloomington: Indiana University Press).

Müller, K., Ryll, A. and Wagener, H-J. (eds) (1999) *Transformation of Social Security: Pensions in Central-Eastern Europe* (Heidelberg: Physica).

Murray Brown, J. and Chote, R. (1999) 'Too much of a good thing', *Financial Times*, June 10th.

Myles, J. and Quadagno, J. (1997) 'Recent trends in public pension reform: a comparative view', in K. Banting and R. Broadway (eds), *Reform of Retirement Income Policy. International and Canadian Perspectives* (Kingston, Ont.: Queen's University: School of Policy Studies).

Navarro, V. (1998) 'Neoliberalism, "globalization", unemployment, inequalities and the welfare state', *International Journal of Health Services*, vol. 28, no. 4, pp. 607–82.

Neal, L. and Barberat, D. (1998) *The Economics of the European Union and the Economics of Europe* (Oxford: Oxford University Press).

Nelson, J. M. (1998) *The Politics of Pension and Health Care Delivery Reforms in Hungary and Poland* (Budapest: Collegium Budapest).

O'Donnell, R. and Thomas, D. (1998) 'Partnership and policy-making', in S. Healy and B. Reynolds (eds), *Social Policy in Ireland: Principles, Practice and Problems* (Dublin: Oak Tree Press).

OECD (various years) *Employment Outlook* (Paris: OECD).

OECD (1981) *The Crisis of Welfare* (Paris: OECD).

OECD (1994) *New Orientations for Social Policy* (Paris: OECD).

OECD (1995a) *Social and Labour Market Policies in Hungary* (Paris: OECD).

OECD (1995b) *Taxation, Employment and Unemployment* (Paris: OECD).

OECD (1997a) *Family, Market and Community. Equity and Efficiency in Social Policy* (Paris: OECD).

OECD (1997b) *Historical Statistics 1960–1995* (Paris: OECD).

OECD (1997c) *Shaping the 21st century – the Contribution of Development Co-operation* (Paris: OECD, Development Assistance Committee).

OECD (1998) *The Battle against Exclusion, Vol 2. Social Assistance in Belgium, the Czech Republic, the Netherlands and Norway* (Paris: OECD).

OECD (1999) *A Caring World: The New Social Policy Agenda* (Paris: OECD).

OECD (various years) *Social Expenditures* (Paris: OECD).

Ohmae, K. (1990) *The Borderless World: Power and Strategy in the International Economy* (London: Fontana).

Ohmae, K. (1996) *The End of the Nation State: The Rise of Regional Economies* (New York: Free Press).

Okun, A. M. (1975) *Equality and Efficiency: The Big Tradeoff* (Washington: The Brookings Institute).

Orgsag, P. R. and Stiglitz, J. (1999) 'Rethinking pension reform: ten myths about social security', Conference on New Ideas About Old Age Security, World Bank, Washington DC, 14–15 September 1999.

Ormerod, P. (1998) 'Unemployment and social exclusion: an economic view', in M. Rhodes and Yves Mény (eds), *The Future of the European Welfare State: A New Social Contract?* (Basingstoke: Macmillan).

Oxley, H. and Macfarlan, M. (1995) 'Health care reform: controlling spending and increasing efficiency', *OECD Economic Studies*, vol. 24, no. 1, pp. 7–55.

Pajarinen, M., Rouvinen, P. and Ylä-Anttila, P. (1998) *Small Country Strategies in Global Competition. Benchmarking the Finnish Case* (Helsinki: The Research Institute of the Finnish Economy).

Palme, J. (1990) *Pension Rights in Welfare Capitalism. The Development of Old-Age Pensions in 18 OECD Countries* (Stockholm: Swedish Institute for Social Research, Dissertation Series 14).

Perron, D. (1999) 'Deconstructing the Maastricht myth? Economic and social cohesion in Europe: regional and gender dimensions of inequality', in R. Hudson and A. Williams (eds), *Divided Europe: Society and Territory* (London: Sage).

Pfaller, A., Gough, I. and Therborn, G. (eds) (1991) *Can the Welfare State Compete? A Comparative Study of Five Advanced Capitalist Countries* (Basingstoke: Macmillan).

Pierson, P. (1994) *Dismantling the Welfare State? Reagan, Thatcher and the Politics of Retrenchment* (Cambridge: Cambridge University Press).

Pierson, P. (1996) 'The new politics of the welfare state', *World Politics*, vol. 48, pp. 143–79.

Pierson, P. (1998) 'Irresistible forces, immovable objects: post-industrial welfare states confront permanent austerity', *Journal of European Public Policy*, vol. 5, no. 5, pp. 539–60.

Pierson, P. (2000) *The New Politics of the Welfare State* (Oxford: Oxford University Press).

Pillinger, J. (2000) 'Redefining work and welfare in Europe', in G. Lewis, S. Gewirtz and J. Clarke (eds), *Rethinking Social Policy* (London, Sage/Open University).

Piven, F. F. (1997) 'Welfare and the transformation of electoral politics', in C. Lo and M. Schwartz (eds), *Social Policy and the Conservative Agenda* (Malden, Mass. and Oxford: Blackwell).

Plovsing, J. (1994) 'Social security in Denmark – renewal of the welfare state', in N. Ploug and J. Kvist (eds), *Recent Trends in Cash Benefits in Europe* (Copenhagen: The Danish National Institute of Social Research).

Polanyi, K. (1944) *The Great Transformation* (Boston, Mass.: Beacon Press).

Poole, L. (2000) 'New approaches to comparative social policy. The changing face of East European welfare', in G. Lewis, S. Gewirtz and J. Clarke (eds), *Rethinking Social Policy* (London: Sage/Open University).

Prais, S. J. and Wagner, K. (1987) 'Educating for productivity: comparisons of Japanese and English schooling and vocational preparation', *National Institute Economic Review*, vol. 119, pp. 40–56.

Przeworski, A. and Wallerstein, M. (1988) 'Structural dependence of the state on capital', *American Political Science Review*, vol. 82, no. 1, pp. 11–30.

Rao, N. (1996) *Towards Welfare Pluralism: Public Services in a Time of Change* (Aldershot: Dartmouth Publishing Company).

Razin, A. and Sadka, E. (1991a) 'Efficient investment incentives in the presence of capital flight', *Journal of International Economics*, vol. 31, no. 1/2, pp. 171–81.

Razin, A. and Sadka, E. (1991b) 'International tax competition and gains from tax harmonisation', *Economic Letters*, vol. 37, no. 1, pp. 69–76.

Reich, R. (1992) *The Work of Nations* (New York: Vintage Books).

Rhodes, M. (1995) 'Subversive liberalism': market integration, globalization and the European welfare state', *Journal of European Public Policy*, vol. 2, no. 3, pp. 384–406.

Rhodes, M. (1996) 'Globalization and west European welfare states: a critical review of recent debates', *Journal of European Social Policy*, vol. 6, no. 4, pp. 305–27.

Rhodes, M. (1997a) 'Globalisation, labour markets and welfare states: a future of "competitive corporatism"?', *European University Institute Working Paper 97/36* (Badia Fiesolana: EUI).

Rhodes, M. (1999) 'The implication of globalization and liberalization for income security and social protection', mimeo; contribution for the ILO Employment Report of 1999–2000, *Income Security in a Changing World* (Geneva: ILO).

Rhodes, M. (1997b) 'The welfare state: internal challenges, external constraints', in M. Rhodes, P. Heywood and V. Wright (eds), *Developments in West European Politics* (Basingstoke: Macmillan).

Rhodes, M. (1998) 'Globalisation, labour markets and welfare states: a future of competitive corporatism?', in M. Rhodes and I. Mény (eds), *The Future of European Welfare State: A New Social Contract?* (Basingstoke: Macmillan).

Robinson, P. (1999) 'Explaining the relationship between flexible employment and labour market regulation', in A. Felstead and N. Jewson (eds), *Global Trends in Flexible Labour* (Basingstoke: Macmillan).

Rodríguez Cabrero, G. (1994) 'La protección social a la familia', in Fundación FOESSA (ed.), *V Informe sociológico sobre la situación social en España* (Madrid: Fundación FOESSA).

Rodrik, D. (1996) *Why Do More Open Economies have Bigger Governments?*, NBER Working Paper No. 5537 (Cambridge, Mass: National Bureau of Economic Research).

Rodrik, D. (1997) *Has Globalisation Gone Too Far?* (Washington: Institute for International Economics).

Rose, N. (1996) *Governing the Soul* (London, Routledge).

Ross, A. (1998) *Real Love: In Pursuit of Cultural Justice* (London: Routledge).

Riih, F. W. (1999) 'Comparing the state of statebuilding. A conceptual framework for the comparison of the post-communist states', manuscript, Collegium Budapest.

Rutkowski, M. (1998) 'A new generation of pension reforms conquers the East – a taxonomy in transition economies', *Transition*, vol. 8, no. 8, pp. 16–19.

Rys, V. (1995) 'Social security development in central Europe: a return to reality', *Czech Sociological Review*, vol. 3, no. 2, pp. 197–208.

Sainsbury, D. (ed.) (1994) *Gendering Welfare States* (London: Sage).

Salminen, K. (1993) *Pension Schemes in the Making. A Comparative Study of the Scandinavian Countries* (Helsinki: The Central Pension Security Institute).

Salvati, M. (1984) *Economia e politica in Italia dal dopoguerra ad oggi* (Milano: Garzanti).

Sandholtz, W. and Stone-Sweet, A. (eds) (1998) *European Integration and Supranational Governance* (Oxford : Oxford University Press).

Sanger, M. (1998) 'The MAI and public and social services', in A. Jackson, and M. Sanger (eds), *Dismantling Democracy : The MAI and Its Impact* (Toronto: James Larimer & Co.).

Sassen, S. (1998) *Globalization and Its Discontents* (New York: The New Press).

Scharpf, Fritz (1991) *Crisis and Choice in European Social Democracy* (Ithaca, NY: Cornell University Press).

Scharpf, F. W. (1999) 'The viability of advanced welfare states in the international economy: vulnerabilities and options', *Max Planck Institute for the Study of Societies Working Paper 99/9* (Cologne: MPIfG).

Scharpf, F. and Schmidt, V. (eds) (2000) *Welfare and Work in Open Economies* (Oxford: Oxford University Press) 2 vols.

Scholte, J. A. (1996) 'Beyond the buzzword: a critical theory of globalization', in E. Kofman and G. Young (eds), *Globalization: Theory and Practice* (London: Pinter).

Sen, A. (1977) 'Rational fools: a critique of the behavioural foundations of economic theory', *Philosophy and Public Affairs*, vol. 6, no. 4, pp. 317–44.

Skocpol, T. (1995) *Social Policy in the United States: Future Possibilities in Historical Perspective* (Princeton, NJ: Princeton University Press).

Skocpol, T. and Amenta, E. (1988) 'States and social policies', *American Review of Sociology*, vol. 12, no. 1, pp. 131–57.

Smith, A. (1776/1976) *An Inquiry into the Nature and Causes of the Wealth of Nations* (Oxford: Oxford University Press).

Social Security in the Nordic Countries (various years). Prepared by the Nordic Social-Statistical Committee (NOSOSCO) (Copenhagen: Nososco).

Statistisches Jahrbuch für das Ausland, 1991, 1995, 1996 (Wiesbaden: Statistisches Bundesamt).

Stenson, K. (2000) 'Recoding social policy as crime control', in G. Lewis, S. Gewirtz and J. Clarke (eds), *Rethinking Social Policy* (London: Sage/Open University).

Stephens, J. D. (1996) 'The Scandinavian welfare states: achievements, crisis and prospects', in G. Esping-Andersen (ed.), *Welfare States in Transition: National Adaptations in Global Economies* (London: Sage).

Stephens, J. D., Huber, E. and Ray, L. (1999) 'The welfare state in hard times', in H. Kitschelt, P. Lange, G. Marks and J. D. Stephens (eds), *Continuity and Change in Contemporary Capitalism* (Cambridge: Cambridge University Press).

Stiglitz, J. (1998) 'Moving toward the post-Washington consensus', in *Wider Angle*, Newsletter of the World Institute for Development Economics Research, The United Nations University, no. 2/97.

Streeck, W. (1997) 'German capitalism: Does it exist? Can it survive?', in C. Crouch and W. Streeck (eds), *Political Economy of Modern Capitalism* (London: Sage).

Streeck, W. (1999) 'Competitive solidarity: rethinking the "European Social Model"', *Max Planck Institute for the Study of Societies Working Paper 99/8* (Cologne: MPIfG).

Svallfors, S. and Taylor-Gooby, P. (eds) (1999) *The End of the Welfare State? Public Attitudes to State Retrenchment* (London: Routledge).

Swank, D. (1998) 'Funding the welfare state: globalisation and the taxation of business in advanced market economies', *Political Studies*, vol. 46, no. 4, pp. 671–92.

Swank, D. (1999) 'Diminished democracy? Globalisation, political institutions and the welfare state in developed nations' (author's typescript, quoted with permission).

Sweeney, P. (1998) *The Celtic Tiger: Ireland's Economic Miracle Explained* (Dublin: Oak Tree Press).

Sykes, R. (1998) 'Studying European social policy – issue and perspectives', in R. Sykes and P. Alcock (eds), *Developments in European Social Policy: Convergence and Diversity* (Bristol, The Policy Press).

Sykes, R. and Alcock, P. (eds) (1998) *Developments in European Social Policy: Convergence and Diversity* (Bristol, The Policy Press).

Tanzi, V. (1998) 'International dimensions of national tax policy', paper given to the Expert Meeting on International Economic and Social Justice, Pocantico Conference Center of the Rockerfeller Brothers' Fund, 12–14 November 1998, United Nations Division for Social Policy and Development, New York.

Tanzi, V. and Zee, H. H. (1997) 'Fiscal policy and long-run growth', *International Monetary Fund Staff Papers*, vol. 44, no. 2, pp. 179–209.

Tanzi, V. and Schuknecht, L. (1997) 'Reconsidering the fiscal role of government: the international perspective', *American Economic Review*, vol. 87, no. 2, pp. 164–8.

Taylor, D. (ed.) (1996) *Critical Social Policy* (London: Sage).

Taylor-Gooby, P. (1996), 'Eurosclerosis in European welfare states. Regime theory and the dynamics of change', *Policy and Politics*, vol. 24, no. 2, pp. 109–23.

Taylor-Gooby, P. (1999) 'Policy change at a time of retrenchment: recent pension reform in France, Germany, Italy and the UK', *Social Policy and Administration*, vol. 33, no. 1, pp. 1–19.

Teague, P. (1998) 'Monetary union and Social Europe', *Journal of European Social Policy*, vol. 8, no. 2, pp. 117–37.

Therborn, G. (1986) *Why Some Peoples Are More Unemployed Than Others. The Strange Paradox of Growth and Unemployment* (London: Verso).

Therborn, G. (1995) *European Modernity and Beyond. The Trajectory of European Societies 1945–2000* (London: Sage).

Tickell, A. (1999) 'European financial integration and uneven development', in R. Hudson and A. Williams (eds), *Divided Europe: Society and Territory* (London, Sage).

UNDP (1998) *Poverty Report 1998. Overcoming Human Poverty* (New York: United Nations Development Programme).

UNICEF (1997) *Children at Risk in Central and Eastern Europe: Perils and Promises*, Economies in Transition Studies, Regional Monitoring Report No. 4 (Geneva: UNICEF).

van Kersbergen, K. (1995) *Social Capitalism* (London: Routledge).

Van Oorshot, W. (1998) 'From solidarity to selectivity: the reconstruction of the Dutch social security system 1980–2000', in E. Brunsdon, M. May and G. Craig (eds), *Social Policy Review 10* (Canterbury: Social Policy Association).

Vandenbroucke, F. (1998) *Globalisation, Inequality and Social Democracy* (London: Institute for Public Policy Research).

Väyrynen, R. (1999) *Suomi avoimessa maailmassa. Globalisaatio ja sen vaikutukset* (*Finland in the Open World. Globalization and Its Consequences*, in Finnish) (Helsinki: Sitra).

Visser, J. and Hemerijck, A. (1997) *'A Dutch Miracle': Job Growth, Welfare Reform, and Corporatism in the Netherlands* (Amsterdam: Amsterdam University Press).

Watson, M. (1997) 'The changing face of macroeconomic stabilisation: from growth through indigenous investment to growth through inward investment', in J. Stanyer and G. Stoker (eds), *Contemporary Political Studies 1997, Volume 2* (Oxford: Blackwell/PSA).

Watson, M. (1999) 'Globalisation and British political development', in D. Marsh, J. Buller, C. Hay, J. Johnston, P. Kerr, S. McAnulla and M. Watson, *Postwar British Politics in Perspective* (Cambridge: Polity Press).

Weaver, R. K. (1986) 'The politics of blame avoidance', *Journal of Public Policy*, vol. 6, no. 4, pp. 371–98.

Weiss, L. (1997) 'Globalisation and the myth of a powerless state', *New Left Review*, 225, pp. 3–27.

Weiss, L. (1998) *The Myth of the Powerless State* (Cambridge: Polity Press).

Wendon, B. (1998) 'The Commission as image-venue entrepreneur in EU social policy'. *Journal of European Public Policy*, vol. 5, no. 2, pp. 339–53.

Western, B. and Beckett, K. (1998) 'The free market myth: penal justice as an institution of the US labour market', *Berliner Journal Für Soziologie*, vol. 8, no. 2, pp. 159–82.

Western, B. and Beckett, K. (1999) 'How unregulated is the US labour market? The penal system as a labour market institution', *American Journal of Sociology*, vol. 104, no. 4, pp. 1030–60.

Western, B., Beckett, K. and Harding, D. (1998) 'Penal systems and the American labour market', *Actes de la Recherche en Sciences Sociales*, no. 124, pp. 27–37.

White, P. (1999) 'Ethnicity, racialization and citizenship as divisive elements in Europe', in R. Hudson and A. Williams (eds), *Divided Europe: Society and Territory* (London: Sage).

Wickham-Jones, M. (1995) 'Anticipating social democracy, pre-empting anticipations: economic policy-making in the British Labour Party, 1987–1992', *Politics and Society*, vol. 23, no. 4, pp. 465–94.

WIDE (Women in Development) (1997) *Gender Mapping the European Trade Policy* (WIDE).

Wilkinson, R. (1996) 'Health, redistribution and growth', in A. Glyn and D. Miliband (eds), *Paying for Inequalities* (London: Institute for Public Policy Research).

Williams, C. (1999) 'Nationalism and its derivatives in post-1989 Europe', in R. Hudson and A. Williams (eds), *Divided Europe: Society and Territory* (London: Sage).

Williams, F. (1989) *Social Policy: A Critical Introduction* (Cambridge: Polity Press).

Wolfensohn, J. D. (1997) Speech at the Annual World Bank Meeting in Hong Kong, September.

World Bank (1991) *Reform of the Social Policy and Distribution System*, Report No. 9349-HU, Budapest: World Bank.

World Bank (1994a) *Reform Issues in Social Policy*, Working Paper. Budapest: World Bank.

World Bank (1994b) *Averting the Old Age Crisis. Policies to Protect the Old and Promote Growth*, Policy Research Report (Washington: Oxford University Press).

World Bank (1996) *World Development Report, 1996: From Plan to Market*, The International Bank for Reconstruction and Development – The World Bank (New York: Oxford University Press).

World Bank (1997a) *World Development Report, 1997: The State in a Changing World*, The International Bank for Reconstruction and Development – The World Bank (New York: Oxford University Press).

World Bank (1997b) *Health, Nutrition and Population: Sector Strategy* (Washington: World Bank, Human Development Network).

World Bank (1999a) *World Development Indicators* (Washington: The World Bank).

World Bank (1999b) 'ECA social protection and labor markets. Challenges and the changes needed', Home page for the World Bank's Europe and Central Asia Social Sector. Reform Agenda. 1999. 17 May. http://www/worldbank.org/w3c//dtd html 3.2//en

World Trade Organisation (WTO) (1998) *Health and Social Services*, Background Paper S/C/W/50, 1st September 1998 (Geneva: WTO Secretariat to the Council for Trade in Services).

Yuval-Davis, N. (1997) *Gender and Nation* (London: Sage).

Zakaria, F. (1997) 'The rise of illiberal democracy', *Foreign Affairs*, vol. 76, no. 6, pp. 22–43.

Zysman, J. (1996) 'The myth of a "global" economy: enduring national foundations and emerging regional realities', *New Political Economy*, vol. 1, no. 2, pp. 157–84.

Index